INTERPRETING OTHERWISE THAN HEIDEGGER

Interpreting Otherwise than Heidegger

Emmanuel Levinas's Ethics as First Philosophy

Robert John Sheffler Manning

DUQUESNE UNIVERSITY PRESS
Pittsburgh, Pennsylvania

Published in the United States of America by
Duquesne University Press
600 Forbes Avenue
Pittsburgh, Pennsylvania 15282-0101

Library of Congress Cataloging-in-Publication Data

Manning, Robert John Sheffler, 1961–
Interpreting otherwise than Heidegger : Emmanuel Levinas's ethics
as first philosophy / Robert John Sheffler Manning.
p. cm.
Includes bibliographical references and index.
ISBN 0-8207-0246-3; ISBN 0-8207-0253-6 (pbk.)
1. Lévinas, Emmanuel. 2. Heidegger, Martin, 1889–1976.
3. Ontology. 4. Ethics. I. Title.
B2430.L484M36 1993
170—dc20 92-45191
CIP

CONTENTS

ACKNOWLEDGMENTS

With all due apologies to all of those whom I hope to acknowledge in future works, this book is dedicated to all of the members of my extended family in Delmont, Pennsylvania, that peculiar place where place and people are one. This work has been written out of the constant memory of those family members who have left us during the long Diaspora of my graduate education—and most especially our sister, Marcia Manning Christian—and out of the constant joy and hope in those who during these same years have been born: Lisa, Rachel and Michelle.

This work on Levinas is especially dedicated to the memory of one who, though unschooled, embodied in my life Levinas's ethical wisdom, my grandfather, James Russell Sheffler, in whose name I will always write. It was he who first imparted to me love and desire for knowledge and wisdom and who taught me that supremely Levinasian lesson, that as much as we desire and seek after knowledge, our ultimate goal is always the wisdom that unites us together as sisters and brothers.

Introduction

> How can one philosophize after Auschwitz? It is this thought that traverses the whole of Levinas' philosophy and that he proposes to us without saying it.
>
> —*Maurice Blanchot*

> The real question is, can we speak of an absolute commandment after Auschwitz? Can we speak of morality after the failure of morality?
>
> —*Emmanuel Levinas*

There is perhaps no philosopher in Europe today more celebrated than Emmanuel Levinas. Many are the books and articles on or by Levinas recently published, hurrying to press, or currently being written on Levinas's philosophy.[1] Levinas's work is also beginning to appear on philosophy course syllabi in universities and colleges, another sign that he is beginning to be granted his place among the other giants of French philosophy contemporaneous with him—Blanchot, Sartre, Foucault, Derrida.

This flurry of interest in Levinas's thought is, I believe, not surprising and is as it should be. Levinas is preoccupied not with the narrow concerns of the professional academic, of interest only to a few dozen colleagues, but with the great events and issues of our century of interest to all who think and care about the world in which we all live so precariously together. Levinas's thought is preoccupied with the brutal and almost (and how much hope is there within this "almost" that Levinas would insist upon?) inevitable reality of violence, and with the possibility of ethics, justice and peace. Even philosophy cannot remain aloof and isolated forever from such concerns. Levinas's thought brings philosophy nearer to them.

Then again, so does the world itself, with its constant epiphanies of violence and horror. Foremost among these in and for our century is the Holocaust. How such a diabolical event could occur in the midst of our own advanced, cultured civilization is a question asked by philosophers and many other people as well. And how could the educated and enlightened, those who should have known better, like the doctors, lawyers, judges, teachers and college professors, participate so willingly in the diabolical? Perhaps this last question presses more heavily upon those of us who would claim the title of philosopher and intellectual now that it is impossible to ignore the Nazism of the one many of us consider the most important philosopher of the century—Martin Heidegger. Levinas's thought is concerned with all these troubling questions.

Perhaps most fundamentally, Levinas's philosophy is addressed to the question Carl Jung posed in an essay on the Holocaust appropriately titled "After the Catastrophe," a question many people, academics and nonacademics alike, have also posed: "Where now is the sanction for goodness and justice, which was once anchored in metaphysics? Is it really only brute force that decides everything?"[2] Or, as Levinas himself has put it, after Auschwitz, "where God let the Nazis do what they wanted . . . what remains?"[3] Levinas insists that another power remains to oppose the brute force of violence. He calls this other power "ethics" or, more rarely, "goodness."

Notoriety outside of his adopted country of France has come to Levinas only after 60 years of laboring in the philosophical vineyard in relative obscurity. It was in 1928 that Levinas left France for The University of Freiburg to study under Husserl and Heidegger. This sojourn resulted in the publication of a series of books and articles interpreting and/or translating Husserl and Heidegger.[4] In fact, in the thirties and forties Levinas was known almost entirely as a translator of Husserl and Heidegger, as the conduit through which German philosophy entered France. In 1940, he was captured by the Germans and spent five years in a prisoner of war camp.[5] His French soldier's uniform prevented him from being sent to a concentration camp. While incarcerated, he wrote the book that initiated the construction of his own philosophy, *Existence and Existents*.[6] This book and the one that immediately followed it, *Time and the Other*, however, brought him very little notoriety and only in the form of a sharp rebuke for being sexist by Simone de Beauvoir in a footnote in her 1947 work, *The Second Sex*.[7]

It was not until 1961, with the publication of *Totality and Infinity*,[8] that Levinas's own philosophy began to attract attention. It was this book, with its severe attack on Heidegger's ontology upon ethical grounds, that provoked the first lengthy analysis of Levinas, Jacques Derrida's 1964 essay "Violence and Metaphysics." In this essay, Derrida concentrates upon Levinas's critique of Heideggerian ontology and asserts that Levinas misunderstands and misrepresents Heidegger's philosophy. Derrida concludes by suggesting that Levinas's discourse is not really philosophy at all, but is actually empiricism, which "has ever committed but one fault: the fault of presenting itself as a philosophy."[9] Derrida's early essay on Levinas did not create nearly so much interest outside France in Levinas as it did in Derrida, and when Langdon Gilkey wrote a commentary on *Totality and Infinity* in 1972,[10] two years after the English version of *Totality and Infinity* appeared, he was only the second person to write an essay on Levinas in English.[11] Even as late as 1975, Harold Durfee could describe Levinas as "quite neglected to date."[12]

Reviewing the literature, one cannot but notice that most of the early discussion of Levinas's philosophy centers upon *Totality and Infinity's* criticisms of Heidegger's ontology on ethical grounds.[13] Levinas's attack on Heidegger is so strident in *Totality and Infinity* that the relation between Heidegger's and Levinas's philosophy is most often interpreted—especially by Heidegger's defenders—as an oppositional and adversarial one.[14] This reading of the Levinas-Heidegger relationship is completely understandable, as Levinas scholarship has tended to interpret Levinas almost solely through *Totality and Infinity*, and Levinas's attack on Heidegger in this work is severe.

Many Levinas scholars, however, seemingly despite themselves, have haltingly and hesitantly suggested that the Levinas-Heidegger relationship may be more complex than it appears to be in some sections of *Totality and Infinity*. Time and again critics have pointed to "similarities" or "convergences" between Levinas's philosophy and Heidegger's that they have labeled "surprising." Luk Boukaert first warned that we should not let Levinas's attack upon Heidegger obscure the fact that there is a certain similarity between Levinas's notion of *il y a* and Heidegger's concept of *es gibt*.[15] F. P. Ciglia says Levinas's philosophy is characterized by "an irremediable opposition to Heidegger," yet also says Levinas's polemic against Heidegger seems to "issue from an analogous inspiration."[16] Guy Petitdemange notes that even in the midst of Levinas's polemic against Heidegger there is "a note of gratitude."[17] According to Allain David, Heidegger in Levinas's eyes is both "admired and impardonable."[18]

Among Levinas's English-speaking critics, Adriaan Peperzak believes that Levinas is in "close affinity with

Martin Heidegger, but at the same time in sharp opposition to him."[19] Similarly, Robert Bernasconi warns us that although Levinas acknowledges only his debt to Husserl, not to Heidegger, "we cannot ignore the Heideggerian heritage that is also operative."[20] David Wood, in the volume of essays on Levinas he edited with Bernasconi entitled *The Provocation of Levinas*, writes of "surprising convergences between Levinas and Heidegger."[21] Andrius Valevicius expresses very clearly the paradoxical nature of the Levinas-Heidegger relationship when he observes that "Levinas attacks Heidegger, and yet we find innumerable influences of the latter on him." Puzzled, Valevicius asks, "What to make of this?"[22] Such consternation on the part of so many critics illustrates the verity of Peperzak's warning that "the exact nature of the relations between Levinas's meditations and Heidegger's is one of the most difficult topics in the field of post-phenomenology."[23]

Levinas's own comments on Heidegger's great work *Being and Time* make this very difficult issue of his relation to Heidegger even more puzzling. In the series of interviews with Levinas conducted by Phillipe Nemo and collected under the title *Ethics and Infinity*, Levinas, the great opponent and the harshest critic of Heidegger's philosophy, states that he considers *Being and Time* "a sovereign exercise of phenomenology" and, as such, one of the four or five greatest works in the history of philosophy.[24] Thus declares Levinas, despite the fact that whenever Levinas criticizes Heidegger's philosophy, his target is almost never the philosophy of the later Heidegger, and almost always the philosophy of 1927, the philosophy of *Being and Time*.

Intrigued by this puzzling issue of Levinas's relation to Heidegger, I chose to pursue it as a way of gaining access to Levinas's philosophy. One of my first discoveries was, in fact, that scholars' describing similarities between Levinas and Heidegger as "surprising" or "puzzling" actually reveals a deficiency quite common in the way in which Levinas's philosophy has most often been interpreted: by beginning with *Totality and Infinity* and then going forward to Levinas's later works. Bernasconi and Critchley have very recently pointed this out by stating that "the initial reception of Levinas's work has been to a great extent determined by *Totality and Infinity*."[25] By beginning with this Levinas work of 1961, critics have tended to forget that *Totality and Infinity* is not at the beginning but is actually in the middle period of Levinas's philosophical production. To ward off misunderstandings that might arise through this mistake, I have instead begun my analysis of the Levinas-Heidegger relation at the beginning of Levinas's philosophical career—with his 1930 dissertation on the philosophy of Edmund Husserl.

Levinas's dissertation makes it obvious that he believes it is Heidegger who has gotten beyond the limitations of Husserlian phenomenology and is exploring the true richness of phenomenology. It is Heidegger who has shown Levinas the true philosophical value of the phenomenological method.[26] Thus, by analyzing Levinas's philosophy from its beginnings, as he interprets Husserl in a profoundly Heideggerian fashion, we begin to see how profoundly Heideggerian Levinas's own philosophical productions are. It is then hardly surprising to discover similarities or convergences between Levinas and Heidegger, or to hear Levinas speak of *Being and Time* in superlatives of respect and appreciation.

The fact that we must insist that it is Heidegger who has shown Levinas the true resources of the phenomenological method does not mean, however, that we are done with this question of the relation between Levinas's philosophy and Heidegger's. Indebted to Heidegger as Levinas is, he is no Heideggerian. If 1930 saw Levinas write glowingly of Heidegger's phenomenological ontology, 1945 saw Levinas declare his urgent need to escape the climate of Heidegger's philosophy, though not for a philosophy that would be pre-Heideggerian.[27] These words indicate what my reading and working through of Levinas's philosophy as it develops has made clear: Levinas's philosophy is neither a simple borrowing from Heidegger's philosophy nor merely a criticism of it. Levinas's philosophy does borrow from Heidegger's, but never without criticizing it, and it does criticize Heidegger's philosophy, but never without borrowing from it and being heavily indebted to it. What, then, of the relation between their philosophies, and how does this issue aid in interpreting the meaning of Levinas's philosophy?

What I have come to understand by thinking these two philosophers together, by reading Levinas with Heidegger's *Being and Time* in mind, is that the relation Levinas's thought bears to Heidegger's is a dialectical one, similar to the relation Kierkegaard's thought bears to the philosophy of Hegel.[28] This means that Levinas's philosophy is a constant arguing against and an interpreting otherwise than Heidegger's phenomenological ontology, but always within the context of and after the manner of Heidegger's phenomenological project in *Being and Time*. *Being and Time* can rightly be seen as both the model and the constant foil for Levinas's own phenomenology. A close analysis of Levinas's early philosophical productions leading to *Totality and Infinity* reveals that every phenomenological description of existence he offers can be seen as a counterpoint to, an argument against, and an interpreting otherwise than a corresponding phenomenological description in *Being and Time*. In other words, Levinas's phenomenology is always a matter of interpreting within but always otherwise than Heidegger's phenomenological ontology. This is what I have attempted to show in chapter 1—"Levinas's Interpretation of Being"—and in chapter 2—"Levinas's Interpretation of Time."

Understanding that Levinas's philosophy is an interpreting within but otherwise than Heidegger enables us to interpret differently Levinas's attack on Heidegger in *Totality and Infinity*. Levinas does attack Heidegger for allegedly giving priority to the knowledge of Being over the ethical relation between persons. However, it is crucial to understand that this is not the point at which Levinas's criticisms of Heidegger's philosophy begin. They begin long before this in Levinas's own interpretations of Being and of human being designed to counter, to argue against, and to displace Heidegger's interpretations of Being and of human being in *Being and Time*.[29] Levinas's criticisms of Heidegger begin, then, within his own philosophical project, which is a different, an other, and in every sense a rival interpretation of Being and of human being. They begin within Levinas's own philosophical project of interpreting otherwise than Heidegger's phenomenological ontology, and they culminate in Levinas's insistence, arguing against Heidegger's version of first philosophy, that it is not the knowledge of Being, but ethics—meaning our responsibility for the other person—that is the true subject of first philosophy.[30]

Levinas's attack upon Heidegger should not lead us to overlook the debt Levinas owes to Heidegger. Levinas proclaims the priority of ethics over ontology because he has found the ethical dimension in human being, and he finds the ethical dimension in human being because Heidegger has taught him to look there, has shown him the resources phenomenology has within itself for describing Being and human being. Yet this should not lead us to overlook the fact that Levinas is always arguing against and interpreting otherwise than Heidegger in order to create a different, an other philosophy, an ethical philosophy. Levinas does find ethics in human existence, but he interprets its significance differently than Heidegger and insists that ethics, and not the meaning of Being, is that which should govern and direct all thought, is that which should always be given priority. Levinas's rhetoric against Heidegger's philosophy must be seen as a moment in his own highly rhetorical philosophy, as a step in his own philosophical project: insisting that ethics is not a branch of philosophy, but first philosophy. This is exactly what I have attempted to do in the third chapter, entitled "The Challenge of Ethics as First Philosophy."

Levinas's interpreting otherwise than Heidegger results, then, in his demand that the process of knowing and the quest for truth be directed by the ethical sense or orientation in but beyond Being. This ethical sense that Levinas claims to find in the intersubjective relation enables him to insist that ethics is first philosophy. The concluding two chapters consider the significance of the ethical sense in the intersubjective relation and the consequent claim by Levinas that ethics is first philosophy, first for religious thought, in chapter 4, then for contemporary philosophy itself, in chapter 5. Both are attempts to evaluate the meaning and the significance of Levinas's ethical philosophy for contemporary thought.

This work as a whole attends, then, not only to the question of how Levinas develops his ethical philosophy by interpreting otherwise than Heidegger, but also to the question of the meaning and the significance of the philosophy Levinas develops. As I have already stated, Levinas's philosophy is a constant arguing against and an interpreting otherwise than Heidegger so as to propose alternative interpretations and to construct an alternative philosophy, an ethical philosophy. As such, it is a highly rhetorical philosophy. One of the characteristics of a rhetorical philosophy is that its meaning should never be studied apart from its method, and vice versa. This is why I have found it absolutely necessary to attend both to Levinas's method and to the meaning of the philosophy he develops in this way.

I had, in fact, been warned not to let my methodological concerns obscure the meaning of what Levinas is saying. Charles Reed wrote his dissertation on Levinas's methodology only to decide that "the question of method is simply the wrong entrance into Levinas's thought. Methodology can never discover why Levinas induces trembling in those who read him."[31] Levinas's philosophy is designed, as Derrida has said, to make us tremble because it is not merely trying to explain something to us.[32] Rather, it is trying to argue against something and to argue for something else. It is trying to get us to rearrange our priorities in a certain way, trying to compel us to commit ourselves to something—our ethical responsibility for the other person. "One doesn't respect a text," says Levinas, "if it doesn't solicit one."[33] Levinas *is* trying to solicit us; his arguing against Heidegger is in the service of arguing for ethics as first philosophy. Steven Smith testifies to the undeniably rhetorical nature of Levinas's philosophy: "it is precisely to the problematic appreciation of rhetoric that Levinas makes a great contribution, for his entire philosophy is deliberately and self-consciously rhetorical."[34] Thus, to attend to the way in which Levinas constructs his highly rhetorical philosophy, to ask how the rhetoric proceeds, without attending to the meaning of the rhetoric, without asking what the rhetoric is directed toward, without asking what the rhetoric is meant to bring about, would not only be to fail to understand Levinas's philosophy. It would also be to fail to do it justice.

In interpreting Levinas's philosophy, I have also attended to the facts of his personal history. In doing so, I have followed not only my own belief that texts and ideas are deeply rooted in a world, in a certain place and in a certain history, but also Levinas's own notion that the task of the critic is not to repeat the words of the text, but is to link the text to the real history of the person who created it.[35] Consequently, in interpreting his philosophy I have borne in mind that Levinas, this Jewish prophet of ethical responsibility for the other person, witnessed firsthand the violation of the Other in the Holocaust. Had he not been a French soldier, and had the Nazis discovered his Jewish identity, he himself perhaps would not have survived the war. While Levinas was spending the war at hard labor in a German prisoner of war camp, nearly every member of his family in his native Lithuania was murdered in concentration camps.[36] During the same time, his Jewish wife sought refuge in certain convents in France and survived only because those who protected her saw their own responsibility in the naked and vulnerable face of the stranger.

Levinas's philosophy is based on a description of an ideal situation wherein responsibility for the Other is recognized. Yet Levinas is no idealist. He knows that every intersubjective encounter is not one of realized responsibility and peace. His early phenomenological descriptions of the "horror of being," "night," "insomnia," "fear of being," etc., illustrate this clearly.[37] In fact, I contend that Levinas's ideal accounts of the intersubjective relation not only recognize relations of violence and oppression, but that relations of violence and oppression are always in the background of Levinas's discourse. The Holocaust and the other horrors of the twentieth century Levinas refers to must be understood, I contend, as the constant background noise from which emerges the appeal of the Other, which founds ethics: "Don't kill me."[38] It is, in fact, this background noise, the history of violence to the Other, that fuels Levinas's rhetoric and gives it such a sense of urgency and such rhetorical force that, as Derrida and Reed observe, it makes us tremble.

By interpreting Levinas's philosophy in relation to his world and his history, I have heard these voices, have heard this background noise. That I am not the first to have done so is confirmed by Jean Greisch's belief that Levinas's thinking in *Totality and Infinity* "is entirely dominated by the problem of violence."[39]

Levinas's close friend, Maurice Blanchot, provides further insight into how one particular epiphany of violence, the Holocaust, casts its shadow over Levinas's thought: "How can one philosophize after Auschwitz? It is this thought that traverses the whole of Levinas's philosophy and that he proposes to us without saying it."[40] Whether I have interpreted Levinas correctly by hearing this background noise and these voices within the night of insomnia Levinas describes, or have simply imagined things in the darkness, I must let the reader decide.

I am fully aware that the way of access to Levinas's philosophy that I have chosen—its relation to Heidegger and the method and the meaning of Levinas's own philosophical project—is not the only way to approach Levinas. There are others, and they are perhaps just as valid, just as necessary. One could study Levinas's relation to the Bible and to the Talmud, or his relation to his Eastern European background, or his relation to other great Jewish philosophers who have influenced him profoundly—Herman Cohen, Franz Rosenzweig, Martin Buber. I look forward to lengthy analyses of Levinas's philosophy from all these different angles, for they all very much still need to be undertaken. I make no claim for the ultimacy of my approach. More modestly, I believe that by thinking Levinas and Heidegger together, I have made more clear how Levinas's philosophy is related to the philosophy that came before it, and I have also explicated the challenge Levinas's philosophy presents to philosophy now and to philosophy yet to come. By doing so, I hope to clarify what Levinas means by ethics as first philosophy and why he insists that this is the best way to philosophize responsibly at the end of philosophy and in the shadow of the Holocaust.

Part I

Interpreting Otherwise than Heidegger

Levinas's Interpretation of Being

> All civilizations which accept Being, the tragic despair of which it consists and the crimes it justifies, merit the name of barbarian.
> —*Emmanuel Levinas*

> If at the beginning our reflections are in large measure inspired by the philosophy of Martin Heidegger, where we find the concept of ontology and of the relationship which man sustains with Being, they are also governed by a profound need to leave the climate of that philosophy, and by the conviction that we cannot leave it for a philosophy that would be pre-Heideggerian.
> —*Emmanuel Levinas*

By the time Emmanuel Levinas embarked upon his own unique philosophy with the publication of "De l'evasion" in 1935,[1] he had already secured a reputation as an astute expositor of the phenomenology of Edmund Husserl and the phenomenological ontology of Martin Heidegger.[2] The different versions of phenomenology offered first by Husserl, then by Heidegger, provided the impetus for Levinas's own philosophical project. Levinas has always insisted, in fact, that his philosophy, from the earliest to the most recent, follows in the phenomenological tradition of his two great mentors, Husserl and Heidegger.[3] Thus, to understand Levinas's philosophy, it is necessary to understand its relationship to these two giants of early phenomenology.

Jacques Derrida was one of the first to attempt to explicate the relationship between Levinas's work and the work of Husserl and Heidegger. In his "Violence and Metaphysics: An Essay on the Thought of Emmanuel Levinas," Derrida states that ". . . Levinas, uncomfortably situated in the difference between Husserl and Heidegger—and, indeed, by virtue of the history of his thought—always criticizes the one in a style and according to a scheme borrowed from the other . . ."[4] To believe this assertion that Levinas is uncomfortably situated in the difference between Husserl and Heidegger is to misconceive both the genesis and the development of Levinas's philosophy. Levinas's early work on Husserl and Heidegger makes it clear that, rather than being in the difference between the two, Levinas's own philosophy will follow Heidegger in rebelling against Husserl's phenomenology of pure consciousness.

By focusing attention on Levinas's dissertation thesis, *The Theory of Intuition in Husserl's Phenomenology*, I shall show that Levinas sees the primary value of Husserl's transcendental phenomenology in the fact that it lays the foundation for Heidegger's phenomenological ontology. It is clear that Levinas views Heidegger as Husserl's true heir and logical successor in that Heidegger has correctly grasped what is essential in Husserlian phenomenology and, just as importantly, has correctly cast aside that which must be cast aside if the true potential of phenomenology is to be fulfilled. Levinas, in fact, very directly parts from Husserl in the same places and for the same reasons that Heidegger does, and he indicates very clearly that his own phenomenology will follow not Husserl's phenomenology of pure consciousness, but Heidegger's phenomenological ontology. Thus, far from situating himself uncomfortably between Husserl and Heidegger, Levinas quite clearly situates himself alongside of Heidegger, and it is there that he grows uncomfortable.

This insight into how Levinas's philosophy is related both to Husserl and to Heidegger will enable us to comprehend more fully the genesis and development of Levinas's philosophy as phenomenology. From the very beginning of his own independent philosophical productions, Levinas is not doing phenomenology as defined by Husserl nearly as much as he is offering an interpretation of the meaning of Being after the manner of Heidegger's *Being and Time*.[5] Levinas's early works, "De l'evasion," *Existence and Existents* and *Time and the Other*, make it clear that he develops his own unique phenomenology of the meaning of Being and of human existence in constant dialogue with phenomenology in its Heideggerian rather than in its Husserlian form. Contra Derrida, I hope to make it evident that to understand Levinas's philosophy correctly, one must realize that from the point at which Levinas parts with Husserl's transcendental phenomenology in the company of Heidegger, his phenomenology is a constant attempt to interpret the meaning of Being differently from Heidegger. In other words, far from being between Husserl and Heidegger, Levinas's philosophy is a constant attempt to answer differently and in his own way distinctively Heideggerian questions.[6]

Levinas on Husserl via Heidegger

In 1928 Emmanuel Levinas journeyed from France to Freiburg to study phenomenology with the movement's founder, Edmund Husserl. From the two semesters he spent at Frieburg, he produced an article reviewing Husserl's philosophy entitled "Sur *Les Ideen* de M. E. Husserl" in 1929,[7] a co-translation of Husserl's

Cartesian Meditations in 1931, and his doctoral thesis in 1930. Although Levinas audited two of Husserl's courses and became personally acquainted with his teacher during his two semesters at Freiburg, it was actually Levinas's confrontation with a book that most profoundly influenced him during his stay at Freiburg. The book was written not by Husserl, but by his most celebrated younger colleague, Martin Heidegger, and it was the book Levinas came to regard as one of the four or five finest works in the entire history of philosophy—*Being and Time*.[8]

1928–29 was a year of transition at Freiburg. Husserl had retired, but he still taught, and he had recommended for his chair of philosophy his most brilliant assistant and younger colleague, Martin Heidegger, apparently in the hope that this might induce Heidegger to construct his own phenomenology in a more strictly Husserlian fashion than heretofore.[9] Indebted as Heidegger readily admitted he was to Husserl, by 1928 he had already exhibited a stubborn independence from Husserl's phenomenology which Husserl seems to have underestimated. Even as early as 1919–20, Heidegger was teaching courses in which he took phenomenology in a decidedly un-Husserlian direction.[10] In 1927 Heidegger published *Being and Time*, which took phenomenology further along in that direction. Husserl apparently did not fully realize this when he recommended Heidegger, but only a few months after Heidegger assumed the chair in the fall of 1928, the split between the two professors became much wider, especially as Husserl studied *Being and Time* more closely.[11] Heidegger's sure and serious departures from Husserlian phenomenology must certainly have rankled Husserl, especially because he viewed his own philosophical productions as merely laying the foundations for an exact and scientific philosophy that depended for its realization on the meticulous and determined efforts of his collaborators.[12] The differences between Husserl and Heidegger are also made evident by the difficulty they experienced in collaborating on an article for the *Encyclopedia Britannica* on the definition of phenomenology.[13]

Such was the uneasy situation that Levinas entered in 1928. He could not but have felt the growing tension between Husserl and Heidegger over the future direction of phenomenology, and this tension is evident in *The Theory of Intuition*. Andre Orianne suggests that since the differences between Husserl and Heidegger had not yet become fully apparent by 1928, "it was difficult (if not at times impossible) to separate, in what Levinas had learned in Freiburg, Husserl's own teachings from Heidegger's interpretation of them."[14] There is, however, no evidence in Levinas's text to support this contention.[15] It seems much more plausible that *The Theory of Intuition* includes both Husserlian and Heideggerian perspectives not because Levinas was confused about which teachings were Husserl's and which Heidegger's, but because the book was written out of and cognizant of the growing tension between the two over the true value of phenomenology's past and the direction of its future. Indeed, rather than being a confusing mixture of Husserl's and Heidegger's perspectives, *The Theory of Intuition* is a clear presentation of Husserl's phenomenology involving an obvious polemic. Levinas desires to demonstrate not only that Husserl's phenomenology is not nearly so opposed to Heidegger's investigation of Being as it may appear, but also that it actually lays the important groundwork for Heidegger's phenomenological ontology. It is, however, necessary for us to examine more closely the phenomenology of both Husserl and Heidegger in order to understand more clearly how and why Levinas presents Husserl's transcendental phenomenology as a precursor and foundation to Heidegger's ontological project.

Heidegger dedicated *Being and Time* to Husserl "in friendship and admiration," and at the end of his introduction he declares that "the following investigation would not have been possible if the ground had not been prepared by Edmund Husserl, with whose *Logische Untersuchungen* phenomenology first emerged."[16] Yet he never mentions Husserl again except in footnotes, and even in the passage cited above, he is quick to assert his independence from him by stating that the value of phenomenology is in its potential, not in the way in which it has thus far been actualized by Husserl.[17] He also states that phenomenology is a method to be employed, not a set of doctrines to which one is obligated to subscribe,[18] and he makes it clear that what he is doing in *Being and Time* is very different from what Husserl is doing in his phenomenology: "it is one thing . . . to tell about entities, it is quite another to graps entities in their being."[19]

It is, of course, the question of the meaning of Being that Heidegger wishes to explore in *Being and Time*. That he takes this project to be something quite other than Husserl's idea of phenomenology is apparent when he criticizes Husserl's phenomenology for circumventing the question of Being.[20] Heidegger certainly also has Husserl (among many others) in mind when he says that the question of the meaning of Being "has become quite forgotten" in philosophy.[21] Indeed, in Quentin Lauer's view, Heidegger thought Husserl was ". . . concerned only with that which is, not at all with Being, with the true, not at all with the truth."[22] Heidegger's investigation of the meaning of Being is, at least on the surface, so different from Husserl's phenomenology that Gilbert Ryle, one of the first reviewers of *Being and Time*, went so far as to say that Heidegger's project was certainly not what Husserl meant by phenomenology, and perhaps it wasn't even phenomenology at all.[23]

What, then, did Husserl mean by phenomenology? Doubtless Husserl regarded phenomenology primarily as a scientific methodology aimed at "the things themselves."[24] This does not mean, however, that phenomenology according to Husserl should be concerned with proving the existence of things. In fact, the prospect of proving the existence of things outside the self was for Husserl extremely problematic. How can it ever be proven that things outside of us actually do exist? This uncertainty was particularly troublesome to Husserl because he thought that any philosophy that involved uncertainty did not merit the name of philosophy.[25] His goal was to create a philosophy based upon that which was absolutely certain, so that philosophy "will be able to represent itself as science."[26] Thus, as Descartes had done before him, Husserl sought as the foundation of his phenomenology that which could not be doubted. Obviously, Husserl's phenomenology as strict science had to be something quite other than an investigation of the nature of the thing-out-there as it is in itself.

Husserl found the absolutely certain foundation for which he was searching in consciousness. We cannot be certain that the thing-out-there actually exists, but we are certain that we have consciousness of a thing-out-there. Like Descartes, Husserl identified the *cogito,* or the consciousness, as that of which we can be absolutely certain. Unlike Descartes, however, Husserl did not stop there. He maintained that we can be certain not only that we have consciousness, but also that we have consciousness of something. That every act of consciousness is always consciousness of something is what Husserl means by the *intentionality of consciousness.* Paul Ricoeur has pointed to intentionality as the "great discovery" of Husserlian phenomenology, i.e., "the priority of consciousness of something over self-consciousness."[27] Husserl presented his theory of intentionality in his *Logical Investigations*[28] and in his *Ideas Pertaining to a Pure Phenomenology and to a Phenomenological Philosophy.*[29] As he says in *Ideas,* "universally it belongs to the essence of every actional cogito to be consciousness of something."[30] Thus, as Levinas says, intentionality for Husserl is not just one property of subjects, but is "what makes up the very subjectivity of subjects."[31]

If for Husserl phenomenology must be based on the absolutely certain, and if the only thing we are certain of is that consciousness is always consciousness of something, then great care must be taken to ensure that that of which we cannot be certain does not corrupt the absolute validity of the phenomenological method. This is the point behind the series of reductions Husserl introduces in *Ideas*. The importance of the reductions in Husserlian phenomenology has led Alfonso Lingis to describe *Ideas* as Husserl's "great manifesto."[32] The reductions are so vital because they are the means by which he ensures that phenomenology stays within the realm of absolute certainty.

The eidetic reduction, for example, reduces consciousness of something to that aspect of perception of which we can be certain by defining as the essence of something not what it is in itself, but rather our mental construction of it. The essence of a tree, to use Husserl's own example, is not the thing in nature, the existence of which we cannot prove and which may be here today but burn down tomorrow.[33] Rather, the essence of a tree is the concept of "treeness" that we have in our minds and which is an aspect of our consciousness as consciousness of something. Thus, intentionality is the intuition not of things in themselves but of essences, and it is not dependent for its validity on the actual existence of the things themselves:

> Positing of and, to begin with, intuitive seizing upon, essences implies not the slightest positing of any individual factual existence; pure eidetic truths contain not the slightest assertion about matters of fact.[34]

This leads to the more fundamental reduction that Husserl terms the phenomenological *epoche*. The existence of the world outside consciousness, the thing-out-there, is, as we have seen, quite problematic for Husserl.

Consequently, theses concerning the existence of the thing-out-there as it is in itself are excluded, are put in parentheses, are not included in the project of phenomenology. The word Husserl chooses to express this phenomenological reduction, *epoche,* means to refrain from voicing an opinion, and this is exactly the attitude Husserl maintains toward the world outside of consciousness:

> We put out of action the general positing which belongs to the essence of the natural attitude; we parenthesize everything which that positing encompasses with respect to being: thus the whole natural world which is continually "there for us," "on hand," and which will always remain there according to consciousness as an "actuality" even if we choose to parenthesize it.
>
> If I do that, as I can with complete freedom, then I am not negating this "world" as though I were a sophist; I am not doubting its factual being as though I were a skeptic; rather I am exercising the "phenomenological" epoche which also completely shuts me off from any judgment about spatiotemporal factual being.[35]

The phenomenological epoche enables Husserl to restrict his phenomenological analyses to that about which we can be absolutely certain. As Ricoeur puts it, the epoche ensures "the conquest of an empire of sense from which any question concerning things-in-themselves is excluded."[36] By excluding the question of things-in-themselves, Husserl aims to explore what really is the true region of his phenomenology because it is what he takes as absolute—the existence of consciousness:

> . . . Consciousness has, in itself, a being of its own which in its own absolute essence, is not touched by the phenomenological exclusion. It therefore remains as the "phenomenological residuum," as a region of being which is of essential necessity quite unique and which can indeeed become the field of a science of a novel kind: phenomenology.[37]

Thus, via the phenomenological epoche Husserlian phenomenology achieves the return to pure consciousness, which is, according to Husserl, what all philosophy seeks.[38] And because it restricts itself to consciousness, phenomenology is the one science that is absolutely certain and, thus is able to criticize all other sciences. Phenomenology is, in fact, according to Husserl, "the secret longing of the whole philosophy of modern times"[39] because it has for its foundation the absolute certainty of consciousness.

If Husserl restricts phenomenology to the study of consciousness and its intentionality, then Heidegger's project of uncovering the meaning of Being—in what he calls fundamental ontology—would seem to constitute a radical departure from Husserlian phenomenology.[40] It seems quite reasonable to wonder, with Ryle, just how *Being and Time* can claim to be in the tradition of Husserlian phenomenology, or how it can claim to be phenomenological at all. Yet this is precisely the problem Levinas endeavors to solve in *The Theory of Intuition*.[41] Levinas attempts to show not only that Heidegger's *Being and Time* deserves the title of phenomenology, but even that in taking phenomenology as a methodology for his own ontological project of the analysis of Being, Heidegger is still loyal to the most fundamental meaning of Husserlian phenomenology. Levinas attempts to demonstrate not only that Heidegger's ontology is phenomenological, but that even despite the many ways in which Heidegger's project is different from Husserlian phenomenology, yet it "is to some extent only its continuation."[42]

But in what way is Heidegger's ontology a continuation of Husserl's phenomenology? Levinas asserts that Husserl's phenomenology is itself an ontology, a theory of Being, and this ties together Husserlian phenomenology and Heideggerian phenomenological ontology.[43] According to Levinas, Husserl's notion of intentionality means that a conscious subject is not something that first exists and then relates to things-out-there, but that its interaction with things comprises its very being: "A subject is a being which, inasmuch as it exists, is already in the presence of the world, and this is what consitutes its very being."[44] Hence, the phenomenological *epoche* is crucial to Husserlian phenomenology because it enables us to obtain that "philosophical residuum,"[45] i.e., consciousness, which is "a region of being"[46] and "absolute being."[47] Levinas asserts that ". . . the reduction has an absolute value for Husserl; he wants thereby to return to absolute being . . ."[48] As Husserl himself says in *Ideas*, by means of the phenomenological epoche, "we have excluded the whole world but have won the whole of absolute Being."[49]

Levinas's point is clear: Husserl's phenomenology is at its heart actually an ontology, a study of Being. As Theodore De Boer puts it, for Levinas "Husserlian phenomenology is to be understood as a new form of ontology."[50] More than, this, however, Levinas argues that by revealing consciousness as absolute Being, there is in Husserlian phenomenology, for the first time, the "possibility of passing from and through the theory of knowledge to the theory of being."[51] The ultimate question Husserl raises in his phenomenology as it is presented by Levinas concerns the nature of Being, and as Levinas points out, this "is an ontological problem in the very precise sense that Heidegger gives to this term."[52] That Husserl himself perhaps did not view his own phenomenology as divorced from ontology can be seen in one concession he made to Heidegger in his attempt to find some common ground with him when the two were collaborating on the *Encyclopedia Britannica* article. In one version of this article, Husserl defines phenomenology as "universal eidetic ontology."[53]

Perhaps it is the disagreement between Husserl and Heidegger over this defining of phenomenology that best clarifies Levinas's contention that Heidegger's ontology is a step through and not around Husserlian phenomenology. In his reply to a draft of Husserl's version of the article, Heidegger agreed with his mentor that the world is constituted in consciousness and that this constitutes human being: ". . . the kind of being which {*Dasein*} is shelters right within it the possibility of transcendental consciousness."[54] Thus, Heidegger got from Husserl the fact that whatever else we can say about human being, or *Dasein*, we can say that it contains the possibility of transcendental consciousness.

Here the most fundamental difference between Husserl and Heidegger becomes apparent. For Husserl, because he restricts himself to what is absolutely certain, the fact that *Dasein* includes the possibility of transcendental consciousness is both the beginning and the end of what we know of the being of *Dasein*. For Heidegger, on the other hand, this is only the first revelation of *Dasein*. As Quentin Lauer says, Heidegger maintains contra Husserl that "consciousness does not constitute Being but is simply the means Being has to reveal itself. Thus, to speak of Being is to speak of an activity whereby what is reveals itself to and in consciousness."[55] In *Being and Time*, Heidegger wishes to explore the other ways in which *Dasein* reveals itself to consciousness over and beyond the fact that *Dasein* constitutes the world in consciousness.[56] Thus, Heidegger agrees with Husserl that the world is constituted in consciousness and that this reveals something about the nature of *Dasein*,[57] but he asks the further question: ". . . what is the kind of being of the entity in which the world is constituted? That is the central problem of *Being and Time*—i.e., a fundamental ontology of *Dasein*."[58]

Levinas expresses a crucial insight when he says that "knowledge of Heidegger's starting point may allow us to better understand Husserl's end point."[59] Husserl and Heidegger are different in that Heidegger begins where Husserl ends, but this also makes them similar, for Heidegger begins his phenomenological ontology in Husserl's "universal eidetic ontology." This allows

Levinas to assert that despite the many differences between Husserl's phenomenology and Heidegger's ontology, the latter is to some extent only the continuation of the former.[60]

Perhaps we can now appreciate more profoundly the significance of Levinas's *The Theory of Intuition in Husserl's Phenomenology* for Levinas's own philosophical project. By demonstrating that at its foundations Husserl's phenomenology is itself an ontology that serves as the basis for Heidegger's phenomenological ontology, Levinas makes evident his own belief that Heidegger is the true heir of and rightful successor to Husserl. Levinas thereby declares that the future of phenomenology lies in the interpretation of Being as it is opened up by Heidegger.

Because this is so, Levinas asserts that his task is to present Husserl's phenomenology as a "living" and "changing" philosophy, which entails that he do more than merely present Husserl's arguments.[61] Rather, he must immerse himself in Husserl's phenomenology and "philosophize" in his own right.[62] Levinas leaves little doubt in *The Theory of Intuition* that he intends to philosophize beyond Husserl's transcendental phenomenology toward and after the manner of the phenomenological ontology of Heidegger.

One can see this clearly by analyzing Levinas's primary criticism of Husserl's phenomenology—that it reaches only theoretical consciousness and, thus, that this is the only being it is capable of revealing:

> . . . for Husserl, being is correlative to theoretical intuitive life, to the evidence of an objectifying act. This is why the Husserlian concept of intuition is tainted with intellectualism and is possibly too narrow. None of Husserl's attempts to introduce into the constitution of being categories which do not come from theoretical life succeeds in suppressing the primacy or the universality of the theoretical attitude.[63]

Because of the primacy of the phenomenological

epoche, Husserlian phenomenology can reveal only a truncated version of human being, one that focuses on the relation of cognition between human being and the world that it constitutes in consciousness at the expense of all other ways in which this relation may manifest itself: "Is our main attitude toward reality that of theoretical contemplation? Is not the world presented in its very being as a center of action, as a field of activity or of care—to speak the language of Martin Heidegger?"[64] The cost of the phenomenological reduction, according to Levinas, is that life is approached only in its cognitive aspect: "The phenomenological reduction has no other goal than to present us with our genuine self, although it presents it only to a purely contemplative and theoretical sight which considers life but is distinct from it."[65] Thus, Husserlian phenomenology in its quest for certainty divorces itself from the fullness of life, the fullness of human being. For Husserl, says Levinas, "philosophy begins with the reduction. This is an act in which we consider life in all its concreteness but no longer live it."[66]

Levinas makes it clear in *The Theory of Intuition* that the true follower of Husserl will follow the master in explicating the meaning of Being, for this according to Levinas is Husserl's essential problem: "'Was besagt dass Gegenstandlichkeit sei'" is . . . the essential problem raised by phenomenology of consciousness."[67] Levinas also makes it clear, however, that the true follower of Husserl will pursue Husserl's question of the meaning of being in a way that is not hampered or limited by the strictures resulting from Husserl's own excessive theoreticism. Only the one who analyzes human being in all its fullness and not merely in its cognitive aspect, only the one who takes seriously human being's rootedness in time and in history,[68] only the one who tackles the existence of human being as it is actually lived, is really raising in its most comprehensive and profound sense the question of the meaning of Being. Levinas states quite clearly who is doing this: "Only Heidegger dares to face this problem deliberately."[69]

Levinas uses the word "deliberately" to point to Heidegger's purposeful rejection of Husserl's phenomenological reduction—which prevents Husserl from pursuing Heidegger's central question, "What is the kind of being of the entity in which the world is constituted?"—in favor of a phenomenological ontology which makes the question of the meaning of Being in all its fullness the sole problem of first philosophy. Levinas thereby unequivocably declares his philosophical allegiance beyond Husserl to Heidegger. He also thereby gives a strong indication that his own phenomenology will be a grappling with the problem of Being and of the being of *Dasein* in its fullness after the manner in which it is attempted by Heidegger in *Being and Time*.[70] As I shall attempt to show, Levinas's own philosophy is both a heavy borrowing from Heidegger's philosophy and also a constant argument against it.

Reading Otherwise than Heidegger—"De l'evasion"

Levinas's 1935 article, "De l'evasion," supports our contention that his philosophy is both heavily indebted to *Being and Time* and also is an attempt to offer a distinctively different answer to Heidegger's problematic of the meaning of being. He begins his article as Heidegger begins *Being and Time*, by criticizing traditional philosophy for basing its conception of being on the "image of being that things offer to us"[71] From this we are led to consider as *being* that which exists, and the fact that things *are* gives birth to the distinction between the perfect and the imperfect. This leads to a "struggle for a better being,"[72] to a preoccupation with an infinite and supreme Being. For Heidegger, this tendency results in philsophy's continually falling back into metaphysics so that the question of the meaning of Being becomes both distorted and actually forgotten.[73] Levinas, too, in substantial agreement with Heidegger, states that Western philosophy has never gone beyond the mistaken notion of being that it derives from the existence of things, and he condemns philosophy for having as its "only preoccupation" the transcendence of finite being embodied in its image of infinite Being.[74] Thus, at the beginning of "De l'evasion" Levinas criticizes or, to use Heidegger's phrase, "destroys" the history of ontology in the same manner and on the same basis as Heidegger. More than this, however, Levinas does this for the same reason and with the same intention as Heidegger: he hopes to raise again "the ancient problem of being as being as such."[75]

Levinas makes it clear that he believes the way to explore the question of the meaning of being is to offer phenomenological descriptions of human existence, which is exactly the solution Heidegger proposes with his "existential analytic of *Dasein,*" or human being in the world.[76] Here Levinas also makes it clear, even in this brief and only suggestive initial essay, that his philosophy will not be merely a repetition of or supplementary to the interpretation of being Heidegger offers through his analysis of *Dasein.* Rather, it becomes obvious here (and more obvious still in his subsequent works, as we shall see) that though it asks the same question and has the same goal as Heidegger's philosophy, Levinas's philosophy will interpret human existence differently from the way Heidegger does in *Being and Time* and, accordingly, will offer distinctively different interpretations of the meaning of being.

That Levinas is both engaged in a Heideggerian project and is at the same time arguing against Heidegger is expressed in the very title of "De l'evasion." Levinas posits here that a fundamental characteristic of human being is its need to escape from being. On the surface this appears to be merely an echo of Heidegger, for Heidegger asserts that fleeing from Being is one of the most fundamental characteristics of *Dasein*. However, it must be pointed out that *Dasein's* fleeing from Being involves for Heidegger his belief that *Dasein* loses itself and its own possibilities for its own authentic existence in its immersion in the world, in the inauthentic sociality Heidegger calls the *they*. Thus, *Dasein*'s fleeing of Being is a fleeing from its own being, from its own *Dasein*: "*Dasein*'s absorption in the 'they' and its absorption in the world of its concern, make manifest something like a fleeing of *Dasein* in the face of itself—as an authentic potentiality-for-Being-its-Self."[77] Also, since for Heidegger *Dasein*'s fleeing means its fleeing from its possibilities to achieve its own authentic being, the aspect of its being which *Dasein* flees most is its death, for death is "that possibility which is its ownmost, which is nonrelational, and which is not to be outstripped."[78] In other words, death constitutes *Dasein*'s greatest opportunity to come to terms with its self and to realize its authentic self as Being-towards-death, and this is why *Dasein* flees death in fleeing its own being: ". . . proximally and for the most part *Dasein* covers up its ownmost Being-towards-death, fleeing in the face of it."[79]

This fleeing of *Dasein* from itself is explicitly not what Levinas means by the escape from Being. He insists that the escape has absolutely nothing to do with death,[80] because the escape Levinas describes is not the escape of the self from itself, from its own potentiality for being, but rather is the self's escape from Being itself, from Being in general. For Levinas, the self does not initially find in Being potentialities for itself either to actualize or to escape from. What the self finds in Being, according to Levinas, is its weight, the heaviness of Being that weighs upon the self and enchains the self to itself. "It is exactly that there is weight in Being that the escape turns away from."[81] Thus, the escape Levinas describes is not from death or from the self, as in Heidegger, but from Being itself. Alfonso Lingis has also noticed how Levinas's interpretation of the escape from being argues against Heidegger's interpretation while borrowing Heidegger's language:

> If our existence has the form of concern, it is first a concern over the being with which one finds oneself affected—and not a concern over the possible nothingness. There is then also in the core of an existent a nostalgia for escape. If our existence is ecstatic and self transcending, it is not so in the pursuit of being, but in a flight from being.[82]

In turning away from the weight of being upon the self, the self also turns away from its self. It is important to notice, however, that for Levinas the self flees itself not in the sense that it flees its possibilities, but that it flees itself as it actually *is*, as that which feels the weight of Being upon it. Levinas makes it clear that this is different than Heidegger's notion of *Dasein* fleeing itself. The following passage is typical of how Levinas treats his relationship to Heidegger in "De l'evasion"; although Heidegger is not mentioned by name, the references to him are unmistakable:

> The need for escape . . . appears . . . as an imprisonment in which it is a matter of getting out. This is identity . . . In the identity of the self, the identity of being reveals its nature of enchainment by which it appears under the form of suffering and invites escape. Also, the escape is the need to leave itself, which is to say to break the most radical, the most irremisible enchainment, the fact that the self is itself.
>
> . . . The self which wants to get out of itself does not flee from itself as a limited being. It is not the fact that life is choice and by consequence sacrifice of numerous possibilities which will never be realized which incites the escape . . . The escape . . . aspires to break the enchainment of the self to one's self. It is being itself, the itself, which it flees from and not at all its limitations. In the escape the self flees not that which is opposed to the infinite which it is not or which it will not become, but in fact even what it is and what it will be.[83]

For Levinas the escape is from what the self is, rather than only from what it may become. The analysis of the escape, then, is a better way to explore and interpret being as such than the way of Heidegger's existential analytic of *Dasein*'s potentiality. Levinas thinks that in the need to escape from being one can get at the pure phenomenon of being as being. As he says, "the need to escape . . . conducts us to the heart of philosophy. It permits us to renew the ancient problem of the being of being as such."[84]

The fact that the self experiences being as a weight from which it needs to escape leads Levinas to interpret several phenomena that Heidegger either overlooks or, in Levinas's view, misinterprets. The phenomena he analyzes in "De l'evasion" include *need, malaise, pleasure, shame* and *nausea*.

Levinas says that *need* has always been considered by philosophy and psychology as a lack in a finite being. The self experiences need because it is finite; it lacks that which is possessed by the infinite, and it is this lack or insufficiency in the self that characterizes need. Quite to the contrary, Levinas describes need not as a lack but as a fullness, as the plenitude of the self that is its constant presence to itself. The self's plenitude, which is the basis of need, is experienced most acutely in suffering. In fact, "need does not become imperious until it becomes suffering."[85] Suffering makes the constant presence of the self to itself insufferable, and one looks for a way out, an escape from one's self, from the plenitude of one's being. Thus, Levinas maintains that need is not the result of a lack in a finite being, but results from the suffering borne by the self constantly present to itself. Need for Levinas is not the self's need to perfect itself, but its need to escape from itself: "It appears as though at the basis of need there is not a lack of being, but to the contrary a plenitude. Need is not directed toward the total accomplishment of a limited being, toward satisfaction, but toward deliverance and escape."[86]

According to Levinas, "the specific mode of suffering which characterizes need is malaise."[87] Levinas uses the term *malaise* to express the restless state of the self. In malaise, the self refuses to stay still and makes a constant effort to escape itself. In malaise, this effort is made without the self knowing where it is to go; in this is an ignorant effort by the self to get out of itself and its enchainment to being, "and this ignorance qualifies the very essence of this effort."[88]

Even in its state of malaise, however, the self can catch a momentary glimpse of the way out of its enchainment to being and to itself. In this glimpse, the self abandons itself, departs from itself in an ephemeral ecstasy, the moment of pleasure: "We contend in pleasure there is an abandonment, a loss of one's self, an escape outside of one's self, an ecstasy. . . . Far from appearing like a passive state, pleasure opens into the satisfaction of need a dimension where malaise glimpses escape."[89]

In *pleasure* the self glimpses the way out of being, but the glimpse is exactly that, merely a glimpse, a momentary relief; the return of the weight of being is inexorable. Thus, pleasure is "an escape which fails."[90] The meaning of pleasure's failure to escape, adds Levinas, "is underscored by shame."[91]

Levinas attempts to define *shame* beyond its moral implications. In nudity, for example, we are not necessarily ashamed of our bodies; the boxer and the ballet dancer are not ashamed of their bodies even though they are not covered with many clothes. Thus, it is not the mere fact of nakedness, but the intimate presence of ourselves to ourselves that is shameful. The failed attempt at escape that constitutes pleasure renders the self even more consciously aware of itself and of its enchainment to being. The fall from pleasure and into shame results from a heightened realization of the impossibility of escape. Thus, what is driven home to us in shame is not our nothingness, but the fullness of our being enchained to being, "the totality of our existence."[92] Shame, then, discovers the self becoming more aware of its being, its weight, and its irremisible presence to itself. As Levinas says, "that which shame discovers is being discovering itself."[93] What being discovers about its own being is its inescapable presence to itself: "That which appears in shame is then precisely the fact of being riveted to itself, the radical impossibility of fleeing to hide itself, the irremisible presence of the self to itself."[94]

The fact of the self riveted to its being and to the weight of being which bears on it constitutes, according to Levinas, the anxiety he expresses by the word *nausea*. Nausea is similar to Heidegger's *Geworfenheit* in that it is the anxious realization that we are thrown into being without anyone having asked us if we wished to be there or having told us where we are going. Levinas's concept of nausea, however, conveys more desperation than Heidegger's *Geworfenheit*, because in nausea the self feels not only that it did not choose its own being,[95] but that the weight of being constantly bears down so that the self needs an escape from being, an escape it can never realize:

> There is in nausea a refusal to stay, an effort to leave. But this effort is already and always characterized as despair . . . And this despair, this fact of being riveted to itself constitutes all the anxiety of nausea. In nausea, which is an impossibility of being what one is, one is at the same time riveted to one's self, inserted in a narrow circle which chokes. One is there, and there is nothing else you can do about it, nothing to add to the fact that we have been brought here entirely, that all is consummated: it is the actual experience of pure being, which we have announced since the beginning of this work. But this "there is nothing to do" attitude is the mark of a limit situation where the inutility of all action is precisely the indication of the supreme instant where there is nothing to do but to get out. The experience of pure being is at the same time the experience of its internal antagonism and the escape which imposes itself.[96]

The fact that Levinas posits the self as weighted down by its own being and by the heaviness of being in general leads him to two fundamental questions: 1) What is the relationship or distinction between being in general and the being of the self? 2) Is there a way to escape from or to pass beyond being? Both of these questions are fundamental to the philosophy Levinas develops by arguing against Heidegger's interpretation of being, and we can now see him moving tentatively toward suggesting solutions that he will work out more fully and will eventually declare quite stentorially in his later works.

The question of the relation between being in general and the being of the self becomes the primary concern of Levinas's next work, *Existence and Existents.* In this work Levinas gives full expression to notions that are only hinted at suggestively in "De l'evasion." Apparently, in 1935 he had not yet developed his concept of the *there is* (*il y a*), which is so crucial to his later philosophy. Although this prevented Levinas from being able to present fully and clearly in "De l'evasion" the relationship between being in general and the being of the self, it is important to note that seminal notions concerning this issue are already present, though in a nascent state.

For example, there is a distinction between the weight of being in general and that which it weighs upon, i.e., the being of the self, which is itself heavy. Despite this distinction, Levinas also points to "the dialectical impossibility" of conceiving the beginning of being. For Levinas, the beginning of being is the moment when being accepts its weight, but this entails that being already exists before its beginning because it already has weight before it is accepted. This "paradox of being" is the "impossibility of dissociating that which accepts the weight of being from the weight itself."[97] Clearly, Levinas is on the way to discussing the emergence of human being from being in general as the solution to the origin of its being, but in "De l'evasion" the issue remains a paradox because he has not yet developed his notion of impersonal being in general, the *there is*, which as we shall see, makes the issue so much more clear in *Existence and Existents*.

The point that is crucial for our purposes is that, even as early as"De l 'evasion," Levinas does not posit as the beginning of the self something like Heidegger's notion of the self projecting itself ahead of itself and actualizing its own potentialities. This is to see the beginning of *Dasein* as active, whereas for Levinas it is essentially passive; the self accepts what it already is, i.e., heavy, that which has weight. The way human being begins is not by actualizing its potential, but is by accepting the weight of being upon itself.

The acceptance of the weight of being leads Levinas to his next question: Is there a way out of or beyond being? It is Levinas's fundamental point in this article that the self has a need to escape being. But can this need ever be fulfilled, or will it always be frustrated? Levinas certainly does not answer this question definitively, but he does point in a certain direction, and we must determine this direction as we follow Levinas beyond "De l'evasion" to his later writings.

Levinas makes it quite clear that the way out of and beyond being must be sought, for merely to accept being as it is is to silence the voices that cry out from and that oppose the violence and cruelty within being: "All civilizations which accept being, the tragic despair of which it consists and the crimes which it justifies, merit the name of barbarian."[98] Levinas points to idealism as the tradition that rises above barbarism in insisting upon going beyond being. He states clearly just how vital and necessary this is when he insists that "in the aspiration of idealism . . . incontestably consists the value of European civilization."[99] However, the problem with idealism is that it goes beyond being by forgetting being, by not taking it seriously. Idealism constantly underestimates the significance of being. Thus, Levinas in "De l'evasion" is left searching for a way out of and beyond being that is true to idealism's aspirations, but avoids idealism's great fault of denigrating concrete being. Levinas is looking for a way to escape from being that is rooted in being itself: "The only path which opens itself from here on in to give satisfaction to the legitimate exigencies of idealism without, however, entering into its error, is to measure all the weight of being in its universality . . ."[100]

Levinas does not explain how it is possible to escape being by measuring the weight of being in "De l'evasion." He says only that this "involves leaving being by a new path," and one can follow this path only by risking the reversal of "certain notions which to the common sense and to the wisdom of many nations seem the most evident."[101] What this "new path" is, and what notions it reverses, are questions that Levinas raises but does not answer in this article. This work leads us to expect, however, that whatever this "new path" is, it will both resemble and be quite other than Heidegger's existential analytic of *Dasein* and his interpretation of Being. Levinas's next work, *Existence and Existents*, confirms this expectation.

EXISTENCE AND EXISTENTS

Existence and Existents appeared in 1947, although Levinas began to conceive it before the war and wrote it while held captive by the Germans between 1940 and 1945. It is, as he says in the preface, only a preparatory work, and many of the themes it introduces are presented much more completely and boldly in his 1961 work, *Totality and Infinity*. *Existence and Existents* is, however, crucial to the understanding of how Levinas develops his philosophy as a direct response to Heideggerian ontology.

In *Existence and Existents,* Levinas states quite clearly

his ambivalent attitude toward Heidegger's philosophy. He sees great value in Heidegger's return to the question of being qua being, and in his critique of Western philosophy as a forgetting of being itself in favor of an investigation of a supreme Being, or a cause of being. Thus, for Levinas, Heidegger showed philosophy where it had gone wrong and pointed to that which it must rediscover, its true area of exploration—being qua being, being not as noun, but as verb. Levinas agrees with Heidegger about the difficulty of this, and about the necessity of it:

> It is as though thought becomes dizzy pouring over the emptiness of the verb to exist, which we seem not to be able to say anything about, which only becomes intelligible in its participle, the existent, that which exists. Thought slips imperceptibly from the notion of Being qua Being, that by virtue of which an existing being exists, to the idea of a cause of existence, a "being in General," a God whose essence will indeed contain existence, but which will nonetheless be "a being," and not the deed, activity, pure event or work, of Being. This latter will be understood in confusion with beings.[102]

In the introduction to *Existence and Existents*, Levinas states quite clearly that his interpretation of "the idea of Being in general" has ensued "from certain positions of contemporary ontology which have made possible the renewal of the philosophical problematic."[103] Thus, for Levinas, Heidegger has renewed philosophy, given it new life and a new direction, and this is why Levinas now claims that his own philosophy is "in large measure inspired by the philosophy of Martin Heidegger."[104]

Inspired as he is by Heidegger's ontology, Levinas is certainly no disciple. As we have seen, by the time he wrote *Existence and Existents*, he had already in "De l'evasion" done something very different from Heidegger's project in stressing the need to escape the weight of being. Yet, in "De l'evasion" his relationship to Heidegger is unmentioned. In *Existence and Existents*, to the contrary, he expresses it quite clearly. His own philosophy is actually an attempt to escape Heideggerian philosophy:

> If at the beginning our reflections are in large measure inspired by the philosophy of Martin Heidegger, where we find the concept of ontology and of the relationship which man sustains with Being, they are also governed by a profound need to leave the climate of that philosophy, and by the conviction that we cannot leave it for a philosophy that would be pre-Heideggerian.[105]

The most fundamental way in which *Existence and Existents* is an attempt to escape Heideggerian ontology is in the way it approaches the question of being. Heidegger's investigation into the meaning of Being in general (*Sein*) quickly becomes the existential analytic of human being-in-the-world, or *Dasein*, because it is through *Dasein* that Being reveals itself and is comprehended. In fact, "understanding of Being is itself a definite characteristic of *Dasein*'s Being."[106] According to George Steiner, *Dasein*'s uniqueness and its privilege over all other being consists in the fact that ". . . man is the one being who questions Being—not only does question Being, but must question Being."[107] Human being, then, quickly becomes the focus of Heidegger's study of Being in general, and what it yields of Being in general is *via* the relation between *Dasein* and Being in general, which according to Levinas is presented in *Being and Time* as primarily one of comprehension.

In "De l'evasion," on the contrary, the relation between the being of the self and being in general is not primarily cognitive. The being of the self does not comprehend being in general as much as it feels its weight and the need to escape from it. In *Existence and Existents*, Levinas expands on this notion to show that the best way to interpret being is to focus on the relationship between the being of the self and being in general. What Levinas intends to explore is not *Dasein*'s comprehension of being, but the very fact that *Dasein* emerges out of the being that precedes it. It is the being's, or the existent's, emergence out of Being itself that is the primary concern of *Existence and Existents*. For Levinas, the central question is not, what does *Dasein* comprehend about its own being and being in general; rather, it is the more fundamental question concerning the emergence of being out of Being, "the meaning of the fact that in Being there are beings."[108]

This is certainly a different way to approach the question of the meaning of Being than Heidegger's existential analytic of *Dasein*, but this should not lead us to overlook the fact that the possibility and the terms of this approach are provided by Heidegger in *Being and Time*. Heidegger, too, posits the existence of Being before the existence of *Dasein*. One of the fundamental characteristics of *Dasein* is that it is thrown into a world that preexists it. The existence of *Dasein* may be necessary for there to be any comprehension of Being, since Being manifests itself only to and through *Dasein*, but the existence of *Dasein* is not necessary for there to be Being. Being is what exists before *Dasein* goes about its work of comprehending it. Being is also that which *Dasein* is thrown into, so before *Dasein* comprehends, it, it is there. Before it gives itself, it already is.

The Being that is there before *Dasein* is thrown into it, and before it gives itself to *Dasein* in comprehension, it revealed by Heidegger's concept of *Geworfenheit*.[109] The fact that Being preexists beings is not nearly as important to Heidegger as is the event of Being giving itself over to the comprehension of *Dasein*. However, the Being that exists before *Dasein* comprehends it is exactly Levinas's focus in *Existence and Existents*, because this is precisely the Being from which beings emerge. This Being is uncharted territory, which it will be Levinas's purpose to explore, but still it is very important to recognize that it is discovered by Heidegger.

Levinas insists that the being that is before human comprehension of it must be presented in impersonal terms. It is the mere fact of being, the fact that there is something. Even if one conceives of the end of everything, there is still an anonymous, shapeless something, a something that is, "which murmurs in the depths of nothingness."[110] Levinas chooses the term *il y a, there is,* to denote the anonymous, impersonal Being that exists before *Dasein* comes to be, that exists before it gives itself to *Dasein.*

The *there is* is different from Heidegger's notion of Being precisely because it does not yield itself and show itself to human being in the way that Being shows itself to *Dasein* in Heidegger. As Levinas and many others have pointed out, the anonymous and impersonal *il y a* is meant to contrast with and to contradict Heidegger's notion of *es gibt, that which gives itself.*[111] Heidegger's notion connotes a fundamental generosity, "a primordial gushing forth,"[112] a donation of Being to the comprehension of *Dasein. Il y a,* the impersonality of Being, on the other hand, means that Being does not initially give itself to human being, but that it *is* before it gives. Before it gives, one does not know what it is, but one knows that it is:

> "There is," in general, without it mattering what there is, without our being able to fix a substantive to this term. "There is" is an impersonal form, like in it rains or it is warm. Its anonymity is essential. The mind does not find itself faced with an apprehended exterior. The exterior—if one insists on the term—remains uncorrelated with an interior. It is no longer given. It is no longer a world. What we call the I is itself submerged by the night; invaded, depersonalized, stifled by it. The disappearance of all things and of the I leaves what cannot disappear, the sheer fact of being in which one participates, whether one wants to or not, without having taken an initiative, anonymously. Being remains like a field of forces, like a heavy atmosphere belonging to no one.[113]

The night is the image Levinas chooses to express the impersonality of the *there is*. In the darkness of the night, one lies awake, unable to sleep. In the night one can see and identify nothing, but one hears something, some something, without being able to say what it is. One experiences nothing in particular, just something, just anonymity, the experience of pure duration. In insomnia, the consciousness is present to itself as conscious of something it is not, some something out there, but which it cannot identify. Something is present to consciousness in an absent form, present without identifying itself. It reveals that it *is*, not *what* it is, but the fact that it is is as present to the consciousness as the consciousness is to itself. In the night, there is the consciousness and something else. Thus, in insomnia, says Levinas, it is not only the self, but the night itself, that watches and waits and rustles within the stillness.[114]

The *there is* does not give itself to be comprehended in the light of day, but rather is a constant, anonymous, nocturnal presence that menaces. By going beyond that aspect of being that reveals itself to *Dasein*—and, thus, is always given over to *Dasein*, so that its essential characteristic becomes "mineness" (*Jemeinigkeit*)[115]—Levinas explores the being that is not only external to us, but, because it does not give itself over to comprehension, never becomes ours. The *there is* does not give itself to human being, but invades it as a foreign power: "Being is alien and strikes at us."[116]

Because Levinas depicts being as essentially alien to the emerging human being, he offers an analysis of fear that is very different from the analysis of fear in *Being and Time*. In the Heideggerian analysis of fear, every instance of fear is "fearing about," and "'fearing about' is 'being afraid for oneself.'"[117] As Heidegger says, "That which fear fears about is that very entity which is afraid—*Dasein*."[118] Since for Heidegger the basic relation between Being in general and *Dasein* is one of comprehension and, consequently, givenness, mineness, every fear is fear about that which is mine, my *Dasein*. Even the fear for the other person is actually a form of fear about my *Dasein*, a "being-afraid-for-onself. Here what one is apprehensive about is one's Being-with the other, who might be torn away from me."[119]

For Levinas, quite to the contrary, because he posits the basic relationship between *Dasein* and being in general as one of exteriority, fear about one's own being is posterior to the fear of being. The most significant aspect of fear for Levinas is not that it makes evident *Dasein*'s concern for, and anxiety about, its self, but that in Being there is something that evokes fear, something about which one is fearful. Fear of being, rather than fear about one's own being, means that one is anxious about one's own being not because human being is finite, but because there is something in being that is threatening. Levinas does not disagree with Heidegger in his insistence that *Dasein* fears for itself, but he tries to explicate what he takes as the more primordial phenomenon, that aspect in Being which is frightening. Anxiety over one's own *Dasein* and its eventual coming to an end can only be because there is first something horrible about being. Horror *of* being is before fear *for* being.[120]

Thus, by the impersonality of the *there is*, Levinas makes the first manifestation of Being an event not of revelation and givenness, but one of separation. The dawning of consciousness is the dawning of the realization of the separation and distance between the being that the self is and the being outside the self. For Levinas, the self is constituted in and by this fact of separation from the *there is*, Being itself. The formation of a being occurs within Being itself, as the rupture of Being itself as it breaks up into beings. This rupture is the very fact that consciousness becomes aware of its separation from Being itself. This consciousness of separation is the awakening of consciousness, the "very upsurge of consciousness against the amorphous *il y a*."[121]

The rupture of Being into beings *via* consciousness of separation opens up for Levinas a region of phenomena to be interpreted otherwise than Heidegger. Whereas for Heidegger *Dasein* is already and always constituted by its immersion in the world so that *Dasein* is always Being-in-the-world, Levinas emphasizes the fact that human being always finds itself separated and at a distance from the world. It is because human being is at the same time already and always its own being and not identical to Being itself, that human being is not only in the world, as Heidegger insists, but is always related to the world "across a distance."[122]

Levinas gives to this event in being, whereby a being emerges out of Being itself and establishes itself across a distance from Being itself, the name of *hypostasis*. Through this *hypostasis*, a position in being is established, and this involves work and effort on the part of a being establishing itself: ". . . being is never inherited but always won in the heat of struggle."[123] A being must struggle not only against the weight of being, but also against itself, in that it must take up the weight of, and the responsibility for, its own being. There is, then, in a being's effort to establish itself over against being itself, an inevitable labor and a contract with oneself. There is gravity and weight within the effort of a being to establish itself not because, as Heidegger thinks, the being has not chosen itself, but because the effort of a being to emerge from being has itself a certain weight, a certain seriousness. This effort is precisely that—effort or labor—not a game or a dream, and it involves an irrevocable commitment to oneself, an enchainment to one's own work of establishing oneself. The being that emerges from Being feels itself as a weight and an encumbrance to itself. Its work of being is always heavy, because the being is always riveted to itself and to its work of being. In freedom from being there is already and always responsibility for being: "A free being alone is responsible, that is, already not free. A being capable of beginning in the present is alone encumbered with itself."[124]

Because Levinas depicts the emergence of a being from being itself as involving labor and effort, he is then led to describe those mental states in which the weight of this effort is felt most acutely. Indolence and fatigue, for example, must be redefined beyond their moral implications as a response on the part of a being to the weight of being. Labor involves a condemnation to continue effort, and the state out of which effort is continued is fatigue. Fatigue involves the recoil before the labor of existence, the moment of hesitation, the "time-lag" before the work of existence is taken up once again. In fatigue there is a heavy reminder of the commitment to the work of existence and, consequently, a desire to escape the work. The aversion to the work of existence constitutes indolence: to be weary of being oneself.[125]

Levinas's analysis of human being as it emerges from Being involves another fundamental difference from Heidegger in that Levinas points to this as the way in which every existent comes to be. This effort is, in fact, what it means to be an existent, and even though this is universal, Levinas insists that it doesn't entail a fall. For Heidegger, on the contrary, the process by which *Dasein* actualizes itself, becomes itself, is quite different. Heidegger begins not with a being who emerges from Being itself, but with *Dasein* that gets lost in the negative collectivity he terms the *they-self.* The initial state of *Dasein* is, for Heidegger, inauthenticity: "*Dasein*'s facticity is such that as long as it remains what it is, *Dasein* remains in the throw, and is sucked into the turbulence of the 'they's' inauthenticity."[126] *Dasein*'s lostness in the *they* constitutes its fallenness; *Dasein* has lost its hold upon itself and its own possibilities and potential for its own authenticity:

> To *Dasein*'s state of Being belongs falling. Proximally and for the most part *Dasein* is lost in its world. Its understanding, as a projection upon possibilities of Being, has diverted itself thither. Its absorption in the they signifies that it is dominated by the way things are publicly interpreted. That which has been uncovered and disclosed stands in a mode in which it has been disguised and closed by idle talk, curiosity, and ambiguity.[127]

Thus, *Dasein* achieves itself or actualizes itself not simply by emerging from Being, but by retrieving itself from its lostness in the *they* by resolutely individualizing itself, which enables *Dasein* to actualize its authentic possibilities. As De Boer points out, *Dasein* can retrieve itself from its fallenness and come to comprehend itself truly only within "the solitude of authentic existence."[128]

Levinas's process of self-actualization is contrary to Heidegger's because Levinas refuses to designate the basic state of human being as fallenness. In fact, as the counterpart to Heidegger's notion of *fallenness* and *inauthenticity* as the basic state of *Dasein,* Levinas posits what he terms the *sincerity* of aspects of life which, though commonplace, have a positive meaning and significance. In the following passage, for example, Heidegger is never mentioned, but it is quite obvious against whom Levinas is arguing:

> . . . in the ontological adventure the world is an episode which, far from deserving to be called a fall, has its own equilibrium, harmony and positive function: the possibility of extracting oneself from anonymous being. At the very moment when the world seems to break up we still take it seriously and still perform reasonable acts and undertakings; the condemned man still drinks his glass of rum. To call it everyday and condemn it as inauthentic is to fail to recognize the sincerity of hunger and thirst.[129]

Levinas's notion of the *sincerity,* rather than the fallenness or inauthenticity of life, leads him to interpret otherwise than does Heidegger the basic relationship between human being and the world—and, most importantly, the relationship between human beings.

When Levinas interprets the relationship between human being and the things or objects it encounters in the world, he is clearly arguing against Heidegger's designation of the things *Dasein* encounters in the world, as *tools* or *equipment* (*Zeug*).[130] Things or objects are for Heidegger "that with which one has to do in one's concernful dealings . . . We shall call these entities which we encounter in concern equipment."[131] Heidegger describes the being such tools possess as *readiness-to-hand* (*Zuhandenheit*), meaning "readiness-to-be-used," because for Heidegger it is their ability to be used or manipulated that determines their being: "Equipment is essentially something-in-order-to. . . . A totality of equipment is constituted by various ways of the 'in-order-to,' such as serviceability, conduciveness, usability, manipulability."[132] Levinas, on the other hand, wants to explicate the sincerity of everyday life by pointing to those things in the world whose being cannot be expressed merely by indicating their utilitarian character. "Not everything that is given in the world," says Levinas, "is a tool,"[133] i.e., can be reduced to their "readiness-to-hand, to their readiness-to-be-used."

Levinas argues that things in the world provide for beings much more than their utilitarian character. In fact, Levinas makes the point that things enable existents to make a home for themselves in being. Levinas expresses his disagreement with Heidegger on this point by the word he chooses to refer to things in the world, a word that clearly counters and argues against Heidegger's *Zeug*. Levinas chooses the word *meubles*: furnishings, belongings, personal property. Alfonso Lingis has seen how this word argues against Heidegger's interpretation: "For Levinas, Being-in-the-world does not reduce to Being-among-things. . . . Then for Levinas not the concept of *Zeug*, implement, but that of *meuble*—"movable goods," furnishing—names the ontological essence of things."[134]

Levinas demonstrates that the essence of things is not expressed simply by their utilitarian character through the *meubles* he chooses to explicate: shelter, clothing and food. The being of a home can never be fully expressed by the mere fact that it is used as shelter, for a home gives to a person so much more than protection from the weather. This is expressed by that old, sexist, but still revelatory saying, "a man's home is his castle." Clothing, too, has a much deeper aspect to its being than its merely utilitarian quality: "To say that clothing exists for covering oneself up is not to see how clothing frees man from the humbleness of his naked state."[135] Food, too, does more than merely keep us alive, for, according to Levinas, it also represents a desire that can be satisfied. Food, thus, represents the satiation to be found in life.

Levinas presents shelter, clothing, and food to show that human life in the world possesses always and already a natural sincerity, an innate region of meaningful being that Heidegger overlooks. Levinas implies that it is because Heidegger thinks *Dasein*'s basic state is fallen and inauthentic that he reduces the being of things in the world to their merely utilitarian character. Levinas argues that thereby Heidegger misses out on the meaning, as he puts it, the sincerity that life already contains, even before *Dasein* begins actualizing its own potentialities.

Levinas also makes the point that Heidegger's concepts of fallenness and inauthenticity lead him to misconceive our relationship with others, or the social relation. At first, it may appear as though Heidegger is immune to this charge, for in *Being and Time* he posits that a basic state of *Dasein* is that it already and always is Being-With-Others (*Mitseinandersein*) so that *Dasein* already and always possesses understanding of others: "Being-With is such that the disclosedness of the *Dasein*-With of others belongs to it; this means that because

Dasein's Being is Being-With, its understanding of Being already implies its understanding of others."[136] By insisting that, as Being-With, "Dasein is essentially for the sake of Others,"[137] Heidegger attempts to offer a view of sociality more primordial and fundamental than one based upon empathy. As he says, "only on the basis of Being-With does empathy become possible."[138] Thus, Heidegger seems to be well protected against Levinas's charge that *Being and Time* presents an inadequate view of the social relation.

However, Levinas's argument is not with the understanding of the other that the self possesses, but rather with the fact that, due to Heidegger's notion of fallenness and inauthenticity, his analysis of authentic sociality takes as its subject solitary *Dasein*: ". . . in Heidegger sociality is completely found in the solitary subject. The analysis of *Dasein*, in its authentic form, is carried out in terms of solitude."[139] Levinas refers to the very blatant fact that in *Being and Time*, sociality is almost exclusively presented as an aspect of *Dasein*'s fallenness, and solitude is presented as the way whereby *Dasein* can achieve authenticity. For Heidegger, *Dasein*'s inherent aspect of Being-With is what gets it in trouble; *Dasein* becomes lost in the inauthentic potentialities for itself that the social collectivity, the *they*, presents to it. It is only by turning away from the *they* and by turning to itself *via* a process of individuation that *Dasein* has any hope of achieving authenticity:

> . . . *Dasein* knows what it is itself capable of, inasmuch as it has either projected itself upon possibilities of its own or has been so absorbed in the "they" that it has let such possibilities be presented to it by the way in which the "they" has publicly interpreted things. The presenting of these possibilities, however, is made possible existentially through the fact that *Dasein*, as a Being-With which understands, can listen to others. Losing itself in the publicness and the idle talk of the "they," it fails to hear its own Self in listening to the they-self.

> If *Dasein* is to be able to get brought back from this lostness of failing to hear itself, and if this is to be done through itself, then it must first be able to find itself—to find itself as something which has failed to hear itself, and which fails to hear itself in that it listens away to the "they."[140]

Heidegger clearly presents the choice between the inauthenticity of the *they-self* and the authenticity of one's own individual self as an either/or: "As something that understands, *Dasein* can understand itself in terms of the world and others or in terms of its ownmost potentiality for being."[141] Clearly, in Heidegger the way to authenticity is the way away from sociality, which is primarily a polluting and distorting influence, and toward solitude and invidualization: ". . . individualization brings *Dasein* back from its falling, and makes manifest to it that authenticity and inauthenticity are possibilities of its own being."[142] This is why Levinas says in Heidegger authentic *Dasein* is informed primarily by solitude rather than by the social relation. According to Levinas, as much as Heidegger retrieves the pre-Socratics, this places Heidegger in the Platonic tradition, which posits a "silent dialogue of the soul with itself."[143]

Levinas, in rejecting Heidegger's notion of fallenness and inauthenticity, also rejects Heidegger's analysis of sociality, which Levinas describes as a "collectivity of comrades." Levinas interprets sociality explicitly otherwise than Heidegger does—i.e, in terms of the solitude of the self—in favor of analyzing the relation between the self and the other. He labels this relation the *I-you collectivity*. Again, Levinas seeks to get beyond the distinction between authenticity and inauthenticity, beyond the level in which *Dasein* can be said to be fallen, to the more primordial state in which a being first emerges from Being and encounters other beings: He seeks to uncover "the fearful face-to-face situation of a relationship without intermediary, without mediation."[144]

In this primordial relation, the self experiences the other not only as an other self, but also as a self entirely different from the self: "The other as other is not only an alter ego. He is what I am not."[145] Levinas finds in the social relation not the authenticity or inauthenticity of the self, but the primordial experience of the self before it can be said to be fallen: the self encounters the genuinely other. The Other does not merely have other qualities than the self has; the Other is itself the quality of otherness. In the social relation the self encounters and is encountered by the otherness of the Other, the very fact of alterity itself. Heidegger might have realized this fact, but in assuming that the basic state of *Dasein* is fallen, he sees the importance of the social relation to lie in the fact that it helps or hinders *Dasein* in its solitary task of actualizing its own possibilities. Quite to the contrary, Levinas insists that the importance of the social relation consists in the more primordial fact that the self encounters and is encountered by the Other.

Levinas suggests that the otherness of the Other is experienced most acutely in the erotic relationship. Even in this, the most intimate of all relationships, the otherness of the Other does not disappear. Levinas insists that love is not fusion; even the loved one remains other, and this constitutes for Levinas the "pathos" of love. Even the most intimate embrace is still the embrace of two people who remain separate, no matter how great is their desire to be one. In love, the "absence of the other is precisely his presence qua other."[146]

Eros is absolutely central for Levinas's philosophy. Not only does it show that even the beloved cannot truly be made into the self, but even more importantly, in eros the other shows him/herself openly to the self. The beloved reveals him/herself to the lover even to the depths of his/her otherness, and this eros moves the lover out of him/herself to embrace the beloved in his/her nakedness and otherness. The lover realizes that in eros there is a power capable of transporting the self beyond him/herself to the beloved who is other. Thus, "it is in eros that transcendence can be conceived as something radical, which brings to the ego caught up in being, ineluctably returning to itself, something else than this return, can free it of its shadow."[147]

Here one can see that the problem of *Existence and Existents* is also the problem of "De l'evasion," which is not only the interpretation of Being, but also the way to escape from Being. In both works, human being is portrayed as irretrievably encumbered with and enchained to the weight of its own being. By showing the emergence of beings from Being, *Existence and Existents* has not changed but deepened and expanded the basic interpretation of being provided in "De l'evasion." In "De l'evasion," Levinas stresses the need for escape from being and states that if this is possible at all, it must be by some mysterious "new path." In *Existence and Existents*, he refers to this escape from the weight of being as *salvation* and *liberation*. How this liberation is procured he doesn't say, but he does say that what is necessary for liberation from the weight of being are "time and the other".[148] Levinas gives us a clue as to what he means by this in his analysis of eros as the radicality of transcendence, but to explain how time and the other constitute liberation from being is not the purpose of *Existence and Existents*. This matter, he says, will be the concern of his next work, appropriately entitled *Time and the Other*.

Time and the Other

Time and the Other, published in 1947 and following closely on the heels of *Existence and Existents*, reiterates many of the themes of the earlier works. The *there is, hypostasis, solitude, the weight of being, salvation, eros*—all reappear in *Time and the Other*. In this work, however, Levinas does make much more evident how he is developing his philosophy by arguing against Heidegger. He also begins to elaborate his own interpretation of time, and, more importantly for our purposes now, he adds certain significant nuances to his interpretation of being that enable him to criticize *Being and time* at a still more fundamental level.

The *there is,* for instance, is interpreted in the manner of *Existence and Existents.* It is this presence in absence that remains even if we imagine the destruction of everything. Thus, the *there is* is the pure verb of existing from which existents emerge, and it is characterized by its anonymity. What he does in *Time and the Other* that is new is to show how this idea of an impersonal existence that precedes the existent is a logical conclusion drawn from Heidegger's notion of *Geworfenheit,* or being-thrown-into existence. This entails he says, an existence independent of the existent, which must already be for the existent to be thrown into it. Also, since the existent comes to be after that which it is thrown into, the existent can never entirely become the master of existence.

Levinas, then, concludes from this the need to escape, which, as we have seen, is so central to his philosophy: "It is precisely because of this that there is desertion and abandonment."[149] As we have seen, Heidegger did not himself deduce this from *Geworfenheit,* and he did not interpret what he termed "fleeing" in this way. This passage is particularly interesting not because it changes Levinas's interpretation of the *there is,* but because here Levinas makes much more obvious than he usually does how his interpretation of the meaning of being both borrows heavily from Heidegger, while constantly arguing against him.

In *Time and the Other,* Levinas also makes more distinct his notion of *solitude* as opposed to Heidegger's notion of solitude. In fact, he states quite clearly that he intends to interpret solitude in an un-Heideggerian fashion: ". . . from the start I repudiate the Heideggerian conception that views solitude in the midst of a prior relationship with the other."[150] He thereby denies Heidegger's contention that solitude is realized by the individual *Dasein* who, as always already Being-With, has been summoned by the call of his/her individualized conscience back from lostness in the *they* and, by this process of individualization, has also realized that his/her authenticity lies in solitude rather than in a negative sociality. Levinas calls this revelation of solitude that the individualized *Dasein* experiences a "privileged experience,"[151] and he advances instead his definition of solitude, which is a universal, rather than a particular, experience. For Levinas, solitude is the very fact of the relationship the self has with itself before it has a relationship with the Other, "the indissoluble unity between the existent and its work of existing."[152] The Other does not bring solitude to the self, but the self is itself solitary in its work of existing. The essence of solitude resides in the fact that already and always

> . . . I am not the other. I am all alone. It is thus the being in me, the fact that I exist, my existing, that constitutes the absolutely intransitive element, something without intentionality or relationship. One can exchange everything between beings except existing. In this sense, to be is to be isolated by existing. Inasmuch as I am, I am a monad.[153]

Levinas's contention that the self is constituted by solitude leads him to criticize again—and this time more explicitly—Heidegger's notion of sociality. Levinas protests that though the relationship with the Other is part of the very constitution of *Dasein,* the social relation plays "no role in the drama of being" by which *Dasein* actualizes itself.[154] "All the analyses of *Being and Time,*" says Levinas, "are worked out either for the sake of the impersonality of the everyday life," in which the social relation is portrayed as playing only a negative role, "or for the sake of solitary *Dasein*," in which the bad influence of the social relation is to be avoided. Even if it be admitted that the authentic possibilities *Dasein* achieves by listening to itself must necessarily come from the Other since *Dasein* is already and always Being-with, this doesn't change the fact that the social relation itself is presented so negatively in *Being and Time*. However, Levinas makes it clear that he wishes to do more than to counter Heidegger's portrayal of the social relation as fundamentally negative and deleterious. Rather, his attack on Heidegger is even more radical: he also wants to analyze the social relation at a deeper level than can be characterized as Being-with: "it is not the preposition *mit* that should describe the original relationship with the other."[155]

Here Levinas's most basic challenge to Heidegger's philosophy is revealed. If the social relation is interpreted in terms of individual *Dasein*, the social relation involves the understanding that the self already and always possesses of the Other, because the self knows the other as another self. Thus, from the standpoint of individual *Dasein*, the being of every human being already and always entails an understanding of the Other. *Dasein* is *Dasein-mit*. Hence Levinas's complaint that "it is in terms of solitude that the analysis of *Dasein* in its authentic form is pursued."[156] However, if the analysis of *Dasein* is done from the standpoint of the social relation itself—which is exactly what is not done in *Being and Time*, even though the notion of Being-with makes it appear to be so—then the preunderstanding the self has of the Other is subordinate to the social relationship itself. It is not that the self is entirely without preunderstanding of the other, for Levinas admits that the other is alter ego, but that it is more than alter ego.

If the focus of the analysis is not on individualized *Dasein*, but on the social relation itself, then the fundamental phenomenon that the social relation reveals always bursts through and expands and exceeds this preunderstanding, revealing it as nothing compared to the mystery of the Other. The fundamental fact revealed in the social relation is that "the Other as Other is not only an alter ego: the Other is what I myself am not."[157] Thus, the social relation is a relation not with what is known, but rather with what is refractory to all knowledge: "the relation with the other is a relationship with a Mystery. The other's entire being is constituted by its exteriority, or rather its alterity."[158]

Thus, Levinas in *Time and the Other* criticizes Heidegger on an even more fundamental level than heretofore. It is not only that Heidegger overlooks the need to escape from Being, or that he describes Being-in the-world and Being-with-others incorrectly because of his notion of "fallenness" and "inauthenticity." Levinas agrees with Heidegger that the question philosophy should pursue concerns the meaning of being, but he also makes it clear that Heidegger's most fundamental and, hence, most crucial error is his assumption that this question can best be answered by conceiving of *Dasein* in terms of solitude. It is, rather, in the analysis of the social relation, the self's encounter with the Other, that the question of the meaning of being can best be answered.

Of course for Levinas, as we have seen, the question of the meaning of being involves the way to escape from being. In "De l'evasion" this way is a "new path," and in *Existence and Existents* we are told that "time and the Other" are necessary for liberation from being. *Time and the Other* presents the social relation as a relation with a mystery, and it hints that perhaps the self can escape being by its relation to this mystery, the otherness of the Other. To understand how this is so, we must turn to Levinas's later works, especially *Totality and Infinity*. However, according to *Existence and Existents*, time is also necessary for the liberation from being.

In *Time and the Other,* Levinas deepens his criticism of Heidegger through his interpretation of time. It is, then, to Levinas's interpretation of time, which he develops by borrowing from but also constantly arguing against Heidegger's *Being and Time,* that we must now turn.

CHAPTER TWO

Levinas's Interpretation of Time

> It is not the finitide of Being that constitutes the essence of time, as Heidegger thinks, but its infinity.
> —*Emmanuel Levinas*

> Time is not the achievement of an isolated and lone subject, but . . . is the very relationship of the subject with the other.
> —*Emmanuel Levinas*

When Heidegger in *Being and Time* turned to the explication of the meaning of Being via the existential analytic of *Dasein,* he was compelled to also raise the question of the meaning of time. The interpretation of Being, Heidegger maintained, is inseparable from the interpretation of time: "the central problematic of all ontology is rooted in the phenomenon of time."[1]

In *Being and Time,* Heidegger presents two fundamental reasons why ontology, or an interpretation of the meaning of Being, must also involve an interpretation of the meaning of time: 1) *Dasein* is intrinsically temporal, is inscribed in time, and thus has time as its very structure; and 2) *Dasein* always conceives of Being in terms of and through time: "whenever *Dasein* understands and interprets Being, it does so with time as its standpoint."[2] Thus, Being and time are for Heidegger so inextricably linked together that he announces as the "provisional aim" of *Being and Time* "the interpretation of time as the possible horizon for any understanding whatsoever of Being."[3]

In situating himself within Heidegger's problematic of the meaning of Being, by raising the ontological question through the analysis of the existent, Levinas, like Heidegger, cannot avoid the question of time. Levinas, too, following Heidegger, will insist on the temporal nature of the existent. Indeed, Levinas's interpretation of time is a fundamental aspect of his philosophy, and it is as true of Levinas as it is of Heidegger to say that it is impossible to understand what he is saying about Being and human existence without understanding what he is saying about time.

Levinas's interpretation of time in all three of its dimensions—present, future and past—illustrates again the dialectical relationship his thought bears to the thought of his great mentor, Martin Heidegger. By carefully analyzing Levinas's interpretation of time in all three of its dimensions, we will show how he develops his interpretation of time by borrowing heavily from Heidegger while also constantly arguing against him. Thus, Levinas's interpretation of time, inseparable from his interpretation of being and of human existence, provides further support for our contention that Levinas interprets after the manner of but constantly otherwise than Heidegger.

We will analyze separately Levinas's interpretation of the three aspects of time in the order that he presents it—beginning with the present, then the future, then the past—to show how he develops each by arguing against Heidegger. It will become clear that Levinas's most fundamental objection to the way in which

Heidegger interprets time is that Heidegger interprets time through the solitary *Dasein*, whereas Levinas insists that time must be interpreted through the relationship between the subject and the Other. By interpreting time through the intersubjective relation, Levinas develops a conception of time as something other than and more than Heidegger's notion of time as the structure of finite being. Levinas attempts to show that the meaning of time is not merely in its relationship to finite being, but that time has a meaning of its own. Although Levinas agrees with Heidegger that being is in time, he concludes from his own phenomenological analysis that time itself is not circumscribed in being, that time is not merely the structure of being, that time bears a meaning beyond being. In other words, Levinas declares with Heidegger that the meaning of time must be explicated with the meaning of being, but he insists, against Heidegger, that the meaning of time is not restricted to its relation to being. As Alphonso Lingis says, despite Levinas's similarities with Heidegger, "a new analysis of time commands all of Levinas's analytic work."[4]

Levinas's reflections on time's three divisions can be separated into three clearly distinct periods of his thought. In his very earliest works, and especially in *Existence and Existents*, he interprets the present. In his middle and more mature period, initiated by *Time and the Other* and culminating in *Totality and Infinity*, he analyzes the future. Lastly, in his most recent works, especially in *Otherwise Than Being*, he is chiefly concerned with the past. It must be understood that since Levinas insists that time entails the relationship between the present moment and another, genuinely new moment, his discussion of time itself begins not with his analysis of the present in *Existence and Existents*, but only with his analysis of the future as connected to the present in *Time and the Other*. Nevertheless, to comprehend fully Levinas's concept of time, all three of time's divisions must be taken into account. Thus, we turn first to Levinas's interpretation of the present.

Levinas on the Present

Levinas's conception of the present is tied to his analysis of being, which we have already discussed. As has been shown, Levinas rejects Heidegger's analysis of *Dasein* as always and already Being-with-another and Being-in-the-world in favor of the analysis of human being at a more primordial level. Whereas Heidegger is not interested in exploring the existence that exists before human being, Levinas focuses his attention on the existence of existence before human existence, and he calls this primordial, impersonal existence the *there is*. This focus enables Levinas to describe the emergence of human being out of being in general, and from this phenomenon he derives his concept of the present.

The instant at which beings emerge from being in general Levinas defines as the *present*. Thus, "the present is the beginning of a being."[5] The instant at which beings emerge from being in general is still momentary, still bears the evanescence of an instant, but this should not trick us into thinking that the present receives its meaning only from its relatedness to other instants.[6] Levinas maintains that however instantaneous the present may be, there is still a point at which the existent becomes the subject of its own becoming. This point, this instant, is for Levinas the present. Thus, the existent has a present when its self is distinct from being in general from which it emerges, when it assumes its own being, its own substance. Levinas's term *hypostasis*, which he chooses to express the substantiality of the subject, entails that the present is that instant in which a being emerges from being, the very event through which the subject becomes a being, becomes substantive:

> The true substantiality of a subject consists in its substantivity: in the fact that there is not only, anonymously, being in general, but there are beings capable of bearing names. An instant breaks the anonymity of being in general. It is the event in which, in the play of being which is enacted without players, there arise players in existence, existents having being as an attribute. In other words, the present is the very fact that there is an existent. The present introduces into existence the preeminence, the mastery and the very virility of the substantive.[7]

The subject/being/existent that emerges from being in general not only has a present, according to Levinas, but it is also locked into its present. By being locked into its identity, which comes to it *via* its separation from being in general, a being is also locked into its present. What Levinas terms the *absolute character* of the present is the inexorable presence of the present; the subject, in being unable to escape from itself, is also unable to escape its presence to itself in the present. For Levinas, the presence of the present brings the subject inevitably back to itself because the present is an absolute presence:

> The presence of the present is due to its irremissibility, its inevitable return to itself, its inability to detach itself from itself. That is not to define the present by the present, but to catch sight of a relationship with itself in the present. The present refers only to itself, but this reference, which should have dazzled it with freedom, imprisons it in an identification. The present, free with respect to the past, but a captive of itself, breathes the gravity of being in which it is caught up. For there is a gravity in the heart of the present, despite its break with the past. The fatality which bears down upon the present does not weigh it down like heredity, and is not imposed on it because it was born without having chosen its birth. The present is pure beginning. But in its initiating contact, an instantaneous maturity invades it; it puts its pin in itself and is caught in its own game. It weighs itself. It is a being and not a dream, not a game.[8]

It is important to understand that for Levinas the existent that emerges from being in general and that is thus locked into its own being, identity, and present, is anterior to the world and, consequently, to the social relation. It is the individual being who emerges as a solitary, separate entity from being in general. At this primordial level, the only movement on the part of the solitary being is an inevitable return to itself. Levinas's images of a prisoner enchained to itself,[9] and of "a winter landscape where frozen beings are captives of themselves"[10] illustrate his notion that a being is locked into the present. This means that the initial movement of a being, before the advent of another being, can only be a return to itself and to its own present, and not an ecstatic movement out of itself toward a moment genuinely new. Thus, Levinas says,

> To the notion of an existence, where the emphasis is put on the first syllable, we are opposing the notion of a being whose very advent is a folding back upon itself, a being which, contrary to the ecstaticism of contemporary thought, is in a certain sense a substance.[11]

Here Levinas makes obvious just who and what he is arguing against. Heidegger analyzes a being not at the level at which it emerges from being in general, but only at the later level at which the existence of an existent is contemporaneous with the world and with others: *Dasein* is already and always Being-in and Being-with. Because for Heidegger the existence of a being is already and always an ecstasy, a movement outward toward the world and toward others, and since for Heidegger time is the structure of Being, Heideggerian temporality is also already and always ecstatic. The present is already and always connected to another moment, to an other's moment, which is to say that the present is already and always connected to the future. The initial movement of a being is always toward something else, toward another moment, and this ecstatic movement constitutes temporality. This is why Levinas maintains that for Heidegger the very event of existence is ecstasy.[12] For Levinas, what Heideggerian ecstatic temporality misses is the significance of the present, the point at which the existent assumes its own being and its own substance: "Modern philosophy has sacrificed for the sake of the spirituality of the subject its subjectivity, its substantiality."[13]

By beginning his analysis of being at an entirely different point—i.e., at the emergence of a being from being in general—Levinas offers an interpretation of the present that is quite consciously opposed to Heidegger's ecstatic temporality. Isolated, without a world and without others, a being emerging from being in general cannot direct itself outward out of itself and its present. The present is, in fact, according to Levinas, the very impossibility of this outward movement. Before the relation to the other person, a being has a present, but does not have a genuinely new moment. Without the Other there is nothing but the present. Since there is nothing but the present, strictly speaking there is not yet time, for time entails the relationship between the present and a genuinely new moment. Therefore, a being initially has a present without having time. As Levinas states, "the definitiveness which comes to pass in the present is not then initially connected with time: it is an intrinsic mark of the present."[14] This is why in *Existence and Existents,* which deals exclusively with the present, there is no section about time, but only one entitled, "On the Way to Time."

Thus, with Levinas's concept of the present, he makes it clear that without the relationship to the Other, a being or an existent cannot have time. For time in its full sense is constituted only as the existent breaks out of its bondage to itself and to its presence to itself and is granted the possibility of a genuinely new moment. The need to escape from being, announced in "De l'evasion," is presented in *Existence and Existents* as the need to escape from the present, which is to say, the need for time. Levinas refers to this escape from the present as a *liberation.* It is an escape and a liberation that the existent is powerless to achieve by itself. The solitary subject does not have the ability ecstatically to project him/herself toward a time beyond the present, and so does not have time. Only the Other can bring something more than the subject's present, can bring a genuinely new moment, can bring time in its full sense. This is why Levinas says that "time is not the achievement of an isolated and lone subject, but . . . is the very relationship of the subject with the other."[15] To understand how this is so and what this means, we must turn to Levinas's analysis of the future.

The Future

Levinas's discussion of time *per se* begins with *Time and the Other* (1947) and continues with *Totality and Infinity* (1961), both of which are solely preoccupied with the future. It is not, in fact, until much later, and especially in *Otherwise than Being* (1974), that he turns his attention to the past. As we have seen, Heidegger interprets time in *Being and Time* almost exclusively in terms of its futural dimension. This does not mean, however, that Levinas simply echoes Heidegger's interpretation of the future. In fact, Levinas's interpretation of time in all three of its dimensions—and especially in the dimension we are about to take up now, the future—shows clearly how Levinas develops his own unique philosophy by constantly borrowing from but arguing against Heidegger.

Heidegger's analysis of the future in *Being and Time* quickly takes him into an explication of the phenomenon of death. For Heidegger, death reveals the essence of the future and of time itself. Thus, an analysis of the future event of death is at the heart of Heidegger's interpretation of the future. Similarly, and as we would perhaps suspect by now, Levinas develops his own interpretation of the future by also interpreting the meaning of death. Levinas's treatment of death, however, is a detailed and careful polemic against the interpretation of death Heidegger proposes in *Being and Time.*[16] Levinas counters Heidegger's claim that death reveals the essence of the future and of time itself. What truly reveals this, asserts Levinas, is not death, but love. Thus, Levinas is not only echoing the Song of Songs and Franz Rosenzweig, but he is also opposing Heidegger when he argues that love is as strong as death.[17]

For Heidegger, death is the end of *Dasein.* He does not wish to engage in any speculation about life after death.[18] By restricting himself to what can be known, he defines death as the phenomenon whereby *Dasein* ends, whereby it comes to nothingness. Death is, for Heidegger, that phenomenon whereby *Dasein* becomes "no-longer-*Dasein.*"[19] Thus, Levinas says that in Heidegger death is the approach of nothingness, the end of *Dasein.*[20]

In *Being and Time,* the phenomenon of death as the end of *Dasein* is interpreted in two ways because there are two basic forms of *Dasein,* authentic *Dasein* and inauthentic *Dasein.* Authentic *Dasein* interprets death in one way, and inauthentic *Dasein* interprets it in quite another. Actually, it is more accurate to say that inauthentic *Dasein* has death interpreted *for* it in quite another way, for it is precisely this that makes *Dasein* inauthentic—that it listens to and believes the interpretation of things provided by the *they.*

In the case of death, the *they* convinces inauthentic *Dasein* that while death certainly comes to everyone some day, this day is far off in the future, so far off that it is not worth giving thought to it. Thus, the *they* convinces inauthentic *Dasein* that even the certainty of death is uncertain because it is so far away. The *they* says, "'Death certainly comes, but not right away.' With this 'but . . . ,' the 'they' denies that death is certain."[21]

The *they* convinces inauthentic *Dasein* that the only deaths that are actually real and meaningful are the deaths we actually experience and encounter all the time—the deaths of other people. Thus, death gets defined by the *they* as what happens to others, and the meaning of death as *Dasein*'s own death gets covered over. In short, *Dasein*'s death is no longer a concern, because death is either the death of someone else, or it is too far away to worry about: "One of these days one will die too, in the end; but right now it has nothing to do with us."[22] Thus, the *they* tricks inauthentic *Dasein* into thinking that it is actually facing and understanding death properly, while it is actually fleeing from the profound significance of the end of *Dasein*. This is why Heidegger says that inauthentic *Dasein* "is a constant fleeing in the face of death."[23]

Authentic *Dasein*, on the other hand, in wrenching itself away from the *they*, comes to a proper understanding of death and of itself. Thus, Heidegger's interpretation of death must be understood through the way in which death is appropriated and authentically interpreted by authentic *Dasein*. This leads to several very important interpretations of death.

First, authentic *Dasein* realizes that death is its own possibility, even that death is never completely understood until it is understood as *Dasein*'s own death. Authentic *Dasein* understands that death cannot be interpreted through the deaths of others, but only through its own death. The Heideggerian term *Jemeinigkeit, mineness*, is a constitutive characteristic of death: "by its very essence, death is in every case mine, insofar as it is at all."[24] Death is that possibility that each and every *Dasein* has to take over for itself.[25]

Secondly, since authentic *Dasein* realizes that death is its own, it sees itself as headed toward that reality. Thus, *Dasein* is Being-toward-death: ". . . just as Dasein is already its 'not-yet,' and is its 'not-yet' constantly as long as it is, it is already its end too. The 'ending' which we have in view when we speak of death, does not signify *Dasein*'s Being-at-an-end, but a Being-towards-the-end of this entity."[26] Authentic *Dasein* thereby comes to stand before itself as itself, as a being directed toward possibilities for itself, which it can actualize in the time that is its own as a Being-toward-death: "With death, *Dasein* stands before itself in its ownmost potentiality-for-Being."[27] Thus, according to Heidegger, in facing up to the reality of its own death, authentic *Dasein* is able to see possibilities as its own and to use its future to realize them.

Thirdly, since authentic *Dasein* comes to see death as the potential that is most clearly and definitely its own, it comes to define itself by its own terms, rather than by the terms given it by the *they*. Death reveals to authentic *Dasein* its identity as a separate and unique individual. Heidegger stresses the fact that the authentic appropriation of death initiates a process of individuation. Death individualizes *Dasein* by calling it back from its lostness in the *they* to realize itself as a solitary being. Heidegger goes so far as to say that when *Dasein* stands before death as its ownmost possibility, "all its relations to any other *Dasein* have been undone."[28]

Fourthly, authentic *Dasein* appropriates death not only as its own possibility, but as the possibility about which it can be most certain. Although the when of death is unknown, it is always certain that death will come, and what *Dasein* gains from death it does so only by holding fast to this certainty. Authentic *Dasein*, then, knows death to be its ownmost certain certainty. Heidegger declares that "death must be conceived as one's ownmost possibility, nonrelational, not to be outstripped, and—above all—certain."[29]

The significance of death for Heidegger is supreme. It is only when authentic *Dasein* receives death as its ownmost, nonrelational, not to be outstripped, and most certain possibility that it becomes aware that it has a future of its own to anticipate and to which it may project itself to actualize its own authentic possibilities. Death reveals to authentic *Dasein* its own identity as a temporal being, as a being thrown into time and projected ecstatically toward the future. Thus, for Heidegger, it is death that bestows a future upon authentic *Dasein,* and it is death that reveals the very essence not only of the future, and, consequently, of time itself, but also of *Dasein* as Being-toward-death. Alfonso Lingis expresses well the supreme significance of death for Heidegger: "The sense of my imminent impotence is a Power. It brings me forth into all the potentiality for Being that I am [and] is the very basis of all power in me."[30]

In Levinas's interpretation of death, he considers all these aspects of Heidegger's analysis of death and argues against them at every point. For Levinas, the fact that we are certain that death will come means nothing compared to the fact that we don't know—and have no way of knowing—what death is and means. Rather than emphasizing the certainty of death, Levinas stresses the ways in which death is supremely uncertain, and he interprets death as mystery. Death is not, then, that about which we are most certain, but is that which always evades our attempts to grasp and to understand it. The fact that we can only conceive of death *via* the deaths of others does not for Levinas say something about us. It does not reveal to us that our existence is inauthentic and that we flee death. Rather, it says something about death itself: "The fact that it deserts every present is not due to our evasion of death and to an unpardonable diversion at the supreme hour, but to the fact that death is ungraspable . . ."[31] In exact opposition to Heidegger, Levinas not only denies that death is the most certain thing in life, but he insists that it is the "absolutely unknowable," that which is "foreign to all light."[32]

If death is the absolutely unknowable, then it is also that which can never be possessed. The Heideggerian category of mineness (*Jemeinigkeit*) does not even begin to express the reality of death, according to Levinas, for death is not only that which someday will be mine, but it is also that which can never be made mine because it has its own reality. Death is something other than myself, something I do not understand and which comes at me. As Lingis says, in Levinas the self does not exist toward death as much as against death, against an opposing power.[33] Death is a power other than my own power that overcomes me, seizes me and takes me away against my will. This is why Levinas's example of death, contrary to Heidegger's model that comes eventually at the end of one's life, is most often violent death, murder, which catches me offguard: "In death I am exposed to absolute violence, to murder in the night."[34] Thus, the consciousness of death does not bring for Levinas a feeling of power, but rather a feeling of vulnerability. As Lingis puts it, "The anticipation of death is not power but lassitude, a passive exposedness to a death that comes prematurely, a violence."[35] The will to oppose death is mine, but the power that seizes me in my death is supremely other than mine, is quintessentially a power external to me. In death, "the subject is in relationship with what does not come from itself. We could say it is in relationship with mystery,"[36] a mystery that opposes and threatens me.

Since death is truly that which is other than and foreign to me, what it reveals is not my own individual, authentic possibilities, but the fact that there is something other than myself. For Levinas, the meaning of death resides in the fact that the subject, locked in itself and in its present, is encountered by what the subject is not, cannot be, and cannot even understand. In death, the subject meets the other, absolute alterity. By being always already in relation to death, the subject is in relation to something other than itself and its present:

> This approach of death indicates that we are in relation with something that is absolutely other, something bearing alterity not as a provisional determination we can assimilate through enjoyment, but as something whose very existence is made of alterity.[37]

Whereas Heidegger posits that the most fundamental aspects of death are its certainty and its mineness as *Dasein*'s ownmost and most certain possibility, Levinas posits that death's most fundamental characteristic is its otherness. Death itself is other to my being and to my present. For Levinas, death's alterity makes manifest to me two basic aspects of human existence: 1) it shows that existence is plural; 2) it reveals to me a future that exceeds the present.

Through an understanding of death, I become aware that even my own existence includes a foreign agent, an external force that breaks into my solitary existence precisely by revealing to me that my existence is not solitary. Through death, "a plurality insinuates itself into the very existing of the existent . . ."[38] The fact of death makes me aware that there is my existence and something else, something other. Existence itself entails duality; this is the lesson of death. Death is otherness itself, and when it forces itself into the existing of the existent, the existent is driven to recognize plurality. For Levinas, once the subject realizes that in being related to death it is related to something absolutely other, "right away this means that existence is pluralist."[39] Quite otherwise than Heidegger's notion that death individuates, Levinas contends that "my solitude is not confirmed by death but broken by it."[40]

Death also reveals to me a future that goes beyond my own present. It is crucial to realize, however, that this future has nothing in common with the future that, according to Heidegger, death gives to authentic *Dasein*. This future has nothing to do with my expectations and projections, as it does in Heidegger, for since death is absolutely other, it is exactly that about which I can have no expectations or projections.[41] I can expect and project only that which I draw from myself and my present. An expected and projected future, as in Heidegger, is not pure future, but is merely the future of the present, or the present in the future. But this is precisely what the future that death brings is not, because death is not a projected or anticipated future, but a "strange" future, a "foreign" future. The future that death brings to the subject is absolute future; I cannot seize it or anticipate it out of my own present. Quite to the contrary, death as the absolute future seizes me:

> Anticipation of the future and projection of the future, sanctioned as essential to time by all theories from Bergson to Sartre, are but the present of the future and not the authentic future; the future is what is not grasped, what befalls us and lays hold of us.[42]

Because the absolute future death brings is refractory to all anticipation and projection, it possesses an alterity, a "strangeness," which I cannot overcome or make my own. Thus, Levinas insists that even though death presents to me a future, it is a future that I cannot connect to my present: "There is an abyss between the present and death, between the ego and the alterity of mystery."[43] Because there is this abyss between my present and the absolute future of death, I dwell in the present and am aware of a future, but I have no way of connecting the two. Without this connection, I have a present and am cognizant of a future, but I do not yet have time. As Levinas says, "the future that death gives, the future of the event, is not yet time. In order for this future, which is nobody's and which a human being cannot assume, to become an element of time, it must also enter into relationship with the present."[44]

As has already been shown, Levinas asserts that to make this connection between the future and the present is to have time. Unlike Heidegger, for Levinas this cannot be accomplished merely when the subject learns of the "strange" future of death. Levinas insists that the subject has a comprehension of time only when it encounters and is encountered by that otherness that is not death, but human otherness, the other person, the Other. This leads Levinas to analyze what he chooses as his model for the relation between the subject and the Other, eros.

Levinas turns to the phenomenon of *eros*, the lover-beloved relationship, because in *eros* the Other gives to the subject a future that connects to the subject's present. Through his phenomenological analysis of *eros*, Levinas makes clear his own contention that it is the relation between the subject and the Other, and not the subject's individual appropriation of its own death, that opens the mystery of time to the subject.

It is important to note that Levinas sees in *eros* not a quantitatively different or absolutely unique relationship between the subject and the Other. Rather, he believes that the erotic relationship reveals more clearly and acutely the basic relationship between the subject and the Other, the true nature of the relationship. As Richard Cohen argues, "the erotic relationship serves as the prototype of the encounter with the radical alterity of the other person."[45] Levinas chooses eros as the prototype because eros brings the subject and the Other into closest proximity,[46] so that they not only become lover and beloved, but they also desire to be no longer subject and Other. They desire to be no longer separate, to be no longer two, but to be united by their love into one being. Levinas refers to this desire for the Other as *voluptuousness*. He presents voluptuousness as a hunger for the Other, a longing for the Other that thrusts itself toward the Other.[47] It can never be satisfied but can only increase, according to Levinas, can only engender more desire, precisely because the lover can never possess the beloved, can never become united with the beloved: "nothing is further from *eros* than possession."[48] Even the most desired and pursued beloved remains in some way other. As Lingis says, "erotic existence projects itself unto an alterity approached without being conceived or comprehended, an alterity that touches, afflicts, obsesses, and remains incessantly out of reach."[49]

In fact, in love the otherness of the Other is felt most keenly as an inextinguishable and inexhaustible otherness because of the intense desire for union.[50] Love reveals the otherness of the other person as absolute otherness, reveals the Other as absolutely other, as the Other. Love reveals that the otherness of the Other cannot be extinguished, even by love. This is why, for Levinas, love is not a fusion, but is:

> . . . a relationship with what always slips away. The relationship does not *ipso facto* neutralize alterity but preserves it. The pathos of voluptuousness lies in the fact of being two. The other as other is not here an object that becomes ours or becomes us; to the contrary, it withdraws into its mystery.[51]

Thus, what becomes apparent in love is the plurality within existence, the fact that there exists an otherness that the subject can never convert into "mineness." Levinas's example or illustration of this plurality is sexual difference.[52] The feminine appears as what is different from, other than the male. Sexual difference does not mean that the feminine is contradictory to the male; the male cannot know the female simply by knowing what it itself is not. Neither is the relationship between male and female one of complementarity, for there is no preexisting whole to be regained. Sexual difference means that reality is multiple because the relationship between the male and the female is one of pure difference. Thus, the relationship between the two, even in love, is always across a distance.

This distance is crucial to understanding what Levinas terms the *feminine*. He is not trying to group one set of characteristics as male and another as female.[53] Rather, the feminine is his image for the otherness of the Other, which always preserves itself across a distance from the subject: "Femininity . . . is the very quality of difference."[54] Thus, the otherness of the Other is the feminine in the sense that it never fully reveals itself. Its manifestation is also a retreat, a hiding, a manifestation of modesty. "Hiding is the way of the feminine"[55] means that the other reveals itself as other without fully revealing its otherness. The feminine can be called nothing else but mystery because it consists in preserving its otherness: "Alterity is accomplished in the feminine."[56]

Because the feminine accomplishes alterity, never gives up its otherness, what it gives to the subject in love is not all of itself, but the very fact of its otherness. Levinas posits that the erotic relationship differs from the relationship of knowledge or power, in which the subject obtains what it seeks and is satiated. There is no satiation in love, however, because the subject seeks what shows itself as unobtainable. Love interpreted as a relationship with the feminine means a relationship with the otherness of the Other, which can neither be grasped nor exhausted, and so is infinite. In love, "the discovered does not lose its mystery in the discovery, the hidden is not disclosed, the night is not dispersed."[57] The beloved is always revealed/concealed as an absent presence and a present absence. As Levinas says, the relation with the feminine "is a relation with its absence, an absence on the plane of knowledge—the unknown—but a presence in voluptuosity."[58] Even the most near other, the beloved, is never fully there, but is there only in his/her mystery. Proximity to the beloved does not disclose knowledge, but rather reveals that which exceeds all knowledge—the infinite otherness of the Other.

What shows itself in voluptuousness, but which is also concealed in that it cannot be made present, is that the Other, the beloved, has a future of its own. The voluptuousness that craves to be united with the beloved is confronted with the fact that the beloved can never be possessed because there is always more of the beloved still to come. This still-to-come quality of the Other constitutes a future—but not the strange future of death and totally foreign to the present-in-the-future of the subject's own projections and expectations. Voluptuousness encounters the pure, absolute future, the future emptied of all content, "the very mystery of the future."[59] Because voluptuousness is a relationship with alterity, it is also a relationship

> . . . with mystery—that is to say, with the future, with what (in a world where there is everything) is never there, with what cannot be there when everything is there—not with a being that is not there, but with the very dimension of alterity.[60]

The relationship to the Other, then, bestows on the subject a time that is more than either the subject's own present or the strange future of death. This is why, for Levinas, time cannot be conceived in its full sense in terms of the individual subject, but rather must be conceived as the achievement of the social relation.[61] Without the Other, the subject is locked into its own present; its own time is not real time, but is merely a return of the present, a return of the same. The social relation, on the other hand, opens up time in its full sense; the Other opens up to the subject its absolute future, its own future as mystery and surprise.[62] As Lingis says, "In making contact with alterity, my existence opens upon a futurity which is no longer the correlate of, the possibility projected by my powers, but is veritable futurity in its ungraspableness, its essential surprise."[63] The social relation, thus, bestows upon the subject an entirely new beginning, a future that exceeds the parameters of what is foreseeable and possible in the present.

This future the Other gives to the subject Levinas refers to as *fecundity*. Considered biologically, the notion of fecundity expresses the fact that the erotic relationship produces something new: "the same and the other are not united but precisely—beyond every project, beyond every meaningful and intelligent power—engender the child."[64] Considered more broadly, beyond its biological context, the notion of fecundity reveals something about time—that time itself is fecund. Time always recommences, is always born anew.

Levinas draws three very important conclusions about time from the fact that it is fecund: first, the fact that time always begins anew means that the essence of time is, according to Levinas, pardon; second, it means that time is infinite; and third, it means that time must not be conceived, as Heidegger does, merely as the dispersion of being.

Time as fecundity means that the time of recommencement and, thus, of youth, triumphs over the time of aging being. The absolute future of the other comes to the present of the subject and renews it, reinvigorates it, purifies it by giving it new life. This is what Levinas means by saying that *pardon* is the work of time.[65] Pardon expresses the fact that the essence of time does not lie in impersonal instants that link indifferently together. The essence of time, rather, is that it flows from the other to the subject and releases the subject from the weight of its present, thus performing the work of pardon.

The fact that time always recommences also means that time as fecundity is infinite time. The relationship with the child, in which what is impossible for the subject is made possible, establishes a relationship with a time beyond the time of the subject, with a future that is continually reborn so that it expands indefinitely, or, as Levinas says, infinitely: "The relation with the child—that is, the relation with the other that is not a power, but fecundity—establishes relationship with the absolute future, or infinite time."[66] Infinite time, which is engendered by the erotic relationship and by fecundity, means that value and goodness can be defined as something other than merely that which triumphs in today. Without infinite time, goodness would either be folly or subjectivity. Without the infinite time of fecundity, says Levinas, "the time necessary for the manifestation of truth behind visible history (which is still time) would be impossible."[67] Infinite time, however, means that the folly of goodness of today is not infinite folly. In fact, "time's infinite existing ensures the situation of judgment, condition of truth, behind the failure of goodness of today."[68] Thus, infinite time makes it possible for a subject to live for the realization of good in a time beyond the subject's own time.[69] We are not duped by morality, we are not fools when we live for good, only because fecundity, the relationship between the subject and the Other, gives to time the structure not of finitude, but of infinity.[70]

Levinas's notion of the infinite time of fecundity leads him to dispute Heidegger's analysis of the relation of time to being. Heidegger interprets time as the dispersion of finite being, as the structure of finite being. Fecundity, the recommencement of being in time, means that time is not merely that through which being is dispersed. Time is what gives to being its continual rebirth. Thus, Levinas declares that "resurrection is the principal event of time."[71] Of course, in fecundity what is resurrected is also something new. Lingis says that the resurrection involved in the time of fecundity is transsubstantiation, for fecundity expresses the fact that "our existence ex-ists to the point of transsubstantiation."[72]

Since time renews and resurrects and transsubstantiates being, Levinas maintains against Heidegger that time is not merely the dispersion of being, but that "time adds something new to being, something absolutely new."[73] What time adds to being, in fact, is newness itself, the continual resurrection and recommencement and transsubstantiation of being beyond the finite and beyond the possible. Time imparts to being its own infinite newness, its own infinity. Levinas makes it very clear who he is arguing against when he conceives time as infinite: "it is not the finitude of being that constitutes the essence of time, as Heidegger thinks, but its infinity."[74]

The Past

Just as Levinas's interpretation of the future opens time forward toward an infinite future beyond all human projections and possibilities, his interpretation of the past opens time backward toward an infinite time beyond all human recollection and comprehension. Levinas develops his conception of the past by once again arguing against Heidegger's *Being and Time*, now in its interpretation of the past.

Heidegger explicates the meaning of the past in the same way that he explicates the meaning of the future, through individual *Dasein*. For Heidegger, the meaning of the past is in how *Dasein* interprets its own individual past. Of course, *Dasein* can interpret its past in an authentic or an inauthentic manner. Inauthentic *Dasein* interprets the past inauthentically in that it interprets it solely in terms of the present; it sees only what is immediately in front of it and is blind to the authentic possibilities within its own past.[75] Authentic *Dasein*, on the other hand, aware of its capacity to actualize its own authentic potentialities, sees in the past something more than what has been and either is or is no more. Authentic *Dasein* can see in the past possibilities for itself that it can choose to actualize through "resolute repetition."[76] Thus, the past is open to authentic *Dasein*, offering authentic possibilities because *Dasein* is already open to the future, already projects itself ahead of itself toward its authentic future and its authentic possibilities. This for Heidegger is the fundamental meaning of the past, that it can provide authentic *Dasein* a greater understanding of its own possibilities toward which it ecstatically projects itself in the future.

Levinas, quite otherwise than Heidegger, interprets the past not in terms of the individual subject, but again in terms of the social relation. The past is not the past of the subject, but the past of the Other. In Levinas's analysis, the past of the Other, rather than opening up possibilities for the subject, as in Heidegger, actually closes them off. In the face-to-face encounter, the subject and the Other are present together in the present. Even so, they are never contemporaries, for the other presents him/herself out of the depths of a past which is his/her own. As Richard Cohen argues, key to Levinas's theory of time is the fact that "the other person encountered face to face is not the subject's contemporary, that they do not meet one another at the same time."[77] The noncontemporaneity of the encounter is a result of the fact that the other person has a dual identity: S/he is not only the you in the social relation, the one present here now, but is also the he or she, the third person, who has a past that is not identical to mine.[78] The dimension of the Other as third person is expressed in the term *illeity*.[79]

Not only is the past of the third person not identical to mine, but it is also that which can never be entirely recaptured through my effort, can never be made entirely present. The depths of the Other's past are unfathomable. The past of the Other is "already too old for the game of cognition,"[80] which is the attempt on the part of the subject to render everything present. Thus, the past of the Other is "an immemorial past which no memory could reassemble."[81] The very otherness of the Other ". . . is the past which cannot be caught up with."[82]

According to Levinas, what the immemorial past of the other opposes is the time of consciousness, the time of the subject. Consciousness constantly attempts to gather all of the past into the present, constantly tries to make all of time its own time. Consciousness is, in fact, "the very impossibility of a past that would never have been present, that would be closed to memory and history."[83] Consciousness does this through employing linguistic systems; Levinas names this process and its result the *Said*. In the Said, all of time "is synchronized into a time that is recallable, and becomes a theme."[84] In the Said, all time is represented as present, as presence—time is reduced to the structure of being. Thus, the Said is not only the realm of synchrony, but it is also the realm of ontology.[85]

But what disrupts the Said, the synchrony of remembered time, is proximity, the nearness of the Other. In the face-to-face encounter, the Other reveals him/herself out of the depths of an immemorial past, a past that can never be reassembled into the Said. Even when the subject realizes this, however, the past of the Other is still not present, cannot be made present, and even has never been present in the time of the subject. Thus, the past of the Other is always past. Since it is always past, even when revealed in the social relation, it is not revealed as a presence, but only as an absence. This is why Levinas says that the immemorial past of the Other shows itself not as a presence, but only as a *trace*, the mark only of its never having been there, and it is this trace that invades the perfect synchrony of the Said and disrupts it:

> . . . a real trace disturbs the order of the world. It occurs by overprinting. Its original signifyingness is sketched out in, for example, the fingerprints left by someone who wanted to wipe away his traces and carry out a perfect crime. He who left traces in wiping out his traces did not mean to say or do anything by the traces he left. He disturbed the order in an irreparable way. He has passed absolutely. To be *qua* leaving a trace is to pass, to depart, to absolve oneself.
>
> . . . in a trace has passed a past absolutely bygone. In a trace its irreversible lapse is sealed. Disclosure, which reinstates the world and leads back to the world, and

> is proper to a sign or a signification, is done away with in traces.
>
> . . . A trace is a presence of that which properly speaking has never been there, of what is always past.[86]

The trace is a disturbance in that, in the face-to-face relationship, the subject becomes aware of a presence that has already been there, but has not been there in the time of the subject. The trace has been there in a time that can never be recovered:

> . . . it is in the trace of the other that a face shines: what is presented there is absolving itself from my life and visits me as already absolute. Someone has already passed. His trace does not signify his past, as it does not signify his labor or his enjoyment; it is a disturbance imprinting itself (we are tempted to say engraving itself) with an irrecusable gravity.[87]

The trace of the Other's immemorial past does not reveal something about the power of memory. Rather, it reveals the nature of time—that it passes, that it lapses irretrievably. Aging is the very nature of time. Lingis explains, "The trace opens up something that has come to pass, which is not an intentional modification of any present—the immemorial past, pure lapse of time. . . an irrecuperable loss of time."[88] Levinas concludes from this that the structure of time is not synchronic, but diachronic:

> . . . the lapse of time is irrecuperable, refractory to the simultaneity of the present, something unrepresentable, immemorial, pre-historical. Before the synthesis of apprehension and recognition, the absolutely passive synthesis of ageing is effected. Through it time passes (*se passe*). The immemorial is not an effect of a weakness of memory, an incapacity to cross large intervals of time, to resuscitate pasts too deep. It is the impossibility of the dispersion of time, a beyond the Said. It is diachrony that determines the immemorial; a weakness of memory does not constitute diachrony.[89]

Thus, for Levinas, the trace of the Other's immemorial past testifies to a past that is beyond all memory and all history, a past not circumscribed in being because it can never be recalled as presence, a past that disappears back into infinity, leaving only the trace of itself. Hence, the relationship between the subject and the Other reveals a past before the time of consciousness, before the time of representation and order, and before the time of ontology, a past that cannot be recollected as the foundation of the Said—an anarchical past.

Levinas insists that what also comes from and exists in the trace of the Other's anarchical past is the sense of responsibility the subject feels for the Other in the face-to-face encounter. In the social relation, the Other not only reveals his/her otherness, but the subject in some way feels responsible for the Other. The subject, in fact, feels responsible even before the Other summons the subject to responsibility. The origin of this feeling of responsibility is paradoxical " . . . in that I am obliged without this obligation having begun in me, as though an order slipped into my consciousness like a thief, smuggled itself in . . . "[90]

But from where, then, does this order, this obligation, this feeling of responsibility come? Levinas answers that it comes from the anarchical and infinite time before consciousness, history and meaning:

> The responsibility for the other can not have begun in my commitment, in my decision. The unlimited responsibility in which I find myself comes from the hither side of my freedom, from a "prior to every memory," an "ulterior to every accomplishment," from the non-present par excellence, the non-original, the anarchical, prior to or beyond essence.[91]

Levinas refers to this order that precedes meaning and history—the work of consciousness that he terms the Said—as the *Saying*. This primordial saying of responsibility for the Other is *Ethics*. The ethical saying bears testimony to the fact that time is not circumscribed in being: "The personal order to which a face obliges us is beyond being."[92] There is a time beyond being—infinity—and from infinity comes the trace of the Other's past, which says the ethical saying, the order of responsibility. Hence, Levinas states that the Saying testifies to the Infinite:

> Saying as testimony precedes all the said. Saying before setting forth a said, is already the testimony of this responsibility—and even the saying of a said, as an approach to the other, is a responsibility for him. Saying is . . . an obedience that precedes the hearing of any order. A pure testimony, it does not testify to a prior experience, but to the Infinite which is not accessible to the unity of apperception, non-appearing and disproportionate to the present.[93]

Because Heidegger interprets time not in terms of the social relation, but only in terms of the individual *Dasein*, his phenomenological ontology cannot witness to the infinite and unrecallable depths of the past. Because Heidegger sees the meaning of the past strictly in terms of the individual *Dasein*'s appropriation of its own past, he only considers that aspect of the past which can be reassembled into the present. Heidegger can only consider time as synchrony, not as diachrony. This is why, for Levinas, "Heideggerian philosophy marks the apogee of a thought in which the finite does not refer to the infinite."[94] Thus, in Levinas's terminology, Heidegger's analysis of the past of the individual *Dasein* remains on the level of the said. Because it does not interpret time through the social relation, it cannot witness to that dimension of the past that is infinitely past, the past of the Other, infinitely refractory to human memory and comprehension, and infinitely speaking itself in the trace of its ethical saying.

Conclusion

Clearly, Levinas develops his own interpretation of time in all three of its dimensions—present, future, and past—by constantly arguing against Heidegger's interpretation in *Being and Time.* By insisting that time must be conceived not in terms of the solitary subject, but rather in terms of the social relation, Levinas develops an interpretation of time diametrically opposed to Heidegger. Levinas's intention is to use phenomenology to show that time is something more than merely the structure of being. His interpretation of the future—which opens up time forward toward an infinite future beyond human projection and possibility—and his interpretation of the past—which opens up time backward to an immemorial and infinite past no human memory can recall and reassemble—illustrate clearly that Levinas sees in time something much more than that through which being is dispersed, something much more than the structure of being. But what, then, is time, according to Levinas?

Levinas challenges Heidegger's notion that time is the way in which we understand being, the way in which being becomes meaningful, not by denying this altogether, but by showing that this is not an adequate way to conceive of time. The infinite future of fecundity and the trace of the Other's infinite past demonstrate that time has a meaning of its own. Time has a meaning beyond being. Time is a reality that exceeds the ontological categories by which we attempt to define it. The meaning of time bursts through human powers of comprehension. The infinite time of fecundity and the immemorial past of the Other have meaning, but it is not a meaning circumscribed in being. It is a meaning beyond being, otherwise than being.

Thus, the meaning of time is mystery, but this mystery is due not to the lack of meaning, but to its surplus.

Time is the surplus of meaning that overflows human comprehension because time itself is the relationship with what cannot be assimilated by experience. Because Levinas interprets time not through the individual *Dasein* but through the social relation, he insists that time is more than the structure of finite being. Time is through being, but it leads from being to infinity. Thus, for Levinas, time itself is the way through being to escape from being. This is true, however, only because time in its full sense is for Levinas already and always the achievement of the social relation, the work of the relationship between the subject and the Other.

The Challenge of Ethics as First Philosophy

A philosophy of power, ontology is, as first philosophy which does not call into question the same, a philosophy of injustice. . . . Heideggerian ontology, which subordinates the relationship with the Other to the relation with Being in general, remains under obedience to the anonymous, and leads inevitably to another power, to imperialist domination, to tyranny.
—*Emmanuel Levinas*

Morality is not a branch of philosophy, but first philosophy.
—*Emmanuel Levinas*

Levinas's early philosophical productions, "De l'evasion," *Existence and Existents* and *Time and the Other*, attracted very little critical attention. The publication in 1961 of his major work, *Totality and Infinity*, occasioned the first lengthy critical study of Levinas's philosophy, Jacques Derrida's 1964 essay entitled "Violence and Metaphysics." In 1969, *Totality and Infinity* became the first of

Levinas's works to be translated into English, and thus it was mainly through this translation and through Derrida's essay that English-speaking readers were introduced to the philosophy of Emmanuel Levinas.[1]

Totality and Infinity is certainly Levinas's most direct attack on Heidegger's ontology. Much of the first part of the book is a harsh critique of Heidegger's philosophy on ethical grounds. In his introduction to the English translation of *Totality and Infinity,* John Wild states that the book "constitutes one of the most basic attacks on the thought of Heidegger that has yet been formulated."[2] *Totality and Infinity* rendered Heidegger, in Richard Cohen's words, "Levinas's great antagonist."[3] F. P. Ciglia calls Levinas's polemic against Heidegger "ruthless."[4] Similarly, Guy Pettitdemange refers to Levinas's attack on Heidegger as a "denunciation which turns to derision and which perhaps does not render justice to Heidegger."[5]

The secondary literature on Levinas has focused on *Totality and Infinity,* on Levinas's sharp criticisms of Heidegger, and on the question of whether Levinas has understood and been fair to Heidegger. The criticism of Levinas's philosophy thus far has tended to see Levinas's relation to Heidegger primarily as an adversarial one, and has failed to take into account the truly dialectical relation Levinas's thought bears to Heidegger's.

The present chapter aims to correct this critical blindness by evaluating *Totality and Infinity*'s ethical critique of Heidegger in terms of the development of Levinas's philosophical project as a constant interpreting in but otherwise than Heidegger's philosophy. It is only by doing this, I would argue, that we can understand the actual grounds upon which Levinas indicts Heidegger's philosophy and, therefore be able to evaluate the validity of Levinas's indictment. We must understand not only how Levinas determines that Heidegger does not assign ethics its rightful place, but we must also understand what it means for Levinas to regard ethics not as a branch of philosophy, but first philosophy. In other words, in order to evaluate Levinas's criticisms of Heidegger, we must understand Levinas's own constructive philosophical project.

Levinas's Attack on Heidegger

In no uncertain terms in *Totality and Infinity,* Levinas proclaims himself opposed to Heidegger when he insists that ethics, and not ontology, is first philosophy.[6] However, as we have seen, this does not mean that Levinas refrains from interpreting being. Levinas's own philosophical project is, to some extent, an ontology; it involves a thinking of being. Levinas quite consciously directs himself toward those regions of being that he thinks Heidegger either interpreted incorrectly or altogether failed to take into account.[7] This interpreting of being does not begin, but rather culminates in, the priority of ethics over knowledge of being, over ontology.[8] Levinas's indictment of Heideggerian ontology should not lead us to forget that if Levinas posits ethics as primary, it is because he finds the ethical dimension in being.[9] As Steven Smith correctly insists, for Levinas "the infinite overflows in being, not elsewhere. Morality is entirely of this world."[10] And, more importantly, if he finds the ethical dimension in being, it is because Heidegger taught him to look there, taught him that the method and the task of philosophy is the analysis of being. If ethics leads *beyond* being, as Levinas insists, it is also equally true that it does so only by going *through* being. And the only valid way to go beyond being, as Levinas insists in "De l'evasion," is through being, and this necessarily means that the relationship between Levinas and his teacher, Martin Heidegger, is not merely one of simple opposition, as it sometimes seems to be.

The knowledge of this much more complex, dialectical relationship between Levinas's ethical phenomenology and Heidegger's phenomenological ontology will enable us to evaluate more justly and profoundly both the validity and the true import of Levinas's ethical critique of Heideggerian philosophy. Levinas's ethical critique of Heidegger's ontology has to be evaluated in terms of Levinas's own philosophical project, in terms of his own counteroption to Heidegger's ontology that Levinas continually offers. Levinas's critique of Heidegger's ontology has to be understood in light of Levinas's own phenomenological analysis of being, which finds in being that which is beyond and more important than knowledge of being—the Good, the ethical relation between persons, or ethics itself. Most importantly, perhaps, Levinas's criticisms of Heidegger's ontology on ethical grounds have to be evaluated in light of Levinas's own insistence that ethics is not a branch of philosophy, but first philosophy.[11] Only if we do this can we understand Levinas's criticisms of Heidegger's phenomenological ontology on ethical grounds.

This attack on Heideggerian ontology is presented in somewhat diluted form throughout *Totality and Infinity*. It receives its most concentrated expression, however, in the section entitled "Metaphysics Precedes Ontology." Here, Levinas's polemic against Heidegger's philosophy is expressed most succinctly and forcefully:

> The primacy of ontology for Heidegger does not rest on the truism: "to know an existent it is necessary to have comprehended the Being of existents." To affirm the priority of Being over existents is to already decide the essence of philosophy; it is to subordinate the relation with someone, who is an existent, (the ethical relation) to a relation with the Being of existents, which, impersonal, permits the apprehension, the domination of existents (a relationship of knowing), subordinates justice to freedom. If freedom denotes the mode of remaining the same in the midst of the other, knowledge, where an existent is given by interposition of impersonal Being,

contains the ultimate sense of freedom. It would be opposed to justice, which involves obligations with regard to an existent that refuses to give itself, the Other, who in this sense would be an existent par excellence. In subordinating every relation with existents to the relation with Being the Heideggerian ontology affirms the primacy of freedom over ethics. To be sure, the freedom involved in the essence of truth is not for Heidegger a principle of free will. Freedom comes from an obedience to Being: it is not man who possesses freedom; it is freedom that possesses man. But the dialectic which thus reconciles freedom and obedience in the concept of truth presupposes the primacy of the same, which marks the direction of and defines the whole of Western philosophy.

The relation with Being that is enacted as ontology consists in neutralizing the existent in order to comprehend or grasp it. It is hence not a relation with the other as such but the reduction of the other to the same. Such is the definition of freedom: to maintain oneself against the other, despite every relation with the other to ensure the autarchy of an I. Thematization and conceptualization, which moreover are inseparable, are not peace with the other but suppression or possession of the other. For possession affirms the other, but within a negation of its independence. "I think" comes down to "I can"—to an appropriation of what is, to an exploitation of reality. Ontology as first philosophy is a philosophy of power. It issues in the State and in the nonviolence of the totality, without securing itself against the violence from which this nonviolence lives, and which appears in the tyranny of the state. Truth, which should reconcile persons, here exists anonymously. Universality presents itself as impersonal; and this is another inhumanity . . .

A philosophy of power, ontology is, as first philosophy which does not call into question the same, a philosophy of injustice. Even though it opposes the technological passion issued forth from the forgetting of Being hidden by existents, Heideggerian ontology, which subordinates the relationship with the Other to the

> relation with Being in general, remains under obedience to the anonymous, and leads inevitably to another power, to imperialist domination, to tyranny. Tyranny is not the pure and simple extension of technology to reified men. Its origin lies back in the pagan "moods," in the enrootedness in the earth, in the adoration that enslaved men can devote to their masters. Being before the existent, ontology before metaphysics, is freedom (be it the freedom of theory) before justice. It is a movement within the same before obligation to the other.[12]

In this long passage, several of Levinas's charges against Heidegger are compressed together. In order to analyze each more carefully, I have separated out five related but distinct accusations, all of which depend upon the first, because they all depend upon the notion of primacy.[13]

1. Heideggerian ontology gives priority to Being over existents. This means that the relationship between persons is subordinated to the relationship of knowledge of Being. For Levinas, to make the knowledge of Being primary is to decide that ontology is the essence of philosophy, is to make the analysis of Being first philosophy.

2. Because Heideggerian ontology gives priority to knowledge of Being over the relation between persons, it thus gives priority to the subject's understanding of the other's being over the subject's obligations toward the other. In Heideggerian ontology, the cognitive content of the subject's understanding of the other's being always has priority not only over whatever cognitive content the ethical relationship between the subject and the other may have, but it has priority over the ethical relationship itself. Because it subordinates ethics to knowledge of Being, Heideggerian ontology allows the subject to maintain its freedom over any obligations it has toward the other.

3. To say that the relationship of knowledge of Being has priority over the ethical relationship entails not only that the other is always given to the consciousness of the subject through interposition of impersonal Being, but it is also to say that the other is always comprehended within the always already established boundaries of Being. Heideggerian ontology, therefore, always in some way neutralizes the alterity of the other. Heideggerian ontology understands the other in terms of Being, which means that it understands the other in its own terms. Thus, Heideggerian ontology does not relate to the other in the full extent of the other's alterity, but rather reduces the other to more of the same.

4. Thematization and conceptualization are part of the process by which ontology not only grasps and comprehends the other, but also masters and controls the other. This means that ontology as first philosophy—as philosophy that has priority over competing versions of first philosophy, such as ethics—is really a philosophy of power, wherein the subject dominates and controls the other.

5. As a philosophy of power and control through knowledge, ontology insulates and protects itself from the other's capacity to criticize and to challenge it. It is related, then, to the adoration slaves can feel for masters, to the often severe reality of command and obedience. Thus, ontology as first philosophy by definition is unjust. Much more than this, however, Levinas maintains that the injustice of Heideggerian ontology not only has philosophical, but also political consequences. Levinas insists that Heideggerian ontology "leads inevitably" to the tyranny and injustice of the state.[14]

But do these accusations have any validity? Is Heidegger guilty on any or all counts? We shall use a two-step process to answer this important question. First, we shall closely analyze arguments from Heidegger's own texts that his apologists put forth to prove that Levinas's accusations are groundless. Secondly, we shall consider Levinas's criticisms of Heidegger's ontology in light of Levinas's own ethical philosophy, in light of Levinas's own insistence that ethics is first philosophy.

Levinas's critics, in defense of Heidegger, have stated that Levinas's charges indicate that he is attacking a "straw man" rather than the real Heidegger,[15] or that he has an "allergy" to Heidegger's thought.[16] If we look closely at the arguments, however, I believe it will become apparent that they constitute much less a valid and sufficient defense of Heidegger than an inability to comprehend the depth of Levinas's understanding of Heidegger, the severity of his criticisms of Heidegger, and the radicality of his own philosophical project.[17]

In Heidegger's ontology, his apologists insist, ethics cannot be subordinated to knowledge of Being because within the knowledge of Being as Heidegger depicts it there is a distinct ethical moment such that Heideggerian ontology includes very significant ethical content. Derrida, Steven Gans, C. D. Keyes, Richard Cohen, Alfonso Lingis and many others all insist that Heideggerian ontology as the thought of Being necessarily means that ontology not only comprehends Being, but that it also respects Being, that it allows Being to be. Certainly, Heidegger insists in *Being and Time* that the phenomenological method consists in letting Being show itself. Heidegger says that he "has no right to resort to dogmatic constructions" but "must rather choose such a way of access and such a kind of interpretation that this entity can show itself in itself and from itself."[18] Heidegger insists that the term "phenomenology" means nothing else than "to let that which shows itself be seen from itself in the very way in which it shows itself."[19] So defined, phenomenology is not only a methodological approach among others, but is also respect for and attention to Being as it actually manifests itself.

This manifestation of Being is, in Heidegger's view, truth itself. In proposing a view of truth more primordial than the *adequatio intellectus et rei* of the philosophical tradition,[20] Heidegger asserts that "Being-true [Truth] is Being-uncovering."[21] This means that truth is the uncovering of entities as they are in their Being, which entails respect for Being in the sense of letting Being be. Because Heidegger maintains that phenomenology as respect for Being is not only a methodological approach but expresses the very essence of truth itself as respectful uncovering of Being, he does not declare that phenomenology is the best way to undertake ontology, but rather he insists that "only as phenomenology, is ontology possible."[22] Ontology is possible only via a respectful letting Being be, a letting Being show itself in that way that it shows itself from itself.

Thus, it is Heidegger's absolute insistence upon this respect for Being that has led Levinas's critics to assert that Levinas is either blatantly unfair to Heidegger's philosophy or willfully distorting it in saying that it subordinates ethics to ontology. C. D. Keyes, for example, states that Heidegger's ontology respects the freedom of the other as much as Levinas's ethics does.[23] Gans points out that Heidegger's notion of truth as "letting be is a process which enables the other and otherness to emerge,"[24] and he concludes from this not only that Heidegger's ontology "is akin" to Levinas's ethics but even that it is "the *sine qua non* of ethics."[25] An even more staunch defender of Heidegger is Derrida, who insists that Heidegger's thought of Being as respect for Being not only is "as close as possible to nonviolence,"[26] but it actually makes ethics itself possible,[27] and, hence, "could not possibly occur as ethical violence."[28]

Even critics much more sympathetic to Levinas, like Lingis and Cohen, insist on the importance of the ethical dimension in Heidegger's thought. According to Lingis, Heidegger's respectful thought of "the recovery of the meaning of Being requires, according to Heidegger, authenticity" and thus amounts to "a promotion of responsibility."[29] Cohen is even more adamant about the ethical nature of Heidegger's thought of Being:

> While Heidegger claims his own task is neither to support nor to oppose this or that worldly morality, it becomes clear that with the end of traditional philosophy, the task of genuine thinking is itself an ethics. What becomes most needful is a responsibility for the world, a caring for what is as it is, a shepherding, a letting be, an allowance for being's generosity, an attunement to the gift giving of words. Ontology becomes indebtedness to what is, a quiet listening vigilant against its own interference, cautious of its own interventions, careful not to disturb. In a word, thinking becomes lovingkindness.[30]

The question arises then: How can Levinas rightly accuse Heidegger of subordinating ethics to ontology if Heideggerian ontology by definition is itself a relation to Being that could be considered ethical?[31] Isn't it true that to accuse Heidegger of this, Levinas has to be either totally unaware of Heidegger's respect for Being, or he has to refuse it take it into account?

The fact is, however, that neither is true, for Levinas illustrates that he is aware of what could be considered the ethical component of Heidegger's ontology when he states quite clearly that "to broach an existent from Being is simultaneously to let it be and to comprehend it."[32] Levinas recognizes that Heidegger's "pure disclosure" of Being respects the being of the other person; what he accuses it of is not respecting the being of the Other *enough*. Many of Levinas's critics assume that, since Heidegger's ontology already includes respect for Being, this necessarily invalidates Levinas's claim that Heidegger subordinates ethics to ontology, but for Levinas this is not so. This suggests that much of Levinas criticism fails to understand the precise point at which Levinas is attacking Heidegger.

Levinas clearly realizes that Heidegger's ontology entails respect for Being and so includes what some would consider an ethical component. Levinas, however, has his own ideas about what ethics is, and because he wants to rhetorically distance his own view of what ethics is from Heidegger's notion of respect for Being, he refuses to refer to the latter with the term ethics. But the issue Levinas raises is not whether Heidegger's ontology includes within it a dimension that could be called ethical. Levinas does not accuse Heidegger's ontology of having no ethical substance (as Heidegger himself, and not Levinas, would define ethics), but rather he raises the question of priority: If the relationship with Being includes both knowledge of Being and respect for Being, is the knowledge of Being primary in the sense of most important and thereby most central in defining the essence of philosophy, or is respect for Being most important and, consequently, most central to philosophy's essence? In short, is the relationship of knowledge of Being, even if this knowledge of Being involves respectfully letting Being be, most important and thereby at the heart of philosophy, or is it ethics itself that is first philosophy? The whole attack Levinas makes on Heidegger's ontology swings on the notion of priority. As Derrida so correctly points out, though he at times tends to forget this in his own analysis of Levinas, "the notion of primacy, employed so frequently by Levinas, well translates the gesture of his entire critique."[33]

The Priority of the Ethical Relation

If the issue depends upon the notion of priority, it is difficult—if not impossible—to see how Heidegger's ontology does not do exactly what Levinas accuses it of—making the comprehension of Being, a relationship of knowing, more important and, hence, more central to the definition of philosophy itself than the ethical relation. Heidegger, after all, states quite clearly in *Being and Time* that his task is "to interpret the meaning of Being."[34] The interpretation of the meaning of Being remains Heidegger's primary concern throughout his later works. As perhaps Heidegger's most important German student, Hans-Georg Gadamer, says: "For Heidegger, the basic relation is not man's relation to himself but his relation to and immersion in the event of being in which beings manifest themselves."[35]

Heidegger's notion that "entities should be grasped in their Being"[36] reveals that he is both arguing against and standing in the philosophical tradition that precedes him. He is not saying that the goal of his ontology is to do something other than to comprehend. He does not say that he is arguing against the priority of knowing in the philosophical tradition, or that philosophy should have a *telos* as something other than knowledge that would define its essence. He does say quite clearly, however, that to show the difference between his own ontology and the philosophical tradition, it is necessary for him to clarify "the kind of Being which belongs to knowledge itself."[37] He then states that the philosophical tradition defines the truth that is known as the adequation of the intellect and of the thing. Heidegger wants to replace this definition with a knowing that "remains related solely to the entity itself."[38] The knowing and the truth related only to the entity itself is the uncovering of the Being of the entity: "Being-true (Truth) is Being-uncovering."[39]

Since Heidegger's argument with the tradition is not with the primacy of knowledge, is not with the essence of philosophy as knowledge of something, but rather with what philosophy thinks it knows and hence takes as truth, he says that his conception of truth as Being-uncovering means that he has not "shaken off" the philosophical tradition but has "appropriated it more primordially."[40] It is difficult to see how Heidegger's more primordial appropriation of the philosophical tradition could entail a rejection of philosophy's essence as a knower sufficient to satisfy Levinas.[41]

It may still be pointed out, however, that part of Heidegger's departure from the philosophical tradition is his insistence that truth as uncovering of Being necessarily involves the letting be of Being. Thereby, Heidegger makes what could be considered an ethical imperative an element of his philosophy, and of the uncovering of Being, and of truth itself. It must be admitted that Heidegger's notion that Being must be respected and permitted to show itself as it actually is makes his ontology not as foreign to what might be considered ethics as Levinas's rhetoric against Heidegger in *Totality and Infinity* makes it appear.

Because Levinas's critique of Heidegger is on the basis of primacy or priority, however, what might be considered the ethical component of Heidegger's ontology does not repudiate but actually confirms Levinas's point that Heidegger's ontology subordinates ethics to ontology. Heidegger affirms that knowledge includes what might be taken to be an ethical component—the requisite respect for Being as it shows itself. Even so, ethics is then an aspect of knowing. Respect for Being is a facet in the larger project of comprehending Being.[42] Heidegger himself insists in his *Letter on Humanism* that his existential analytic of Being attempts to interpret a region of phenomena more primordial than the level of moral distinctions, which Heidegger says is secondary and derivative.[43] Even the terminology in *Being and Time* that is usually associated with ethics—such as authenticity and inauthenticity, guilt, resolve, etc.—should not, asserts Heidegger, be understood in terms of morality.[44] As William Richardson says, Heidegger

> conceives his question about being as far more radical than any question about the oughtness of human acts . . . In raising a question about the Being of finite *Dasein,* Heidegger feels that he is getting deeper than the ethical problem as such. This comes into focus when he is dealing

> with the question of *Dasein*'s guilt. Though this notion normally appears in the context of morality, for Heidegger it expresses *Dasein*'s ontological indebtedness, the sum total of its finitude, and nothing more.[45]

If ethics is a facet, even an integral one, in the more comprehensive and more important project of comprehending Being, then ethics is conceived of as subordinate to ontology. This is, after all, precisely what Levinas accuses Heidegger of.

Before we discuss the ramifications of making the knowledge of Being primary on the conception of the relationship between people—which is the issue Levinas is most concerned with in all of his accusations against Heidegger enumerated above—we must first consider another argument made in Heidegger's defense to show that his ontology does not subordinate ethics to itself. This argument does not, I believe, provide an adequate defense of Heidegger nearly so much as it underestimates Levinas's understanding of Heidegger and fails to evaluate Levinas's criticisms of Heidegger in the light of his own philosophical project.

C. D. Keyes states that because for Heidegger the uncovering of Being also always involves the concealment of Being, Being itself cannot be rightly conceived of as opening itself to full presence.[46] In support of this, he quotes *Being and Time*: "Truth (uncoveredness) is something that must always be wrested from entities. Entities get snatched out of their hiddenness. The factical uncoveredness of anything is always, as it were, a kind of robbery."[47] For Keyes, since Heidegger insists that the disclosure of Being is never total but always involves concealment, this means that Heidegger's ontology is not a totality, is not an impersonal term that encompasses all: "Heidegger's ontology cannot totalize because Being's disclosure and concealment are too closely connected to become a plenum capable of swallowing the other. Disclosure comes as a blinking of the eye."[48] He implies that Levinas does not understand this, and this is why Levinas can mistakenly accuse Heidegger of subordinating ethics to ontology.

Levinas, however, never states that Heidegger's uncovering of Being entails full presence. His critique of Heidegger does not center upon the extent to which Being manifests itself or conceals itself. Being may always, in fact, hold something of itself back in manifesting itself so that the uncovering of Being is always at the same time the concealment of Being, and yet the meaning of Being as revealed/concealed can still be taken to be the essence of philosophy. If the meaning of Being as revealed/concealed is the essence of philosophy, then it is judged to be more important and more central than ethics. Ontology, even conceived as manifestation and hiding together, can still be given priority over ethics, and this is precisely the force of Levinas's argument against Heidegger.

This returns us to Levinas's other accusations against Heidegger, all of which depend upon the first, the subordination of ethics to ontology in Heidegger's philosophy. What ramifications does this have on his conception of the relationship between persons?

Heidegger, Being-With, and the *They*

Heidegger's treatment of the social relation in *Being and Time* is dominated not by ethical considerations, but by the question of the meaning of Being. When Heidegger discusses the relationship between people, he does so in terms of the understanding of the being of individual *Dasein* and of the other. Not only this, but the social relation is portrayed almost entirely negatively, and its negativity resides in the fact that *Dasein*'s association with the social collectivity, the *they*, hinders it from gaining an authentic understanding of its own being.

In his discussion of the social relation, Heidegger insists that *Dasein* always already possesses some understanding of the being of the other because it always understands its own being as always already Being-with: "Being-with is such that the disclosedness of the *Dasein*-with of Others belongs to it; this means that because *Dasein*'s Being is Being-with, its understanding of Being already implies the understanding of Others."[49] Heidegger is quick to point out that this understanding is not derived from interaction with others, but is "a primordially existential kind of Being" that makes knowledge possible. Because *Dasein* is always Being-with, the other is a matter of *Dasein*'s concern. *Dasein*'s concern for the other can manifest itself in various ways. *Dasein* can "take hold" of this concern "with, for, or against the others."[50] Heidegger maintains that "a lively mutual acquaintanceship" with the other depends upon the extent to which "one's essential Being-with has made itself transparent and has not disguised itself."[51] He insists that "the dominant modes of Being-with" are "unsocial" and "indifferent"—"the indifference of passing one another by."[52] This is because a "genuine understanding [of *Dasein* as Being-with] gets suppressed."[53]

But why does *Dasein*'s genuine understanding of its own Being as Being-with, necessary for a "lively mutual acquaintanceship" between the individual *Dasein* and the other, get suppressed? Heidegger answers that our Being-with includes "constant care" about how and what one is compared to the others who are at a distance. This Being-with-one-another he calls *distantiality*, which actually means that *Dasein* becomes subject to others, takes its orders and its understanding of its own being from others. This negative sociality, the *they*, exercises a certain "dictatorship" over the individual *Dasein*. The *they* tells *Dasein* what to enjoy, what to read, how to judge literature and art, etc. It is from the *they* that the individual *Dasein* "draws its preontological way of interpreting its Being."[54] Because *Dasein* gets its being interpreted for it by the *they* and, hence, does not understand its own being correctly, *Dasein*'s "way of

Being is inauthenticity and failure to stand by one's self."[55] Thus, for Heidegger, *Dasein* is inauthentic because it doesn't understand its own being.

Heidegger poses the problem of the social relation in terms of *Dasein*'s understanding of its own being and of the being of others, and he offers the solution also in terms of the meaning of Being. *Dasein* becomes authentic by taking hold of its self and its world in its own way. This "authentic Being-one's-self" is a process of individuation. It does not entail detachment from the *they*, for this is impossible, but rather entails "an existentiell modification of the they."[56] In other words, *Dasein* achieves authenticity when its understanding of itself given it by the "they" is combined with and modified by the understanding of itself that comes from itself, so that it genuinely understands its own being.

Clearly, the understanding of Being is much more at the center of Heidegger's discussion of sociality than is ethics.[57] As Peter Elliston says in *Heidegger's Existential Analytic*, "In Heidegger's view, it is the comprehension of Being that most profoundly characterizes the Being of man."[58] If there is for Heidegger a problem in the relationship between persons, it is not because *Dasein* denies its ethical responsibilities to the others, but is because *Dasein* doesn't understand its own being, and it is put right when *Dasein* listens to itself and thereby understands its own being. Thus, Heidegger's discussion of sociality *supports* Levinas's charge that Heidegger's ontology subordinates ethics to knowledge of Being. But does this mean that Heidegger is guilty of all the other accusations as well? Does the fact that, in his discussion of the social relation as well as in his entire ontological project, he gives priority to the understanding of Being over ethical obligations mean that Heideggerian ontology serves to maintain the freedom of the subject over the other? Does it mean that it always reduces the other to the same? Does it mean that

Heidegger's ontology is a philosophy of power that masters and controls the other? Finally, does it lead to a tyrannical and unjust political order?

Ethics Over Ontology

The true grounds for these accusations against Heidegger are seen most clearly in the light of Levinas's attempt to use phenomenology to describe the relationship between the subject and the other in such a way that philosophy is forever changed; philosophy discovers in knowledge of Being something that goes beyond and is much more important than knowledge of Being—the ethical relationship of responsibility for the Other. Levinas refers to this as the good beyond being. As we have already seen, Levinas develops his phenomenology by interpreting within Heidegger's philosophy while also constantly interpreting against and otherwise than Heidegger's own phenomenological ontology. Levinas's rhetorical strategy is to purposefully dichotomize his own philosophy against Heidegger's philosophy, so that his own philosophy becomes a counteroption to Heidegger's, a competing interpretation of Being and of human being. Thus, Levinas's highly rhetorical philosophy desires to make reading together both his philosophy and Heidegger's not merely a matter of analyzing or comparing the two, but of choosing between them—an either/or.[59] We must choose either Heidegger's philosophy of the primacy and the priority of the knowledge of Being, or Levinas's philosophy that finds in Being that which is supreme over the knowledge of Being, ethics or the Good.

Levinas's accusations against Heidegger concerning the social relation, then, have to be seen in the context of his most fundamental attack—that Heidegger subordinates ethics to ontology. This is because Levinas attacks Heidegger not merely to criticize him, but rather to convince us that it is not knowledge of Being but ethics that is most essential, that ethics alone merits the status of first philosophy. As Levinas says, "the establishing of this primacy of the ethical, that is, of the relationship of man to man . . . is one of the objectives of [*Totality and Infinity*]."[60] It is necessary always to keep this in mind in interpreting Levinas's philosophy and in evaluating his accusations against Heidegger.

Heidegger's and Levinas's accounts of the social relation clearly illustrate this necessity. As we have seen, Heidegger's concern with the social relationship primarily centers upon *Dasein*'s understanding of its own being and of the being of the other. Now, when *Dasein* and the other confront one another, *Dasein* already possesses some understanding of the other, an understanding in terms of the other's being. It is clear, as we have already shown, that Heidegger insists that understanding involves letting the other be, letting the other's being manifest itself. It is equally true that for Heidegger the other never completely manifests its own *Dasein*, for every disclosure of *Dasein* is at the same time a concealment of *Dasein*. So, to be fair to Heidegger is to insist both that *Dasein* comprehends the other only in letting the other manifest itself and that *Dasein*'s comprehension of the other is never, and can never be, total or complete.

There is, then, for Heidegger, always a difference between the other's *Dasein* and the subject's understanding of the other's *Dasein*. This is certainly one of the differences Derrida has in mind when he insists that Heidegger's philosophy does not suppress but rather "permits the emergence of every possible difference."[61] But the question then becomes: What does *Dasein* do with the difference? This is also to ask, what does philosophy do with the difference? What else can *Dasein* do but let the other's Being be in order to comprehend it, however inadequately and incompletely? And what else can philosophy do except know that even though it can never know all of Being, yet Being still reveals itself to the understanding? The disclosing of Being even within its hiddenness is still a knowing of Being, still an understanding of Being, still an opening of Being to the comprehension of *Dasein*. Petitdemange has expressed the consequences of this most clearly: "Remarkable, rigorous, novel, the thought of Heidegger, even when transformed into an interrogative and questioning thought, remains tied to a mode of thinking entirely determined by human ipseity, essentially qualified by the power of initiative and of opening."[62] For Heidegger, doubtless, the disclosure of Being is the essence of philosophy and makes possible authentic thinking. The comprehension of Being as both manifestation and concealedness is for Heidegger both the consolation and the essence of philosophy.[63]

It is precisely at this point (and not before) that Levinas's critical voice enters the discussion of the social relation. Levinas is not trying to deny that there is a preontological understanding of the Other in terms of being. Nor, certainly, is he taking exception to Heidegger's notion that the being of the Other is never fully revealed. Heidegger concludes from this that there is always a difference between the other's being and the subject's understanding of the other's being, and this difference becomes central to Levinas's own thought. In fact, Levinas's objections to Heidegger center around Heidegger's interpretation of what this difference means both for the subject and for philosophy.

Derrida on Levinas

Again, however, Heidegger's defenders misunderstand this crucial point in their analysis of Levinas's attack. Derrida assumes that what Levinas is trying to escape from is the fact that "to know an existent it is necessary to have comprehended the Being of the existent."[64] Even though Levinas calls this statement a "truism," Derrida believes that it is this truism that Levinas believes establishes the priority of Being over the existent. For Levinas, according to Derrida, this truism is not just a self-evident proposition, but one that is "laughably self-evident." Derrida here means the laughter to be derisory, for he also says that for Levinas this is a "criminal truism, which places ethics under the heel of ontology."[65] What Levinas says about this truism, however, is not that it is criminal or that it places ethics under the heel of ontology. Quite to the contrary, he states quite clearly: "The primacy of ontology for Heidegger does not rest on the truism: `to know an existent it is necessary to have comprehended the Being of the existent.'"

Consequently, this truism is not the foundation upon which Levinas establishes his attack on Heidegger's ontology. Indeed, for Levinas this is not a certain kind of truism, but merely a truism—a self-evident truth—just as he had earlier said that Heidegger's notion of *Geworfenheit,* that we are born into a world not of our own making, is also a truism.[66] Clearly, Levinas is not arguing with Heidegger's notion that to know the other it is necessary to conceive of the other in terms of being. Rather, he is admitting the point and stating that the problem in Heidegger's ontology lies elsewhere.

Derrida's misunderstanding of this point causes him to misconceive Levinas's treatment of the social relation and, consequently, the thrust of Levinas's whole ethical philosophy. Derrida thinks that Levinas argues that the subject's understanding of the Other in terms of Being—in terms of anything other than the Other's pure alterity—is itself violent;[67] therefore, Derrida offers instead a conception of the social relationship wherein the Other is not already in some way understood in terms of Being before the social relation, offering a pseudo-phenomenological account of the social relation totally outside of all ontological language. This is why Derrida asks, "Would the experience of the face be possible if the thought of Being were not implied in it?"[68]

Thus, Derrida interprets Levinas's hyperbolic description of the other literally. For Derrida, "absolutely and infinitely other" must mean that the other is at no moment prior to its manifestation of itself already understood in terms of something else, in terms of Being. The Other is not ever taken as an intentional modification of the subject's ego. Derrida then argues that for the Other to appear as other and to be recognized as such, it must be "other than"; thus, the ego must have some understanding of itself that it brings to the social relation and by which it understands the Other.[69] Derrida states that Levinas refuses to acknowledge an intentional modification of the ego because "this would be a violent and totalitarian act for him."[70] By refusing to enter into this "transcendental violence," Derrida maintains, Levinas also refuses to enter into the realm of the actually real and possible, and, thus, "deprives himself of the very foundation and possibility of his own language."[71] Derrida concludes that in his yearning for an absolutely nonviolent thought, Levinas produces a language not only without rhetoric, but also without concept, without phrase, and without the verb "to be."[72] He claims that Levinas's language is not a philosophy rooted in history and in what is, but is a dream for what cannot be:

> It is the dream of a purely heterological thought at its source. A pure thought of pure difference. Empiricism is its philosophical name, its metaphysical pretension or modesty. We say the dream because it must vanish at daybreak, as soon as language awakens.[73]

Derrida makes it clear that if Levinas's thought is "a pure thought of pure difference," it doesn't have the power to criticize Heidegger's ontology or anything else because it is not rooted in history or the real. However, Derrida's mistake is apparent when we realize that, although Levinas refers to the Other as absolutely and infinitely Other, this does not mean that he believes in pure difference any more than Derrida and Heidegger do. Levinas never claims that he can do without ontological language. Derrida makes this mistake because he interprets literally Levinas's hyperbolic language of "absolutely and infinitely other." For Derrida, absolute and infinite otherness must mean "pure difference." However, although Levinas contends that the otherness of the Other is absolute and infinite, he does not deny that the Other is understood in terms of being.

This is, in fact, something Levinas says in a minor key in several places.[74] He admits that there is no such thing as pure difference, admits that there is no comprehension of the Other without ontological language, when he says: "to know an existent it is necessary to have comprehended the Being of the existent" is a "truism." More precisely, although he refers to the Other as infinitely and absolutely other, he also says quite clearly in both *Time and the Other* and *Totality and Infinity* that "the other, as other, is not only *alter ego*. It is what I myself am not."[75] It is clear that Levinas admits that the Other is infinitely and absolutely other not in the sense of purely other. The Other is *alter ego* but is not only this, is always more than this.

Here, Levinas's hyperbolic language takes the place of literal language, and this is what Derrida fails to see.[76] Levinas insists that the Other is not only more than *alter ego*, but is infinitely more, absolutely more. By the term infinitely and absolutely other, Levinas does not mean not that the otherness of the Other is pure difference. He is aware, with Derrida and Heidegger, that pure difference is the stuff of dreams. Yet Levinas still insists that the otherness of the Other is infinite and absolute, not in the literal sense of purity, but rather in the hyperbolic sense that the otherness of the Other is not only beyond me and beyond my powers of comprehension, but infinitely and absolutely beyond me and my powers. According to Levinas, the manifestation of the Other is not a phenomenon in which I am entirely without any prior conception. Rather, the manifestation of the Other is the infinite overflowing of my conception, the overflowing of infinity in the finite,[77] "an exceeding of thought,"[78] "an excess of meaning."[79]

This overflowing manifestation, this excess of meaning infinitely beyond my thought is, in fact, what Levinas expresses by his notion of the *face* of the Other: "The way in which the other presents himself, exceeding the idea of the other in me, we here name face."[80] The face of the other means that the otherness of the other is greater than what I could ever understand or even imagine—and not just greater, but infinitely greater, absolutely greater. As Richard Cohen notes, the face of the Other for Levinas is not just a positivity, but an "emphatic positivity, an excessive positivity, an ultrapositivity."[81]

Levinas's Hyperbolic Rhetoric

Here we see what is so vital to understand if Levinas's philosophy is to be interpreted correctly—that it proceeds by way of exaggeration, by way of the rhetorical trope called *hyperbole*. Levinas's rhetoric magnifies some things to such an extent that it is as if other things didn't exist at all.[82] For instance, it is not that the subject is entirely without any understanding of itself and of the Other before the manifestation of the Other, but compared to the depths of the otherness of the Other, it is as if it were nothing.

The reader of Levinas's philosophy must guard against misunderstandings that arise from this hyperbolic rhetoric, for this is exactly what causes Derrida to misinterpret Levinas. That something is *as if* it were nothing is absolutely different from actually *being* nothing. It must be said, however, that Levinas's rhetoric is designed not to highlight but to obscure this difference. But why does he want to obscure this difference? Why does Levinas want to portray the understanding of the Other as nothing, as though it doesn't even exist, even though he affirms it?

It is because Levinas's rhetoric is in the service of his philosophical project, which, as Derrida has rightly seen, is based upon the notion of primacy. Consequently, he aims to provoke the reader to look and to think somewhere else, and particularly, somewhere else than Heidegger led the reader to look and think in *Being and Time*.[83] Certainly we have some understanding of the Other. Comprehension of the Other's being is, as Heidegger insists, part of our own *Dasein*, and Levinas takes this insight over without ever trying to deny it. What is primary for Levinas, however, is the fact that the Other is *more* than our comprehension of him/her. Levinas wants us to look not at our own understanding, but at the manifestation of the Other itself, at the way in which the infinite otherness of the Other overwhelms and exceeds our powers of comprehension. His hyperbolic rhetoric makes our understanding of the Other look like nothing because it wants us to look not at the finitude of our understanding but at that which infinitely exceeds our understanding, at the Other's *face*.

For Levinas, the face of the Other robs our understanding of its primacy and makes it look as if it were nothing because the face not only looks at us, but *speaks*. This is why the manifestation of the Other's being is quantitatively different from the manifestation of the Being of everything else. The Being of objects is just there to be comprehended, or, rather, to be comprehended to the extent *Dasein* lets it be. The point is that the comprehension of the being of objects is primarily through vision. But the being of the Other is not merely there to be seen and, thus, comprehended by the subject. Levinas insists that the way in which the Other manifests him/herself is qualitatively different because it is not merely manifestation to the comprehension of the subject, but expression. The Other discloses him/herself, comes into contact with me, speaks. Levinas does not deny that the Other is disclosed in the openness of being, but he insists that to say that this is the only way the Other is disclosed "is to say that we are never directly with the existent as such."[84] But because we are with the Other directly, the Other is not only a disclosure of Being but is a face, is its own expression. The face of the Other manifests itself through and by the idea I have of it, but also "it expresses itself."[85]

For Levinas, the fact that the Other attends its own manifestation in the face, so that the face is not manifestation but expression, means that the Other speaks itself, offers itself in language. According to Levinas, the face is the offering of itself, and this offering is the very essence of language: "The vision of the face is inseparable from this offering language is."[86] Every use of language, every language event, Levinas insists, "takes place already within the primordial face to face of language."[87] The fact that the face is expression and not merely manifestation entails three very crucial consequences, all of which make clear how Levinas's own account of the social relation is both rooted in but also consciously trying to interpret otherwise than Heideggerian ontology.

First, because in expression the Other gives to the subject more of him/herself than the subject knows already—exceeds the idea of the Other the subject already has—the Other gives to the subject that which the subject doesn't already know. Thus, the very essence of language, and thus of speech, is not reminiscence, but teaching: "As an attendance of being at its own presence, speech is a teaching."[88] More than this, however, since the Other "comes to me from without by exceeding my capacities," as Lingis says,[89] by teaching me, by introducing "into me what was not in me,"[90] the relationship with the Other is "a relationship with his transcendence."[91] As teacher, the Other is the subject's master and, thus, the Other's face comes from his/her position of transcendence. In Levinas's spatial metaphor, the voice of the Other comes from above the subject, from a height, and "the height from which language comes we designate with the term teaching."[92]

Secondly, Levinas maintains that the expression of the Other not only teaches the subject, but it gives to the subject more than the subject even had the idea of heretofore. Levinas concludes from this that the Other thereby gives the subject the idea of excess, the idea of that which exceeds all ideas, the idea of *infinity*: "to receive from the Other beyond the capacity of the I . . . means exactly: to have the idea of infinity."[93] As Lingis says, the exceeding of any capacity, which the Other brings to the subject, is the very reality of the idea of infinity.[94]

Thirdly, the fact that the Other is present at, directs, and gives itself in its expression beyond the capacity of the subject means that the relationship with the face is a relationship with the Other's transcendence, with the Other's height and mastery. The expression of the Other is not only spoken, but addressed to the subject, and it calls the subject from its position of transcendence. The face of the Other as expression is more than manifestation; it is command from the height. As Lingis says, "the face is not turning a surface but contesting and appealing."[95] In the face, the Other expresses that s/he is, and that s/he has a right to be, and summons the subject to recognize this right. The Other thereby initiates the relation by calling into question the freedom of the subject. Thus, for Levinas the expression of the face is also the ethical command: "Thou shalt not kill."[96] The expression of the face means that before the subject asks about the meaning of the Other's being, the Other has already expressed itself, has expressed its right to be, and called the subject to responsibility.[97] The face of the Other acts upon the subject's freedom, calling it into question with the language of command. This is why Levinas says "true speech, speech in its essence, is commanding."[98]

This command to the subject prompts a "saying to the other" on the part of the subject. This is not an attempt to comprehend the Other, but rather is a recognition of the Other's right to be. As Lingis says, "In his alterity, the other is faced, that is not cognized, but answered by a speaking that is a response. To re-cognize the face of the other is not to grasp, to conceive, but to give."[99] This means that the first saying to the Other is apology, which is at one and the same time an act of assertion—in which the subject justifies itself—and an act of submission—in which the subject recognizes the Other's right to be: ". . . the very fact of being in a conversation consists in recognizing in the other a right over [me}, and hence in justifying oneself. Apology . . . belongs to the essence of conversation."[100] The first saying of the subject is apology because the expression of the face calls the subject into the relationship determined by responsibility, so that the relationship is itself the very institution of ethics.[101] Expression, says Levinas, is the manifestation of being, but it is much more than this: "it is of itself presence of a face, and hence appeal and teaching, entry into relation with me—the ethical relation."[102]

Truth as Respect for Being

The ethical relation wherein the Other calls the subject into responsibility demands, for Levinas, a radical redefinition of truth. It is precisely truth as comprehension of Being that is called into question by the face of the Other. The phenomenon of the face not only reveals the subject's comprehension of the Other as inadequate. Much more important for Levinas is the fact that the appeal and command in the face reveals the subject's comprehension of the Other as a hold, a grasp, an attempt to contain. Thus, truth as comprehension of being involves "... the hand which grasps."[103] Truth as "a grasp on things"[104] means that "knowledge would involve the suppression of the other by the grasp, by the hold, or by the vision that grasps before the grasp."[105] The command of the Other—the call of the subject into responsibility for the Other in the face—is, then, the ethical grasp that halts the subjects's grasp of comprehension by calling it into question.[106] This seizing of the subject by the Other necessitates a conception of truth that is not only different from truth as comprehension of being, but which argues against it, displaces it, overthrows it: "The face brings a notion of truth which, in contradistinction to contemporary ontology, is not the disclosure of impersonal Neuter, but expression."[107]

What, then, according to Levinas, is truth? Truth has to do entirely with the relationship between persons. It is, in fact, produced within the relation between same and Other. It is not a meaning that already exists, which I then must let be, respect and comprehend. Truth is the face of the Other, the Other's expression of him/herself to me, an appeal made to me and a demand made upon me. Levinas insists that the Other's "appeal to me is his truth."[108] But if truth is appeal, then it does not merely exist, but it has to be produced in that it has to be responded to: "My response is not added as an accident to a `nucleus' of his objectivity, but first produces his truth."[109] Truth is produced between the subject and the Other when the Other commands the subject in the ethical relation and the subject responds in responsibility. This means that truth is not merely letting the Other's being be in the process of comprehension. Truth as comprehension of being, even when it respects being, isn't sufficiently respectful, isn't sufficiently ethical, because it still defines truth in terms of the being that is comprehended. Levinas insists, on the other hand, that truth is not the comprehension of being that occurs within the relationship between subject and Other, but is the relationship itself, because in the relationship the subject is commanded into responsbility by and for the Other. Truth is "a modality of the relationship between the same and the Other."[110]

Truth as a modality of this relationship means that truth is inseparable from the just relation between people and, thus, from ethics or morality, or justice. Since Levinas defines truth as the Other's command and the selfsame's response, "truth is thus bound up with the social relation, which is justice."[111] Ethics, morality and justice are not for Levinas somehow subordinate to truth or an aspect of truth. They are the truth of truth, the highest truth. "To be in truth," says Levinas, "is not to comprehend nor to take hold of . . . , but rather to encounter the other without allergy, that is, in justice."[112] Thus, the just relation with the Other is not only the essence of ethics, or morality, or justice, but is the essence of truth as well. Because to be in an ethical relation, to submit oneself to the command of the Other and accept one's responsibilities for the Other in justice is, for Levinas, to be in truth, there is a tie between truth and morality, or ethics, or justice. "Morality," says Levinas, "presides over the work of truth."

Truth, then, is not something in addition to ethics, but is ethics itself. The highest and most important truth is ethical truth, the truth of ethics, which Levinas also refers to as the *good*. Thus, he proposes a version of truth that is not other than but coincidental with the good precisely because the very truth of truth is ethics. As he says, he opposes the hypocrisy of a philosophy that thinks itself devoted equally to the true and to the good while also insisting on their distinction. [113] Richard Cohen explains that Levinas's philosophy "Aims to pronounce this goodness . . . to realign its relation to the true. His thought is a peculiar ethical exacerbation of language which bends the true to the good."[114] And because ethics is the highest and most important truth, and equivalent to the good, Levinas insists that ethics should be given the status of first philosophy: "Morality is not a branch of philosophy, but first philosophy."[115]

But what does Levinas mean by this statement? This is certainly an argument against Heidegger, an interpretation of first philosophy otherwise than Heidegger's establishment of ontology as first philosophy. For Levinas, ethics as first philosophy means that the social relation is that event in being that is not only irreducible to knowledge of being, but is something other than, more than, and better than comprehension of being. Ethics thus overthrows the supremacy of knowledge of being; it puts an end to the "domination of knowledge."[116] Ethics has nothing to do with epistemological power or weakness, but refers to the responsibility that is prior to and the condition of knowing.[117] Ethics is not divorced from knowledge but cannot be reduced to knowledge, and it interrupts the project of knowledge both from within and from above, from the transcendence of the Other, "with a higher call, a more severe condition: responsibility."[118] "It is not that the Other escapes knowing," Levinas asserts, "but that there is no meaning in speaking of knowledge or ignorance, for justice, the transcendence and condition for knowing, is nowise a noesis correlative of a noema."[119] Thus, it is ethics, which interrupts and conditions the adventure of knowledge, and not the adventure of knowledge itself, which is first philosophy.

We can see that Levinas's accusations against Heidegger do not stem from misunderstanding him, or from the desire to have a straw man to rail against. Rather, Levinas's attack on Heidegger stems from his own philosophical project of constantly interpreting otherwise than Heidegger in order to present not only an optional interpretation of being and of human being, but also an optional definition of truth and an optional way of prioritizing between knowledge and ethics. Levinas's proclamations about ethics—and not ontology—as first philosophy, and about justice, ethics and the Good as truth—rather than the comprehension of being—make clear that he understands Heidegger and is, in fact, arguing within Heidegger's ontology while arguing against it to propose a different version of truth itself.

Levinas himself makes this obvious by the very Heideggerian language he chooses. He does not say that truth is not concerned with being, has nothing to do with being, or is entirely outside of the realm of being.[120] Rather, he says: "To account for being, or to be in truth, is not to comprehend or to take hold of . . . , but rather to encounter the other without all allergy, that is, in justice."[121] Similarly, Levinas makes evident how he opposes Heidegger by arguing within Heidegger's own philosophical framework when he asserts that "no thought could better obey being than by allowing itself to be dominated by exteriority."[122] Even when Levinas determines ethics as the essential content of truth and calls it something as un-Heideggerian as *metaphysical truth*, he still reveals that his argument against Heidegger's philosophy is also within Heidegger's philosophy. "The meaning of metaphysical truth," he insists, "is truth as a respect for being."[123]

It is essential to understand what Levinas's own conception of truth as respect for being means. He here argues against an interpretation of respect for being that sees it as a moment, even an important moment, in the comprehension of being, which is defined as truth. Levinas takes the Heideggerian formulation of respect for being and refers to it as the meaning of metaphysical truth, i.e., as ethics itself, as truth itself. For Levinas, then, respect for being is not involved in the project of comprehending being, which is truth. Respect for being is truth itself—the most important, the greatest, highest and best truth. And if respect for being, the ethical relation, is the highest and best truth and, thus, is first philosophy, this means that respect for being always has priority over what we can know of being. Levinas insists that what we can know of the Other is always secondary in importance to the fact that we are responsible for the Other. This is what he means when he says that the ethical relationship not only cannot be dominated by the relationship of comprehension of being, but in fact the ethical relationship commands the relationship of knowledge.[124]

That the ethical relationship has priority over and commands the relationship of knowledge of being, that respect for being commands and presides over knowledge of being, is what Levinas means by "Truth as a respect for being is the meaning of metaphysical truth." This is not, however, what Heidegger means by truth as respect for being; it is, in fact, a certain reversal of Heidegger's notion. Levinas's philosophy ultimately offers both another interpretation of and a counteroption to Heidegger's notion that truth involves respect for being. To evaluate the validity of Levinas's accusations against Heidegger, then, involves not merely analyzing Heidegger's ontology, but becomes a matter of evaluating both philosophers' conceptions of the relation between truth and respect for being and then choosing between them.

Certainly, it is true that Heidegger does not give priority to the ethical in the way that Levinas does, for comprehension of being remains the goal and the essence of Heidegger's ontology. Levinas can therefore rightly say that Heidegger gives priority to knowledge of being over the ethical relation. But is Levinas correct in saying that thereby Heidegger's ontology reduces the other to the same? Does it mean that Heidegger's philosophy is a philosophy of power and is necessarily unjust? Is Levinas correct when he states that by making knowledge of being primary, more important than ethics, Heidegger's ontology "leads inevitably" to the tyranny and injustice of the state? Doesn't Heidegger's notion that truth as the uncovering of being necessarily involves respect for being rule all of this out and make Heidegger immune to such charges? Is it fair of Levinas to accuse Heidegger of all these things merely because the goal of Heidegger's ontology is to comprehend Being rather than to give priority to ethics?

These questions, which we have been discussing throughout this chapter, are best answered by highlighting the difference between how Heidegger and Levinas define the relationship between truth and respect for being. Heidegger insists that to know Being, one has to let it be as it is, and this is what he means by respect for Being. As we have seen, Heidegger insists that without respect for Being it can never be understood, but the comprehension of Being is still for Heidegger the essence of philosophy and of truth itself. He insists that true thought, thought within the truth of Being, is thought that allows and enables Being to appear as it is. For Heidegger, then, philosophy, or what he will call "meditative thinking,"[125] or thinking within the truth of Being,[126] is thought that respects Being in the sense that it lets Being manifest itself as it actually is. Respect for Being, the passive letting be of Being, is a component in the process of comprehending Being, which is truth. The manifestation of Being as it actually is leads to the always partial comprehension of Being, which is truth itself.

Because Heidegger defines respect for being as a moment within the comprehension of being, which is truth, rather than seeing respect for being as truth itself, as does Levinas, Heidegger subordinates ethics to ontology. This means that the grounds upon which to adjudicate between the various manifestations of Being are surrendered to the myriad manifestations of autonomous Being.[127] The manifestation and comprehension of Being is, for Heidegger, truth. Any manifestation of Being, no matter what form it takes, is truth; and ethics, or what we have allowed ourselves to consider as a possible ethical dimension in Heidegger's philosophy—

respect for Being—is not truth itself, but simply amounts to the demand to let Being come to presence as truth in whatever form it may take.[128] To surrender the right to judge between various manifestations of being on ethical grounds, to respectfully attend to being however it reveals itself, is, as Cohen says, "to turn from the ethical exigency to the ontological exigency, for being wants only to persevere in being."[129]

Levinas, on the other hand, arguing from within Heidegger's own terms but much more radically than Heidegger, takes Heidegger's notion of respect for Being, redefines it explicitly in terms of the ethical relationship between persons, and makes it the very essence of truth. True thought, then, is thought that gives up its supremacy and allows itself to be dominated by the highest truth, which is our ethical responsibility for the other person. Thus, Levinas's thought sees in ethics, in the command to responsibility as expressed in the face, the grounds upon which to adjudicate between the various manifestations of being. Whereas Heidegger's ontology includes respect for being, Levinas's ethical metaphysics finds in the thought of being that which exceeds, and has priority over and commands every thought—our ethical responsibility for one another, or the Good.

To Levinas, respect for Being is not sufficiently respectful if it is only a moment in the process of comprehending Being. Respect for Being is not a moment in the process of truth, but is truth itself, the highest truth, the Good. As such, it has priority over all thought, which means that it is the grounds upon which all else is to be evaluated. Thought that merely listens to Being and thinks thereby that it is truth is thought that places itself above the Good. To really be truth, thought must abdicate its place of primacy and subordinate itself to ethics, which means that it must allow itself to be directed by the highest truth, namely the Good. The manifestations of being are not truth itself; truth for

Levinas is ethics, that by which we not only can, but must judge between the various manifestations of being.[130]

It is clear, then, that Levinas's accusations against Heidegger do not constitute a misreading of Heidegger but constitute a radicalization of Heidegger's own notion that truth involves respect for being. Levinas demonstrates that Heidegger's ontology does include respect for Being in the process of comprehending Being. More than this, however, Levinas also attempts to convince us that respect for Being is the highest and most important truth and must preside as sovereign over all thought, or else thought inevitably becomes unjust or at least lends itself to injustice and forsakes its ability to criticize and to correct the real in light of and for the sake of the Good.

This is really the point of Levinas's polemic against Heidegger. Heidegger's ontology makes ethics less important than the comprehension of Being. Here Levinas enters to insist that if anything is made more important than ethics, if ethics is not seen as the highest truth, then thought is at the service of some end other than an ethical one and either becomes unjust or is coopted by what is unjust. For Levinas, because Heidegger's ontology sees ethics only as a necessary aspect of the ontological project of comprehending Being, it cannot render justice to that in which the demand for justice arises—the face of the Other.

Heidegger's *Dasein* may know that it has to respect the other's being in order to comprehend it, and it also may know that it can never know the other's being completely. Heidegger insists on both, as Levinas knows. For Levinas, however, this is not enough, because this does not mean that *Dasein*'s understanding of the other's being is subject to and commanded by the ethical obligation to respect and to protect the other. Levinas insists that if ethics isn't given priority to preside over all thought, then *Dasein* will always be in danger of thinking that its own comprehension of the Other is more important than its relation with the Other. And if *Dasein*'s comprehension of the other's being is what is most important, then that aspect of the other's being that *Dasein* cannot ever comprehend is secondary to the knowledge of the other that *Dasein* can possess. This means that the Other is always in some way reduced to the same when it is comprehended by *Dasein*, reduced to that which *Dasein* can comprehend.[131] And if the relation with the other person is subordinated to the knowledge of the other person that *Dasein* derives from the relation, then the Other—even if the Other is to be known in an ethical manner, in respect—is still essentially something to be known.

KNOWLEDGE, POWER AND THE TYRANNY OF ONTOLOGY

Having made this point, Levinas heightens his rhetoric once again. He insists that a philosophy that conceives of the social relation in such a way that the Other is essentially something to be known will control the Other through this knowledge; this philosophy will necessarily become unjust and will lend itself to the injustice and tyranny of the state. If ethics isn't conceived of as having priority over and commanding thought, then thought will necessarily fail to be ethical in the highest sense and will be unethical and, ultimately, violent. Heidegger's ontology may respect Being, but since its respect for being is at the service of comprehending being, even its respect for being is not only insufficiently respectful, but it is also unethical and potentially violent.

Only a philosophy that gives priority to ethics, exalts ethics not only as a branch of philosophy but as first philosophy, says Levinas, is sufficiently respectful of being. "No thought could better obey being than by allowing itself to be dominated by this exteriority,"[132] by which Levinas means alterity. Only a philosophy that views knowledge as dethroned by the call to responsibility that comes from alterity has within it the capacity to resist and to refute the grasp of comprehension, the first movement toward injustice and, ultimately, violence and tyranny.

If we consider Levinas's accusations against Heidegger in this manner—i.e., as proceeding not from some allergy toward Heidegger's thought nor from some misunderstanding of him, but from Levinas's own philosophical project of interpreting otherwise than Heidegger[133] —it becomes quite obvious that Levinas is going to catch much more of philosophy than Heidegger's ontology in his ethical net. In fact, we may legitimately ask whose philosophy, aside from Levinas's own, would not be subject to his criticism that ethics as first philosophy must direct all thought. This question does not reduce the force of Levinas's accusations against Heidegger, but shows the radicality of Levinas's notion that morality should preside over every thought, event and relation of knowing.

To Levinas, Heidegger represents the culmination of the tendency of Western philosophy to define itself, first and above all, as a knower of what is, as a knower of truth. Heidegger's ontology is for Levinas not a radical challenge to philosophy but much more a restatement of philosophy's definition of its own essence as a knower of what is in terms of the being of what is. Thus, Heidegger's ontology is guilty of the same type of "hypocrisy" that Levinas says typifies most of Western philosophy, which thinks that it can define itself as dedicated to knowledge of truth while the the same time claim that it somehow serves the Good. To serve the Good, for Levinas, means to find in being, to find in truth, that which overthrows and commands the project of knowing. Not to do this, not to see in the Good that which has priority over the true, Levinas insists, is necessarily to dedicate oneself in actuality to the true over the Good, and this is for Levinas the mistake Western philosophy often makes, and which Heidegger's ontology makes explicit.

Of course the fact that Levinas's accusations against Heidegger extend in Levinas's opinion to the main current of Western philosophy does not in some way render his attack on Heidegger's ontology less severe. As I have already said, Levinas's criticisms of Heidegger gain their greatest force if his philosophy convinces us that there is a real difference between ethics as a branch of philosophy and ethics as first philosophy, if there is a difference between a thought that merely listens to Being and lets Being manifest itself in whatever form it chooses and a thought that is commanded by some conception of the Good and so has some grounds to arbitrate between the various manifestations of Being as they appear.[134] Does it make a difference whether or not we let morality preside over the work of truth, over the work of philosophy, or can we have a philosophy devoted to letting Being appear as it is, as long as we remember to respect it and allow it to show itself as it actually is? Is there anything at stake here, socially, historically and politically, or is this merely an internal dispute within the isolated, insular, and for the most part irrelevant world of professional philosophy?

The validity both of Levinas's rhetoric against Heidegger and the rhetoric of his own philosophy proclaiming ethics as first philosophy largely rests on convincing us that there is something at stake here, and that it does make a difference whether we think of ethics either simply as a moment in the more important process of comprehension or as the most important thing we could ever comprehend, so that ethics directs our thinking. Can thinking that gives priority to truth over ethics really have the consequences Levinas mentions? Does it really "lead inevitably" to the tyranny and injustice of the state? Is it really a philosophy of power and domination? Here we can certainly recognize Levinas's hyperbolic rhetoric again. But is this all it is? If Levinas has absolutely no case to make here, if there is no basic fact to exaggerate about the dire social, political and ethical consequences of giving priority to knowledge over ethics, then Heidegger's philosophy is perhaps wrong, but hardly dangerous, hardly tyrannical, and there is no need for us to make the change in priorities that Levinas's rhetorical philosophy is trying to convince us to make.

Troubling Questions Concerning Heidegger and National Socialism

Here, I believe, Levinas's rhetoric makes its silent appeal not only to the event so central and cataclysmic in his own life, the Holocaust, but also to the unstated but well-known fact of Heidegger's Nazism and his apparent indifference to the fate of the Jews. These historical facts provide the greatest force to Levinas's rhetoric and make its hypberbole far from groundless.[135]

Heidegger's complicity with the National Socialists has been known for years. It is only very recently, however, that it has become a central topic of philosophical discussion. Philipe Lacoue-Labarthe's 1987 work, *La fiction du politique*,[136] and Victor Farias's more controversial work that appeared later that same year, *Heidegger et le Nazisme*,[137] uncovered a few new facts about Heidegger, repeated some old ones and served to fan the embers of an issue that had never before really produced much fire in academic circles. As Jurgen Habermas contends, philosophers in Germany have known about Heidegger's relationship to the Nazis, but the issue has always been merely a "specialists'" affair; and, in France, Heidegger was "instantly de-Nazified."[138] Consequently, although Lacoue-Labarthe's and Farias's books do not say a great deal that is new—new at least to philosophers—they are important in that they have brought to the fore the issue of Heidegger's association with the Nazis.

Of course this one issue involves many questions about Heidegger's life, about his politics, and about the relationship, if any, between his politics and his philosophical writings. One of the more strictly biographical questions concerns whether or not he abandoned the Nazi Party in 1934 as he said he did. Karl Lowith's account of his meeting with Heidegger in 1936, in which Heidegger affirmed his faith in Hitler, stated that "National Socialism was the proper path for Germany," and wore a swastika, forces us to extend the dates of Heidegger's Nazism at least a few years.[139]

Another question is, did Heidegger after the war alter his own writings so as to minimize their sympathy with the Nazis? We know that in 1953 Heidegger published under the title *Introduction to Metaphysics* lectures originally given in 1935, in which he speaks of the "inner truth and greatness of the Nazi movement."[140] In the *Introduction to Metaphysics,* he adds parenthetically that by the Nazi movement he means "the encounter between global technology and modern man," and he claims in the preface that this parenthetical remark was included in the original lecture. This claim is contested not only by Lacoue-Labarthe and Farias, but by many Heidegger scholars before them who believe that Heidegger added the parenthetical remark to make the passage more acceptable. This issue may never be completely resolved because the page in question is mysteriously missing from the Heidegger archives.

More important than these biographical questions is the purely textual but still haunting question of whether there is an inner affinity between Heidegger's philosophy, most especially *Being and Time,* and the speeches and essays written in 1933–34 during his rectorship of the University of Freiburg in which he actively advocates Nazism.[141] Derrida recently labored to show that Heidegger's use of the term *Geist* in his Nazi writings—a term he said in *Being and Time* was to be avoided—and the fact that he is speaking of the leadership of the Fuhrer as a spiritual leadership, mean that "even while he runs the risk of placing this thematics of the *Fuhrung* [spiritual leadership] in the service of a determinate politics [i.e., Nazism], Heidegger gives it to be understood that he is breaking in advance with any such service."[142] Similarly, Arnold Davidson says we must admit at least that *Being and Time* and Heidegger's Nazi writings and speeches "cannot be merged" because of the differences between them. He specifically cites the fact that in *Being and Time* the social collectivity, the *they*, hinders authentic *Dasein*, whereas in his Nazi writings "the tension and countertension between authenticity and the they . . . is replaced by absorption in our [German] historical-spiritual mission."[143] Authentic *Dasein* is, in the Nazi writings, no longer the individualized authentic Being-one's-self, but is "our spiritual being as part of a people."[144]

The question of the continuity or discontinuity between Heidegger's philosophical writings and his political writings then becomes: Did Heidegger think that Nazism was the authentic manifestation of the Being of the German people so that the authentic Being of individualized *Dasein* was being authentically expressed corporately through the Nazi movement? That this is a reasonable conclusion to draw is stated by Karsten Harries, who points out that *Being and Time* gives a prominent place to the concept of destiny. "Once we recognize that authenticity demands subordination of the individual to a common destiny," reasons Harries, then *Being and Time* and Heidegger's political writings "aren't opposed."[145] Lacoue-Labarthe is even more bold: "His political involvement of 1933 is neither an accident nor a mistake . . . In contrast to what may have been said, Heidegger's involvement is completely consistent with his thought."[146] Lowith's account, only very recently published, of his 1936 meeting with Heidegger in Rome strongly supports this view. According to this account, Lowith said to Heidegger that he thought

Heidegger's involvement with National Socialism "was in agreement with the essence of his philosophy," and Heidegger in turn "told me unreservedly that I was right and developed his idea by stating that his concept of historicity—*Geschichlichkeit*—was the foundation for his political involvement."[147]

But perhaps the most troubling question about this issue of Heidegger's involvement with the Nazis is how he viewed the Nazis and the Holocaust for which they were responsible after the war and after the atrocities had been revealed fully. Heidegger did refer to the event of the Holocaust a few times, but for the most part he kept silent, and never did he renounce or repudiate the Nazis' genocide of the Jews. Even the accounts wherein Heidegger does mention the Holocaust constitute a grim testimony to how he felt about it. In a letter to Herbert Marcuse, Heidegger equates the mass murder of the Jews with the deaths of the Eastern Germans killed in the war. Even more astounding is the short excerpt of a talk Heidegger gave in 1949 in which he bemoans the fact that the once pastoral and tranquil life of the German peasant slowly tilling his land by hand is rapidly being made a thing of the past by the mechanization of farming. His words here indicate that he can be rightly accused of a certain "ethical indifference"[148] and of having "astounding priorities"[149]: "Agriculture is now a mechanized food industry. As for its essence, it is the same thing as the manufacture of corpses in the gas chambers and the death camps, the same thing as the blockades and the reduction of countries to famine, the same thing as the manufacture of hydrogen bombs."[150] Levinas asks if we cannot perceive in this passage and in the fact that Heidegger never repudiated the Holocaust "a kind of consent to the horror?"[151] And, Levinas asks, if Heidegger could give any kind of consent at all to such a horror, "can we be assured . . . that there was never any echo of Evil" in *Being and Time*?[152]

The foregoing is not meant to be a complete

discussion of even a few questions involved in the very complex issue of Heidegger's affiliation with the Nazis and its effect on how we should read his philosophy. A complete analysis of this problem is far beyond the scope of the present work. This serves only to locate Levinas's criticisms of Heidegger within this discussion that has only so recently caught fire. And if the facts of Heidegger's life and some of what he wrote and said compel us to the conclusion that there is at least a certain indifference to the human in his thought, who more than Levinas has reflected upon the meaning of this indifference? Who more than Levinas has attempted to think through the inadequacies of Heidegger's conceptions of *Dasein* and of Being-with-one-another? Who better than Levinas has tried to explicate the ethical ramifications of Heidegger's ontology? Who better than Levinas has shown that Heidegger's thought of Being makes ethics derivative and subordinate, and who more than Levinas has pointed out the dangers of this?

If philosophy has never fully comprehended Levinas's accusations against Heidegger and has for the most part dismissed them, perhaps it is at least partly because philosophy has never seriously considered the relationship between the thought of Being in Heidegger's philosophy and the thought of the human through and in the light of certain facts regarding what Heidegger was, and wrote, and said and didn't say. "The thought of being," says Derrida quite emphatically, "could not possibly occur as ethical violence."[153] Can we see this bit of rhetoric in Heidegger's defense as any less hyperbolic than Levinas's rhetoric? Can it be maintained if Heidegger's association with the Nazis has to be seen as more than what he himself said it was, a blunder?[154] And if philosophy is now beginning to seriously consider the relationship between Heidegger's association with Nazism and his philosophy, then perhaps it will return to Levinas's accusations against Heidegger and will attempt to evaluate them anew.

This should not lead us to forget, however, that Levinas's accusations against Heidegger are included within Levinas's own constructive philosophical project, and it is this constructive project that is his greatest contribution to philosophy. Making accusations against Heidegger on ethical grounds is not the only thing—not even the main thing—Levinas has achieved. Were this the case, then the discovery that Heidegger himself actually said that the genocide of the Jews was acceptable as an event of Being would render Levinas's philosophy superfluous. We would not need to attend to Levinas's philosophy to convince us of the deficiencies of Heidegger's thought. The point is that although Levinas's philosophy is a constant polemic against Heidegger, Levinas has done much more than question Heidegger's philosophy.

By interpreting within but otherwise than Heidegger, Levinas has developed his own philosophy, one that questions and challenges the nature of philosophy itself. Levinas offers another option to Heidegger not only because Heidegger's ontology is insufficient. Much more pressing for Levinas is the fact that in the light of the cataclysmic events of the twentieth century—the Holocaust foremost among them, which philosophy not only was helpless to prevent but may have even underwritten and partially caused—other options concerning the relation of philosophy to ethics must be found.[155] "The full weight of Levinas's thought," says Steven Smith, "is a question of opposing the philosophy that produced and underwrote the colonial arrogance of Europe and the totalitarian cruelties of Hitler and Stalin."[156] More than this, however, history also provides the reason why Levinas's counteroption, his insistence that ethics is first philosophy, has to be taken seriously as a distinctively post-Holocaust philosophy. As Levinas's lifelong friend, Maurice Blanchot, puts it: "How can one philosophize after Auschwitz? It is this thought that traverses the whole of Levinas's philosophy and that he proposes to us without saying it."[157]

For this is what Levinas's philosopy is—a post-Holocaust philosophy, an attempt to respond in the language of philosophy to that paramount example of the terror and barbarity that has arisen even in the very heart of our very civilized and advanced twentieth century culture, that fact which so much thought pays homage to but which so little thought is actually radically changed by—the fact of the Holocaust. The Holocaust constitutes an absolute crisis for Western thought because the people who carried out the greatest genocide of the century weren't barbarians, but were civilized, educated people, people familiar with the greatest art, culture and philosophy of the West. Thought is stymied by the fact that educated persons were guilty of such an atrocity. How could cultured, educated humans surrender so completely to the diabolical?

The diabolical, says Levinas, "is endowed with intelligence and enters where it will."[158] If, as Heidegger's personal history seems to prove and as the history of his own time and place definitely does prove, even the most educated and civilized hearts and minds can house the darkest evil, then the diabolical may be inscribed even where we least expect to find it—in our greatest and most profound thoughts—so that the diabolical is difficult to discern. To reject the diabolical, insists Levinas, "it is first necessary to refute it. Intellectual effort is needed to recognize it."[159] If this is so, then the greatest wisdom consists not only in knowing, but in knowing the Good above all, and in letting the Good preside as sovereign over all thinking and all knowing. Then we may recognize the diabolical, even when it takes the harmless guise of thought, and may guard ourselves against it. This is the wisdom Levinas's philosophy explores and recommends.[160]

The Holocaust is the fact before which all thinking stops. Emil Fackenheim has described it as the rupture that ruptures philosophy.[161] Jean-Francois Lyotard has stated that Auschwitz raises the problem of what genre of discourse could possibly link up with this name, for a "merely speculative" one is out of the question.[162] Levinas offers one thinking, one philosophy, that attempts to link up with the name of Auschwitz by presenting thought itself as emerging from the horror of the event thoroughly ruptured, thoroughly chastened in the sense of absolutely dethroned. Levinas does indeed argue against Heideggerian ontology, but it is crucial to understand that in doing so he also argues against most of Western philosophy, and he does so to give to philosophy a new direction and a new identity. After the Holocaust, surely philosophy needs to think itself, needs to question itself on how it conceives of the relationship between the true and the good, between knowledge and ethics. Levinas suggests that a proper answer to the Holocaust is to conceive of obedience to the Good, or ethics, as more important than and sovereign over knowledge of the true, conceived either as what is or as the being of what is.

Levinas insists that since the Holocaust teaches us that evil is insidious, we cannot afford to consider ethics a branch of philosophy, but must rather view the good as the truest truth because it is the best, so that ethics presides over truth as first philosophy.[163] And if this is so, then far from being a dream of what can never be, as Derrida charges, Levinas's philosophy is, to use his own metaphor, an insomnia, a night watch, a perpetual vigilance that speaks from the nightmare that actually was.[164] And if our philosophy since the Holocaust has either kept Heidegger's silence about the nightmare or has never found the words to respond to it, then don't we need to listen more closely to Levinas's voice? Even worse, if our philosophy and our thinking since the Holocaust are no more concerned with and directed by ethics, are no more concerned with the devaluation of the human, than they were before the Holocaust,[166] then perhaps we need to begin thinking with Levinas the difference between ethics as a branch of philosophy and ethics as first philosophy, and the difference that difference might make. And if we follow Levinas in thinking this difference, as contrary to Heidegger as our thought will be, still, as Derrida insists[167] and Levinas's philosophy not only admits but makes obvious and exemplifies, we will see, within the very thought of this very difference, the trace of Heidegger.

PART II

Ethics as First Philosophy

Levinas's Contribution to Contemporary Religious Thought

> Not to submit the law of justice to the implacable course of events, to denounce them when necessary as senseless or insane—this is what it means to be a Jew.
> —*Emmanuel Levinas*

> The philosophical problem, then, which is posed by the useless pain which appears in its fundamental malignancy across the events of the twentieth century, concerns the meaning that religiosity and the human morality of goodness can still retain after the end of theodicy.
> —*Emmanuel Levinas*

As we have seen, Levinas's philosophy both exalts ethics and thereby criticizes and attempts to change the essence of philosophy. Our ethical obligation to one another, he insists, means that morality must be considered as more than merely a branch of philosophy; rather, it must be considered first philosophy, must be seen as the most important and the central truth that presides as sovereign over the rest of philosophy. To evaluate Levinas's claim that ethics is first philosophy, it is necessary first to ascertain the grounds upon which Levinas makes this statement. We cannot allow the force of his rhetoric to persuade us of the validity of his philosophy without first evaluating the soundness of the foundation upon which it is built. What are the basic presuppositions that lead Levinas to insist that ethics is not a branch of philosophy, but first philosophy?

It is precisely at this level that Levinas seems to be most susceptible to criticism, for his philosophy certainly seems to depend upon assumptions external to philosophy, namely upon a certain religious vision or upon theological beliefs drawn from his Judaism. Doesn't all of Levinas's talk about the idea of the Infinite and of the Infinite itself at least hint that his presuppositions are not philosophical but religious?[1] Doesn't he show in his Talmudic writings how the eternal wisdom of the Bible contradicts philosophy, especially Heidegger's philosophy, in the same places and for the same reasons as he does in his own ethical philosophy?[2] Isn't the thought of God ever present in, though often in the background of, Levinas's philosophy, and isn't this proven by the fact that the language of Infinity in *Totality and Infinity* becomes God-language in his later work?[3] Certainly we must agree with Alan Megill when he says that although Levinas "employs a philosophical language and method, the dominant preoccupation of his thought arises within the perspective of a certain kind of Judaism."[4]

But if Levinas's philosophy is written from a religious perspective, does this mean that the cogency of his philosophy depends upon *a priori* religious beliefs? In other words, are Levinas's claims that the Other is infinitely Other, and that the face commands one to ethics and, consequently, that morality is first philosophy, grounded in and based upon religious beliefs? To assent to the notion that ethics is first philosophy, is it necessary to share in Levinas's religious presuppositions? Is it necessary to step into the hermeneutical circle in the same way and at the same point as does Levinas? That is to say, does Levinas's claim that morality is first philosophy depend upon a certain form of Judaism, with its certain kind of theology and its certain kind of God?

Jacques Derrida certainly thinks that this is so. When he discusses the similarities and differences between the thought of Levinas and the thought of Blanchot, Derrida points out Blanchot's insistence that Levinas's notion of the dissymmetry between the selfsame and the other "must be maintained independently of the theological context in which it occurs."[5] Derrida then goes on to ask: "But is this possible? Independent of its 'theological context' (an expression Levinas would most likely reject) does not this entire discourse collapse?"[6]

But does Levinas's discourse depend upon its religious presuppositions, upon its "theological context," so that without that context the discourse would collapse? Levinas would certainly deny this, and this is at least part of what he means when he insists that he is a philosopher and not a theologian. The fact remains, however, that in addition to all of his philosophical writings, Levinas is also the author of several essays on the meaning of Judaism and of the Talmud.[7] So how can Levinas the Talmudist bracket out religious presuppositions and write philosophy based not on those presuppositions, but upon claims founded and justified philosophically? This is exactly the issue troubling Derrida when he wonders if Levinas's entire philosophical discourse would collapse independent of its theological context.

It is important to see how Levinas defends himself on this point. Although he in no way says he stops being a religious person when he writes philosophy,[8] he also says he writes philosophy, not theology, and that his philosophy rests upon rightly philosophical, and not necessarily religious, claims. We can see what Levinas means by this if we explore the basis of his contention that morality is first philosophy. This claim depends entirely upon his presupposition that we as human beings are ethically responsible for one another.

The Grounding for Levinas's Claims: Philosophical or Religious?

But upon what grounds does Levinas posit that we as humans are ethically responsible for each other? It is crucial to notice that he does not try to prove this point by appealing to any religious belief or to any sacred text. He insists that whenever a biblical reference occurs in his philosophy, it "never serves as a proof, but as an illustration."[9] He explains the true grounding of his claims when he says that he "would never introduce a Talmudic or biblical verse into one of my philosophical texts to try to prove or justify a phenomenological argument."[10] Here Levinas insists again that what he does in his philosophical work is phenomenology. This means that he claims to find the evidence of our responsibility for one another within the relationship between the selfsame and the Other. Levinas's presupposition that we are ethically responsible for the Other depends for its validity not upon any religious belief but upon whether or not we actually experience ourselves as ethically responsible for each other. In other words, Levinas's claim that ethics is first philosophy, which depends upon the veracity of his presupposition that we are ethically responsible for each other, is not a religious but a phenomenological, or at least a quasi-phenomenological claim.[11] Levinas finds ethical responsibility within the phenomena of human relationships, and this means that Levinas's assertion that morality is first philosophy is founded upon philosophical, and not religious, claims.[12]

This means that the philosophical legitimacy of Levinas's discourse rests upon a phenomenological or quasi-phenomenological claim that we actually experience ourselves as ethically responsible for others. If this claim accords with experience and/or the foundations of consciousness, then Levinas is free to declare that this ethical obligation should have priority over the cognitive content of every other truth. And although our ethical responsibility does indeed have, as we shall see, great religious significance for Levinas, his philosophical contention that morality is first philosophy in no way depends upon this religious significance. However, if we do not experience ourselves as responsible for the Other so that we are not ethically obligated to the other person—if Levinas's phenomenological claim does not accord with experience, is not grounded in the intersubjective relation—then Levinas's philosophy is not what he insists it is, a phenomenology, a description of what is and/or the conditions of what is. If we are in fact not ethically obligated to the Other, then Levinas's philosophy must give up its philosophical pretension and admit that although it is in the guise of phenomenology, it is actually a religious discourse about what should be rather than a philosophical discourse about what is. This would make Levinas's ethical philosophy a sermon, an exhortation, a prophetic word, or even, as Derrida has it, a dream of what can never be.[13] The philosophical legitimacy of Levinas's discourse, then, does not have to do with God or with certain religious presuppositions but depends entirely upon whether or not Levinas is correct when he maintains that our ethical obligation to the Other is within the relationship between persons and, hence, can be discovered and described not only religiously, but also purely phenomenologically.

As we have already seen, Levinas's philosophical project is a phenomenological analysis of human being, and its foundation is his discovery in the social relation of that which Heidegger either overlooked or underestimated—the ethical dimension. Without this ethical dimension of the social relation, Levinas's entire discourse survives as sermon, but collapses as philosophy.

Levinas shows that, for him, our ethical responsibility is a phenomenological fact of human existence independent of any religious or theological proof when he discusses the story of Cain and Abel wherein Cain asks, "Am I my brother's keeper?" Levinas does not introduce this passage in order to prove that we actually are ethically responsible for each other. He states, rather, that this story illustrates that this is already established phenomenologically.[14] As Jean Greisch says, borrowing some words from Wittgenstein, that we are responsible for one another is for Levinas "as clear as a sock on the jaw. In no way does it become a problem."[15]

Whether or not Levinas is correct in stating that humans experience themselves as ethically responsible for one another, whether or not our obligations toward others hit us as unmistakably "as a sock in the jaw," it is clear that Levinas sees this as a properly philosophical claim because it is based on a phenomenological description of existence. It must be said, however, that whether or not this is true, certainly Levinas is not the only one who has found in the phenomenon of human existence an ethical dimension. This ethical aspect of our existence is, in fact, a phenomenon many philosophers have tried to explain and account for. The most obvious example, of course, is Immanuel Kant, someone to whom Levinas bears a certain similarity.[16] It is crucial for our purposes here to note that, in Kant's formulations of the categorical imperative, it is not religion that leads to ethics, but rather ethics that leads to religion. This is, in fact, precisely what Kant says in *The Critique of Practical Reason*: "ethics leads to religion."[17] Thus, the ethical dimension is the foundation of religion for Kant because it is found and experienced in human existence as one of the basic categories of human understanding.

The fact that philosophy has tried to come to grips

with the reality of ethics in human experience is also testified to even by those critics of Levinas who defend Heidegger. They do not maintain that Heidegger denies that there is an ethical dimension to human existence, to human dwelling. Rather, they defend Heidegger by stating that his phenomenological ontology has already accounted for it. His analysis of *Dasein,* they point out, includes a necessary respect for Being, which means that his analysis of *Dasein* already includes an ethical component.

More recently, Derrida has posited the notion of language as a system of differential relations so that language use is really the free play of signifiers. The brilliant semiotician and psychoanalyst, Julia Kristeva, criticizes this view of language, saying it cannot exhaust the meaning of language precisely because it fails to take into account the ethical dimension of human experience in which language is involved and to which it must respond.[18] The analyst, for example, is not free to join the free play of the signifiers and so to say whatever s/he likes because s/he has an ethical responsibility to employ language so as to help the other, the patient. For Kristeva, this ethical responsibility is not something that the analyst assumes only when s/he receives a degree and license, but is a basic aspect of human life that must be included in any account of human being and of language.

Even Derrida himself in recent work admits to grappling with the ethical dimension in human experience. In an essay written in 1980 entitled "The Time of a Thesis: Punctuations," he writes of an "ineluctable responsibility."[19] In the same year, in his essay on Levinas entitled "At this Very Moment in this Work Here I Am," not only does he say that he writes out of an obligation to give something to Emmanuel Levinas, but he also says that his essay is a response to the phrase "il aura oblige"—"he will have obligated."[20] Bernasconi and Critchley say they hope that this essay by Derrida will lead to a greater consideration of Derrida as an ethical thinker.[21] And certainly Derrida's recent works defending Heidegger[22] and Paul de Man[23] from accusations leveled at them because of their association with Nazism illustrate clearly, as Derrida himself says in the de Man piece, that he writes out of "the responsibilities of friendship."[24] It is undeniable in all of these works, and especially in these last two labors of friendship, that Derrida writes not only to disseminate and to endlessly defer meaning, but also to respond to an ethical obligation which, he says in words reminiscent of Levinas, cannot be evaded.

We can see, then, that Levinas is certainly not the only philosopher who has experienced the reality of the ethical in human experience. While this certainly does not prove Levinas's claim as a phenomenological claim, it at least makes more intelligible Levinas's insistence that his philosophy is not grounded in *a priori* religious beliefs but in an ethical dimension to human existence such that we experience ourselves as responsible for the other person. This is the phenomenon of human existence that Levinas, among others, has discovered, described, and to which he has responded in the language of phenomenological philosophy.

Levinas's Philosophy as Religious Discourse

But if Levinas's philosophy is not religious in this sense—does not depend upon religious presuppositions—then in what way is it religious? We can best answer this question by inquiring into the religious significance of the phenomenological fact of our ethical responsibility for one another. Indeed, if we approach the question of Levinas's significance for religious thought in this way, we may well conclude that our ethical obligation to one another is so absolutely central to what Levinas says about religion and God that his philosophy can rightly be seen as the most important retrieval and reinterpretation of the significance of ethics for religion since Kant.

Although the philosophical legitimacy of Levinas's argument that ethics is first philosophy depends upon a phenomenological and not upon a religious basis, it is certainly true that his philosophy "arises within the perspective of a certain kind of Judaism."[25] God is ever present in Levinas's philosophy, but Levinas's God is not the manifest God of natural theology, nor the mysterious but still comprehensible (by some) God of mysticism, nor the God who is understood as the first and most excellent Being. For Levinas, God is the absolutely unknowable, absolutely transcendent, and wholly other God of traditional Judaism. What isn't so traditional about Levinas's God, what isn't so commonplace about Levinas's "certain kind of Judaism," however, is his insistence that God can be known only through the ethical command. Thus, there is no event of God's revelation that is not the experience of being commanded by God.[26] "The attributes of God," says Levinas, "are not given in the indicative, but in the imperative. The knowledge of God comes to us as a commandment, as a Mitzvah."[27]

This priority of commandment opens the way for the great religious significance Levinas attributes to what is for him the phenomenological fact that we are responsible for the Other. This responsibility for and obligation to the Other is the very command of God, and it is through this command, and only through this command, that the absolutely transcendent God comes to our understanding. Levinas insists that in the ethical obligation to the Other, of which we are aware as humans, "there is a meaning, which is that the relationship with the face of the other is where God comes to the idea."[28] It is in the description of the ethical relation between persons "that for the first time I employ the word God as if I were naming a being."[29] In other words, Levinas insists that God actually begins to come to us in the idea, begins to come to a certain meaning, through ethics, through the reality of the ethical command to protect and be responsible for the Other: "We think the idea of the Infinite-in-me—or my relation to God—comes to me in the concreteness of my relation to the other person in the sociality which is my responsibility for the neighbor."[30] Since the idea of God comes only through my ethical relation to the Other, Levinas says that "Ethics isn't the corollary of the vision of God, it is this vision itself. Ethics is an optics,"[31] a "spiritual optics,"[32] the only vision of the invisible God. The only way God comes to our understanding and becomes visible to us is through the ethical relation between persons, which founds justice. "A God invisible," says Levinas, "means a God visible in justice,"[33] for ethics is "the singular epiphany of God."[34]

That ethics is the way in which the invisible God becomes visible does not mean that God is fully comprehensible or becomes fully present to us in ethics. The fact that God comes to the idea in ethics should not, Levinas warns, "be taken as a new proof in the existence of God."[35] Levinas here is not just making a very traditional move, not just preserving the transcendence and the absolute otherness of God in traditional Judaism. He is also making a very distinctive move when he insists that the ethical relation between persons is not the presence but the "trace" of God:

> For ethics, it is only in the infinite relation with the other that God passes (*se passe*), that traces of God are to be found. God thus reveals himself as a trace, not as an ontological presence which Aristotle defined as a Self-Thinking-Thought and scholastic metaphysics defined as an *Ipsum Esse Subsistens* or *Ens Causa Sui*. The God of the Bible cannot be defined or proved by means of logical predictions and attributions. Even the superlatives of wisdom, power and causality advanced by medieval ontology are inadequate to the absolute otherness of God. It is not by superlatives that we can think of

> God, but by trying to identify the particular interhuman events which open towards transcendence and reveal the traces where God has passed.[36]

That God is visible only through the ethical relationship between persons does mean that thought of God cannot be in terms of Being but in terms of ethics. According to Levinas, God-language must be spoken not in an ontological but only in an ethical perspective.[37] "All that I know of God and all that I can hear of His Word and can reasonably say of Him," insists Levinas, "must find an ethical expression."[38] The ethical relation between persons is, for Levinas, "the singular signification of God."[39] The fact that God ". . . can only be understood in the interhuman dimension" means that all true understanding of God is at the same time the understanding of ethics, the acknowledgment of the ethical command.

Levinas confirms his belief in the coincidence of ethics and religion in a recent interview with Edith Wyschogrod.[40] Here Wyschogrod asks if the staging (*mise en scene*) of religion, or the scene in which God appears, is exactly the same as the staging of ethics. Levinas responds: "That's right. It is the same thing."[41]

But it must be asked why Levinas restricts religion to the realm of ethics. Why is all knowledge of God knowledge of ethics? Why does he describe the ethical relation between people as the only place God passes, as the only place where can be found not the presence, or the manifestation, or the evidence, but only the trace of God's passing? Why is the ethical relation between persons "the singular epiphany" and "the singular signification" of God?[42] What does he mean when he states that everything in religion that "can't be reduced to the interhuman relation is primitive religion?"[43] What does he mean by differentiating in *Totality and Infinity* between "the believers of positive religions . . . who accept being immersed in a myth unbeknown to themselves" and those who have "faith purged of myths, the monotheist faith [which] itself implies metaphysical atheism?"[44]

It is apodictic that Levinas's philosophy "arises within the perspective of a certain kind of Judaism."[45] However, what kind of Judaism is this? What kind of Judaism insists that the ethical relationship between persons is the only place where God passes? Although Levinas's Judaism includes the God of the ethical command, where is the God who called Abraham, and who saved Noah from the flood, and who led the Israelites out of Egypt, and who spoke to Moses? Where is the God of the Exodus who is the God of miracles? Where is the God who delivered Jonah from the belly of the whale and Daniel from the fiery furnace? Where is the God who delighted in Jacob and not Esau and who turned Sarah's laughter from cynicism into joy? In other words, where is the God who is ethical and founds ethics but who also reveals Himself in other ways, by acting in history? What kind of Judaism is it that is "purged of myths" and implies "metaphysical atheism?" Doesn't Levinas's retrieval of religion and of God entirely and exclusively through the ethical mean at least the abandonment, if not the death, of God conceived as an all powerful being who rules the world and intervenes in history?[46] Is not Levinas's own Judaism unique indeed?

In his essay "Meaning and Sense," Levinas harshly criticizes the traditional conception of a God who intervenes in history and works miracles. There was a time when we used to believe in such a god, but what has proven this idea a lie, he says, is history itself.[47] Undoubtedly, Levinas's certain kind of Judaism is forever different from Judaism's traditional belief in a God who acts in history, because history itself has made it so. And the historical event that is most significant and most central to Levinas's thought is, as we have already seen, the Holocaust. Consequently, Levinas's Judaism is an explicitly post-Holocaust Judaism.

According to Levinas, God is most often conceived

ontologically by Western philosophy and religions as a Being who does certain things and possesses certain ontological qualities. The conception of God thus takes place within the logic of ontology, within "Being's move,"[48] and God is thereby conceived of in human terms, as a Being we can know and understand: ". . . faith and opinion speak the language of being. Nothing is less opposed to ontology than opinion and faith."[49] Conceived of in this way, God is a character in the great cognitive drama of ontology, in the great unfolding of reality to our minds that Levinas refers to as "the ontological adventure."[50] According to Levinas, our knowledge and understanding of this greatest of all beings enable us to explain and to make meaningful and bearable all human suffering. For Levinas, if God is understood through ontology—and, thus, is implicated in Being's move and caught up in the ontological adventure—then God will ultimately be employed to rationally explain human suffering. This is why Levinas says that theology—thought of God in terms of Being—always ultimately leads to theodicy.[51]

But this is exactly why Levinas conceives the Holocaust as the overthrow of theology, the end of God understood as the greatest of all beings. The Holocaust is that supreme event of suffering that shows once and for all that suffering exceeds any and every attempt to make it bearable and meaningful.[52] The Holocaust brings about once and for all time "the end of theodicy."[53] Thus, it forces us, according to Levinas, to rethink God outside of ontology, outside of "Being's move" in which theodicy and theology take place. Levinas does not mean that the Holocaust is the *only* event that destroys theodicy and the traditional conception of God upon which theodicy is based; rather, he says that the Holocaust is paradigmatic of the catastrophic events in this century, such as the Gulag and Cambodia, which also mean the end of theodicy:

> . . . the Holocaust of the Jewish people under the reign of Hitler seems to us the paradigm of gratuitous human suffering, where evil appears in its diabolical horror. This is perhaps not a subjective feeling. The disproportion between suffering and every theodicy was shown at Auschwitz with a glaring, obvious clarity. Its possibility puts into question the multi-millennial traditional faith. Did not the word of Nietzsche on the death of God take on, in the extermination camps, the signification of a quasi-empirical fact?[54]

Levinas's problem, then, is to interpret religion after the end of theodicy and after the death, or at least the disappearance, of the God conceived ontologically as the supreme Being. Levinas has this problem because he is Jewish, because he takes the Bible, Judaism, and the idea of God seriously, and because the Holocuast means that there is no way to evade this problem. What meaning can the words God, morality and religion have after their absolute denial and betrayal without rescue in the Holocaust? Interestingly enough, Levinas says that the "explicitly Jewish moment" in his philosophical thought is not any appeal to the Bible but is his reference to Auschwitz, "where God let the Nazis do what they wanted."[55] "Consequently," asks Levinas, "what remains?" He asks the same question in more philosophical language:

> The philosophical problem, then, which is posed by the useless pain which appears in its fundamental malignancy across the events of the twentieth century, concerns the meaning that religiosity and the human morality of goodness can still retain after the end of theodicy.[56]

It becomes clear, then, that Levinas's ethical philosophy must be seen as a religious as well as a philosophical and an ethical response to the Holocaust. The failure of morality which was the Holocaust raises for Levinas the question of the validity of the moral law. Even without the promise that fulfilling the moral law will always result in some reward, will always result in a "Happy End,"[57] does the moral law still hold? After the Holocaust, is ethical language still possible, still valid? "Everyone will readily agree," writes Levinas, "that it is of the utmost importance to know whether we are not duped by morality."[58] "The real question is," he says further in an interview entitled "The Paradox of Morality," "can we speak of an absolute commandment after Auschwitz? Can we speak of morality after the failure of morality?"[59]

Levinas not only finds this question within the Holocaust, but he also finds the answer to this question there, for he says it is written on the faces of the Holocaust sufferers. Even without the comfort of theodicy promising a "Happy End" for all those who suffer, the moral law still holds because the face of the sufferer remains, calling us to responsibility. The face of the sufferer expresses the fact that in the Holocaust the moral law was not destroyed, but violated. The moral law stands because the evidence of its violation is still within the face of the sufferer. Thus, the face of the sufferer means that morality survives its violation. Because of this, then, morality is not foolishnes. "It is time," says Levinas, "that the abusive confusion of foolishness with morality were denounced."[60] This can be done because "there is meaning testified to in outcries, before being disclosed in propositions, a meaning that signifies as a command, like an order that one signifies."[61]

And if the Moral Law—our responsibility for the other—is all there is in the absence of the "Happy End" of theodicy and of the God behind all the assurances of theodicy, then God must be in the moral law. Either God is there, or God is nowhere. God must be conceived strictly in ethical terms because this is the only way to think of God, through the face of the sufferer whose suffering is beyond all theodicy. The trace of God, says Levinas, is in the face's commandment to be responsible for and to love the other. This is why God can be known only as "the one who says that one must love the other."[62] Levinas insists that only because there is still this commandment after the Holocaust is there still God after the Holocaust, and he also insists that the fact of the Holocaust means that outside of this commandment there is no trace of God.

Levinas must be considered, then, along with Rubenstein, Fackenheim and others, as a distinctively post-Holocaust Jewish thinker.[63] And one of Levinas's contributions to religious thought, in addition to his contributions to philosophy, is his attempt to seriously rethink the notion of God in light of suffering in history, and especially in light of that ultimate modern experience of suffering and horror called the Holocaust. If the Holocaust is that event in modern history before which all thought must stop and be rethought,[64] if it is the event that ruptures philosophy,[65] and especially if those who were responsible for the atrocities in some way considered themselves religious and ethical,[66] then one thing that must be rethought is the relationship between ethics and religion, morality and God. Levinas, perhaps more than anyone else, has attempted to do this. In fact, Levinas's philosophy achieves its greatest significance for religious thought precisely because it retrieves religion through ethics in the face of the Holocaust.

The Trace of God and the Good

I have no intention of claiming that this definitely limited doctrine of God conceived entirely through the ethical relation either should or should not be maintained. The important thing to be aware of is that, for Levinas, this is the only way God can be conceived of after the failure of the God of ontology in the Holocaust. Other religious traditions must revise their own traditional, ontological conceptions of God in the light of the Holocaust and other epiphanies of evil. It is doubtful, to say the least, that other Jewish thinkers, let alone theologians from other religious traditions, will deduce the very same conception of God that Levinas has adopted, for to argue that God is known only through the ethical relationship between persons would entail a very radical change on the part of all religious traditions.

The question I wish to address is not whether other Jewish thinkers or theologians from other religious traditions would accept Levinas's contention that God is known only through the ethical relation between persons. Doubtless some will think Levinas's retrieval of his tradition incomplete and his conception of God too narrow and minimalistic; others will think Levinas far too sanguine and will insist that no conception of God, and least of all an ethical one, is tenable or even tolerable after the Holocaust.[67] Rather, the question I put to Levinas is whether his contention that God is known only through the ethical relation between persons is supported by and concordant with the rest of his ethical philosophy. This question hinges upon the fact that by Levinas's own definition the ethical relation between persons is not only the sole trace of God, but it is also the Good.[68] In fact, as Steven Smith says, the ethical relationship between persons is so good for Levinas that it has to refer to God, and hence arises the connection between the ethical relationship between persons and the trace of God.[69]

The question that has to be asked of Levinas is, however, whether this is a sufficiently comprehensive definition of the word *good*? Can the good be restricted to the ethical relationship between persons, to the ethical command to protect and to be responsible for the other? Are there not other relationships or events or examples of that which we can and do think of as the good?

I believe that, in the most recent interview with him included in *The Provocation of Levinas*, Levinas's interlocutors were attempting to explore just this suspicion—

that his definition of the good is too narrow. Several times the questioners attempted to get Levinas to respond to the possibility that perhaps not only the face of the other person but also the face of an animal expresses the ethical commandment so that the definition of the ethical relationship—and, consequently, the definition of the good—would have to be expanded beyond only the relationship between persons. I do not wish to appear to sympathize with the specifics of this question, for it illustrates a misunderstanding of Levinas's philosophy. The questioners, foremost among them John Llewelyn, should not be surprised or dismayed that Levinas insists on the absolute distinctiveness of the human face.[70] Levinas's contention that the being of a human being is absolutely different from the being of anything else is, as I have already shown, absolutely central to his interpreting being in but otherwise than Heidegger and, consequently, to the development of his ethical philosophy. Not only this, however, but to ask this question of a Jewish person who has suffered so much from an experience in which his fellow Jews were regarded not only as less than human, but of less worth than dogs and cats (for didn't the masters of the concentration camps feed and care for and pamper their pets while they exterminated their fellow humans?) perhaps reveals a certain insensitivity and forgetting.

Nevertheless, I do feel that the question itself pushes Levinas in the direction in which I think he has to be pushed, toward recognizing a conception of ethics and of the good that is broader than the ethical relation between persons.[71] The best way to accomplish this, it seems to me, is not to propose that the face of the animal expresses the ethical commandment just as the face of the other person does; rather, the best way to expand Levinas's concept of ethics is, I think, to explore his notion that this relation between persons equals the good.

Can we not find another relationship, in addition to

the relationship between persons, wherein an ethical commandment, an order, an obligation is also inscribed? Can we not say that there is an ethical relationship, a relationship wherein the ethical command is expressed, not only between one human being and another, but also between human beings and the whole, the cosmos, the universe?[72] If so, can we not then say that this ethical relationship between humans and the universe, wherein humans are summoned to their ethical responsibility to and for the universe, is also the good? And if this relationship is an ethical relationship and consequently is good, is it not then also true by Levinas's own logic that it has to refer to God?[73] In short, if we can establish that there is some version of the relationship between humans and the universe such that the ethical command is expressed, making this relationship an ethical relationship and, hence, also the good, then doesn't this relationship in Levinas's terminology have to be considered also a trace of God, another trace of God in addition to the trace of God that is the ethical relation between persons?

Again, I am not arguing either for or against Levinas's retrieval of God and religion through ethics, but I am questioning whether God is rightly conceived of as narrowly as Levinas does even if God is conceived of only through ethics. If we know God through the good, and if the ethical relation between humans and the cosmos is good just as the ethical relation between persons is good, then don't we know God through the ethical relation between humans and the universe? To use Levinas's language, isn't God the one who commands us to be responsible for and to love one another and also the one who commands us to be responsible for and to love the cosmos? And if we can hear God's voice also in this ethical command, then doesn't ethics yield us more traces of God than Levinas allows, so that even strictly through ethics we can know more of God and attribute more actions and adjectives to God than does Levinas? If so, then how can the traces of God in the ethical command prevent a slippage—gradual, imperceptible perhaps—toward ontological language? This leads us to the same suspicion about Levinas's God-language that we have already stated about his philosophy as a whole—that Levinas employs rhetoric to make his philosophy appear to be farther away from ontology than it actually is, even while he also admits the difficulty, if not the impossibility, of avoiding the slippage back into ontological language within the very attempt to escape it.

This is not to say that Levinas's God-language is traditional or that it does not constitute an important and much needed contribution to postmodern discourse on religion and on the meaning of religious language. Levinas's greatest contribution to religious thought lies, as I have already suggested, not so much in his conception of God as in his retrieval of religion through ethics, thereby redefining and reappropriating the religious significance of ethics. In the process, he also makes another important contribution to religious thought in that he advances a very interesting, significant and unique reinterpretation of the meaning of religious language.

As we have seen, Levinas insists that even after the death of the God of traditional Judaism and Christianity, there still is the moral law to deal with, to explain, and to respond to. If for some the Holocaust destroyed forever the hope in the God of the Exodus and of the Incarnation, it also makes quite clear that whatsoever else can be said about what happened there, it must be said that what happened there was wrong. The diabolical gives rise both to moral outrage and to thought,[74] and thought knows there would be no moral outrage without some conception of the moral law, without some standard of what is right and wrong, without some concept of the good. This is the inner logic of Levinas's ethical philosophy, that moral outrage leads one back to the moral law. The Holocaust may mean the death of God no matter how God is conceived, and certainly for some it does, but for Levinas it means much more certainly the death of relativism.[75] The death of relativism is the resurrection of the moral law, of the ethical command. And for Levinas, the moral law is not something to be taken for granted, or taken lightly, or considered as a purely human phenomenon. The moral law is, rather, God's call to humans, God's command, God's very voice. No one better than Levinas has explicated the religious significance of the moral law or has expressed so adamantly what Kant felt so strongly—that the moral law is the basis of our devotion to the good and to God.

Religious Language as the Echo of Revelation

Levinas's retrieval of God and religion through the ethical commandment leads him to propose a unique interpretation of the meaning of revelation and, consequently, of religious language. When asked in what way the Bible is revelation, Levinas responds:

> The Law of God is Revelation because it proclaims: You shall not kill. All the rest is perhaps an effort to think that thing—an indeed necessary staging of the scene, a culture where that thing can be understood. It is that which I try to say. "You shall not kill" means of course "You shall do everything so that the other lives.[76]

Revelation for Levinas is, then, the ethical command, which means that all the other elements of the Bible that do not have to do directly with the ethical command are given a secondary status. In fact, they constitute the stage upon which we place God and attempt to comprehend Him. Levinas insists that revelation is not in itself the stage that enables us to think and to conceive of God. Rather, revelation is the ethical commandment: ". . . it is as an ethical kerygma that the Bible is revelation."[77] This revelation qua revelation has priority and authority over every attempt to stage God, to place Him in a setting of our understanding.

This identification of revelation with ethical command has tremendous consequences for Levinas's interpretation of what religious language means and how it should be conceived of and employed. Levinas does not say that language that attempts to conceive of God is distorted and should be avoided. It is necessary and inescapable, but it is also secondary. The highest and the truest religious language does not name God or enable us to understand Him, but echoes the message of revelation, echoes the moral command. The highest and the truest religious language is expressed not in nouns, but in verbs.[78] And verbs come into their verbalness, says Levinas, by ceasing to name,[79] by showing that at the heart of language there is an activity other than naming, i.e., commanding.[80] Certainly, there is a religious language expressed in nouns, but Levinas insists it is secondary precisely because the religious language expressed in verbs emanates from the ethical command and is the echo of revelation: "Thou shalt not kill." The ethical command taken as the content of revelation means that responding to the ethical command in action has priority over the attempt to contemplate and to conceive of God.

Levinas thereby advances a new way both to use and to interpret religious language. He is not denying that there is religious language that conceives of God in ontological terms and that places God in a setting of our understanding. He recognizes this as a necessary kind of religious language. But there is another kind of religious language that is more important than and has priority over the first kind of religious language. This second type of religious language is different from the first because it is not an attempt to think God, to understand God, and makes no attempt to name God, but is the echo of the ethical command.

The important thing to understand about Levinas's interpretation of religious language is not only that there are two different types, but also that the latter type has priority over the former.[81] This is another example of how central the notion of primacy is to Levinas's discourse, as Derrida has astutely pointed out.[82]

Levinas's Contribution to Religious Thought

The fact that Levinas distinguishes two types of religious language and gives one priority over the other enables us to answer two very important questions. First, in what way is Levinas's ethical philosophy a religious philosophy, a religious language? Secondly, what does Levinas's religious philosophy have to say to and contribute to religious thought?

As we have already seen, Levinas contends that his philosophy is not religious in that it does not depend upon religious presuppositions. Neither is it religious in the sense that it is primarily a reflection upon the nature of God and an attempt to understand Him. Our ethical responsibility for the other person is the heart of Levinas's discourse. This means that his philosophy is religious in the sense that it is an echo of the ethical command of revelation.

As we have also seen, Levinas's philosophy begins as a phenomenological ontology, as a description of being and of human existing, but it finds in the relationship between persons that which is beyond being—the ethical command, the moral law, the summoning of the selfsame to responsibility for the Other. Once this occurs, Levinas's philosophy no longer merely describes, but decides, sets priorities, and announces that ethics is beyond being in the sense of better than being. Levinas's philosophy exalts ethics by echoing the ethical commandment, "Thou shalt not kill." As Luk Bouchaert observes, Levinas's philosophy changes from a phenomenological-descriptive to an ethical-orienting language game, and this means that his philosophy becomes "an appeal to the reader" and "a summons" to ethical responsibility.[83] "One doesn't respect a text," says Levinas, "that doesn't solicit one."[84]

To the extent that this philosophy does solicit us, does remind us of our ethical responsibilities to the other person and commands us to recognize and to fulfill them, it is an echo of the ethical command, an echo of revelation. In that sense, in Levinas's own sense, it is a religious philosophy, a religious language of the second and higher order precisely because it echoes the ethical command. Steven Smith quite rightly observes: "Levinas' deductions are themselves moral events: the book *Totality and Infinity* offers itself to the reader as a generalized prototype of just utterance."[85] Because his philosophy is a "just utterance," an echo of the command to justice and ethics, it is *ipso facto* and primarily in this way a religious philosophy.

Levinas's insistence on the two types of religious language and on the priority of the one over the other means that his ethical and religious philosophy is always suspicious of, watchful over, and critical of every movement of theology. Levinas insists that whatever theology—any theology of any tradition—thinks it knows of God must be subordinated to, controlled by, and chastened by the fact that the highest and most essential thing we know of God is that God commands us to be ethically responsible for the Other. Never can any understanding of God have priority over or displace the God who commands us in the Moral Law. Levinas is in this sense as absolutely un-Kierkegaardian as he can be. Any teleological suspension of the ethical is not religious, but diabolical.[86] And the diabolical, says Levinas, is always looking for a chance to sneak in.[87] To reject the diabolical, insists Levinas, it has to be refuted. Levinas recommends to theology that the best way to refute the diabolical is to insist that the God of the ethical command always and in every way has priority over any other possible understanding of God. Levinas knows that with its history of violence and crusades and hatred, theology must once and for all learn this lesson so that it never again will let itself be coopted by the diabolical.[88] Theologies thrive on abstracting a fuller concept of God from God's only trace, ethics, from translating the verb of the ethical command into the nouns of theology, but, warns Levinas, "so do wars of religion."[89]

Levinas's ethical and religious philosophy also insists to theology that ethical action on behalf of the Other is more essential and more primary than understanding and contemplating God. Revelation not as gnosis but as command means that response is not ontological thought but action. For Levinas, theology loses touch with revelation and puts something in revelation's place whenever it thinks that the response to revelation is the intellectual consent to or belief in some proposition about God rather than the acceptance and the performance of our ethical responsibility for the Other. Levinas's philosophy can support, then, only a theology that stresses the absolute primacy of action and ethics over belief and theological concepts and which echoes the ethical command that is the cry for justice. As Levinas says, the Word of God is "Thou shall not kill," which means that revelation is a command not to *know* something but to *do* something. Thus, Levinas says, "'Thou shall not kill' means of course 'You shall do everything so that the other lives.'"[90]

Considering Levinas's insistence on the primacy of action over reflection, it is no wonder that the theologies that have paid attention to and been influenced by Levinas's ethical philosophy are forms of liberation theology.[91] In fact, some of Levinas's statements in his religious writings could lead one to believe that he offers a distinctively Jewish form of liberation theology. Consider, for example, his expression of the Jewish people's solidarity with the outcast and the suffering: "The traumatic experience of my slavery in Egypt constitutes my very humanity, a fact that immediately allies me to the workers, the wretched, and the persecuted peoples of the world."[92] Or, consider his remarks on the relation between justice and economic equality: "Justice can have no other object than economic equality . . . it is illusory to suppose that justice could be maintained outside of economic conditions in a kingdom of pure respect."[93]

Perhaps one of the most important ways in which Levinas's philosophy can contribute to theology is in the contemporary ecumenical discussion among various religious traditions. There are, of course, many academic conferences in which representatives of various traditions dialogue with one another in order to increase their understanding and appreciation of each other. In these ecumenical conferences, the truth claims of the traditions are compared and discussed, and in great contrast to the historical animosity between the religions, a certain peace reigns among the participants of the dialogue. This peace is founded upon the general consensus that no one tradition possesses the entire truth and that all traditions have some claim upon the truth.

This may be an adequate basis for peace among the participants from the various religions at academic conferences, but peace among the religions in general means a great deal more than peace among intellectuals. Peace among the religions is vital not primarily for the purposes of intellectual conferences, but because there can be no world peace without peace among the religions. This is a fact intellectuals often overlook, as they talk about interreligious dialogue as if there were not still hostility and wars among the religions and even as they assert that these ecumenical discussions are the first time the religions have encountered one another. The religions have always encountered one another, and most often not to dialogue but to destroy one another, a destruction that continues to this day.

This is exactly where Levinas can contribute. For Levinas, to concede that the selfsame does not possess the entire truth means something about the selfsame, but more importantly it means something about the relationship between the selfsame and the Other. It means that the Other teaches the selfsame, which means that the relationship between the two is not merely grudging acceptance but an obligation and a summons to ethical responsibility.

Levinas, speaking out of the depths of the violence the religions perpetrate against each other, would insist to all the religions that this ethical responsibility for one another is the truest and the highest Revelation of God and must always have priority over every other truth, every other revelation embraced by any religion.[94] Without this priority, warns Levinas, the peace that reigns in ecumenical discussions will never become peace among the religions. By insisting that the ethical command must be the most important and primary revelation even for the religious traditions that recognize other instances of revelation, Levinas's philosophy not only insinuates itself into ecumenical discussions, but it echoes the command that wars cease and peace be founded among the religions. It is by echoing that ethical command, by echoing "the voice commanding from beyond,"[95] that Levinas's philosophy breaks into theological discussion and itself becomes religious, as well as philosophical, language.

Levinas's Contribution to Contemporary Philosophy

> The moment when philosophy becomes suspect is not just any moment.
>
> —*Emmanuel Levinas*

> I would maintain, against Heidegger, that philosophy can be ethical as well as ontological, can be at once Greek and non-Greek in its inspiration.
>
> —*Emmanuel Levinas*

In the previous chapter, I have attempted to show both the religious dimensions of Levinas's thought and the contributions his ethical philosophy can make to religious thought. I did so at the risk of appearing to confirm Derrida's suspicion that Levinas's philosophy is not really philosophy at all but an ethico-religious discourse. Quite to the contrary, all theological considerations of Levinas's should be seen as theological inquiries into what is a phenomenological philosophy. Levinas has always insisted that he is a philosopher,[1] and I have taken that claim seriously as I have attempted to show that his entire philosophical project has been constructed by interpreting in but against the thought of another philosopher, Martin Heidegger.

When Derrida declared that Levinas, a "non-Greek," could kill Greek speech only by feigning to speak Greek, and that there was no such thing as feigning to speak a language but only actually speaking that language—so that Levinas has to speak Greek in order to kill Greek speech[2]—Derrida might have been discovering something very important for the development of his own deconstructive project, but he was not saying anything with which Levinas would not readily agree. Levinas has never denied he is speaking Greek, nor has he ever stated that he is only pretending to speak Greek. Rather, he has insisted that the Biblical element of his thought does not prevent him from using the Greek philosophical language that all philosophers must use precisely because it is the language of philosophy. Levinas's insistence that "I am Greek, it is Greek thought . . . everything I say about justice comes from Greek thought, and Greek politics as well"[3] is confirmed by his constant appeal to the first Greek of the *grammata*, Plato, and his idea of the Good beyond Being, and by his heavy use of and borrowing from those very Greek non-Greeks: Descartes, Husserl and Heidegger. This is why in this final chapter I turn from discussing the religious dimensions of Levinas's philosophy and the significance of his work for religious thought to a discussion of his philosophy *qua* philosophy in order to evaluate the contributions Levinas's thought makes to contemporary philosophy.

In the first part of this chapter, I intend to situate Levinas's philosophy historically in its proper context within modern continental philosophy. This will involve a brief detour through the problem of the relation between subject and object in modern philosophy. Thus, in this first part I shall very briefly describe the major contributions to this philosophical problem made by

Kant, Hegel, Husserl and the early Heidegger. I do so in order to demonstrate that Levinas both belongs in and transmutes this tradition by interpreting the problem of otherness through the intersubjective relation and, consequently, by putting ethics at the center of this classical philosophical problem.

The latter part of the chapter is an attempt to evaluate the significance of Levinas's contribution to contemporary continental philosophy. By explicating the very real concern for ethics shown in the work of three other contemporary continental philosophers—Theodor Adorno, Jacques Derrida and Jean-Francois Lyotard—I hope to show how Levinas's ethical philosophy can both criticize and augment the ways in which contemporary continental philosophy has felt itself compelled to respond to both historical exigency and the philosophical tradition in a more self-consciously ethical manner.

Kant's Chasm

Perhaps the central figure in the philosophical tradition of the problem of the subject and the other—the philosophical tradition initiated in the West by Bacon and Descartes and in which Levinas rightly belongs—is Immanuel Kant. His "Copernican Revolution in philosophy" began when David Hume awoke him from his "dogmatic slumber"[4] with his question of the origin of the concept of causality.[5] According to Kant, Hume concluded that Reason is deluded in considering this concept "as one of her children," for it is really "nothing but a bastard of imagination, impregnated by experience, which subsumed certain representations under the law of association, and mistook a subjective necessity (custom) for an objective necessity arising from insight."[6] Hume's question of the origin of the concept of causality was the correct one to ask, Kant maintained, but his answer was incorrect because Hume tried to derive it from experience. Concepts such as causality, concluded Kant, were not derived from experience, "but sprang from the pure understanding."[7] Hence Kant's assertion in his 1779 work *The Critique of Pure Reason*[8] that knowledge is two-fold, comprised both of "what we receive through our impressions and of what our own faculty of knowledge (sensible impressions serving merely as the occasion) supplies from itself."[9] Kant labeled the first aspect of knowledge, knowledge derived from experience, *a posteriori*, and the aspect of knowledge that our faculty of knowledge supplies from itself, *a priori*, or "knowledge absolutely independent of all experience."[10]

Kant's concept of *a priori* knowledge led him to reconceive radically the relationship between the subject and knowledge, between the knower and the process of knowing. For Kant, the mind is not merely the passive recipient of sense impressions, but it supplies to sense impressions its own *a priori* structures, and "supplies" them in the sense that sense impressions are experienced through these *a priori* structures. Thus, for Kant, even though the mind is still taught by what is external to it, it does not in the process of knowing have ". . . the character of a pupil who listens to everything that the teacher chooses to say, but of an appointed judge who compels the witnesses to answer questions which he has himself formulated."[11] What we know of nature, then, is not so much a matter of what nature shows us as it is a matter of the questions our *a priori* knowledge prompts us to ask of it.

This is, according to Kant, a revolution in our thinking about the relation between ourselves and the process of knowing just as radical as and analogous to Copernicus's discovery that we revolve around the heavenly bodies rather than that they revolve around us:

> Hitherto it has been assumed that all our knowledge must conform to objects. But all attempts to extend our knowledge of objects by establishing something in regard to them a priori, by means of concepts, have, on this assumption, ended in failure. We must therefore make trial whether we may not have more success in the tasks of metaphysics, if we suppose that objects must conform to our knowledge. This would agree better with what is desired, namely, that it should be possible to have knowledge of objects a priori, determining something in regard to them prior to their being given. We should then be proceeding precisely on the lines of Copernicus's primary hypothesis. Failing of satisfactory progress in explaining the movements of the heavenly bodies on the supposition that they all revolved round the spectator, he tried whether he might not have better success if he made the spectator to revolve and the stars to remain at rest. A similar experiment can be tried in metaphysics, as regards the intuition of objects. If intuition must conform to the constitution of the objects, I do not see how we could know anything of the latter a priori; but if the object (as object of the senses) must conform to the constitution of our faculty of intuition, I have no difficulty in conceiving such a possibility.[12]

But Kant's concept of *a priori* knowledge and, consequently, his contention that objects must conform to our knowledge, have a consequence that even Kant himself labels "startling" and apparently "highly prejudicial to the whole purpose of metaphysics."[13] *A priori* knowledge as such has to do with the process of knowing and imposes its method of inquiry on objects external to the subject, but it does not extend so far as to make any claim to know external objects as they are in themselves. We know things, says Kant, insofar as they are given to us, but we do not know them insofar as they are things in themselves. Kant's "startling conclusion" is that

> . . . objects in themselves are quite unknown to us, and that what we call outer objects are nothing but mere representations of our sensibility, the form of which is space. The true correlate of sensibility, the thing in itself, is not known, and cannot be known, through these representations; and in experience no question is ever asked in regard to it.[14]

Kant's "Copernican Revolution in philosophy" severed the union between subject and object and brought about a chasm between human subjectivity and what subjectivity comes into contact with but that is not identical to itself, its other. Kant's *Critique of Practical Reason* and *Critique of Judgment* are attempts to breach this chasm, but ultimately for Kant the chasm proves unbreachable.[15]

This chasm between the subject and its other not only proved to be central to Kant's work, but it also provided subsequent continental philosophy with its central problematic. Paul Tillich, for instance, confirmed this when he wrote that "the whole history of epistemology" since Kant has been "a cognitive attempt to bridge this [subject-object] split by showing the ultimate unity of subject and object, either by annihilating one side of the gap for the sake of the other or by establishing a uniting principle which contains both of them."[16] Similarly, Levinas writes in "Meaning and Sense" that "the overcoming of the subject-object structures [is] the idee fixee of the whole of contemporary thought."[17] The French title of Vincent Descombes' recent exploration into modern French philosophy is also indicative of this—*Le Meme et L'Autre*.[18] Descombes also confirms that attempts either at overcoming Kant's chasm between subject and object or at overcoming these attempts have dominated continental philosophy since Kant's First Critique: "the humanization of the identity between subject and object [is] the point around which contemporary French philosophy has continued more or less unwittingly to turn."[19] Similarly, in his discussion of modern and contemporary philosophy, which serves as his introduction to *Deconstruction in Context*, Mark Taylor writes that "philosophy begins and ends with the question of the other."[20]

Kant's philosophy was immediately succeeded by a plethora of attempts to bridge the chasm between subject and object that he posited.[21] The philosophers of feeling (Herder, Jacobi, Haaman) and the Romantics (Schliermacher, Coleridge) attacked the theoretical conception of subjectivity in the First Critique by advancing a more holistic view of the subject in which thinking, feeling, knowing and acting are united. The greatest challenge to Kant's notion of the chasm between subject and object, however, came from the German idealist tradition represented by Fichte, Schelling, and most notably by Hegel.

Hegel's Overcoming of Kant's Chasm

Hegel is, of course, the primary counterpart to Kant concerning the question of the relation between subject and object. Kant's reservations about the limitations of thought to comprehend the thing in itself (*Ding an sich*) were based on the fear of an epistemological error, the error of mistaking categories of thinking for categories of being. Hegel, on the other hand, in his *Phenomenology of Spirit*, declares boldly that Kant's epistemological caution, his fear of error, is in reality fear of the truth.[22] Hegel proposes that philosophy should not be an "avoiding of error" but rather should be based upon the "working through error" to truth.[23]

The fundamental error that philosophy must work through, according to Hegel, is the apparent absolute distinction between subject and object. Arguing on Kant's own terms, Hegel points out that to place the thing in itself outside the bounds of knowledge is *ipso facto* the conscious positing of the thing in itself, is its positing within consciousness.[24] Although there appears to be a distinction between subject and object, this distinction is itself within consciousness. There is no thing in itself that is not as such related to consciousness, which means that every thing in itself is also being-for consciousness. In being known, every in-itself "... becomes something that is the in-itself only for consciousness. And this then is the True: the being for consciousness of this in-itself."[25]

Hegel's thesis that every in-itself is always already a being-for-consciousness entails that any disparity "which exists in consciousness between the I and the substance which is its object" should really by understood "as the disparity of the substance with itself."[26] Hegel posited that "consciousness will arrive at a point at which it gets rid of its semblance of being burdened with something alien, with what is only for it, and some sort of other, at a point where appearance becomes identical with essence."[27] In other words, Hegel took the opposite view of Kant and stated that the chasm between subject and object was only illusory and that thought would eventually overcome the division between the subject and its other. Absolute knowledge would then eliminate or supercede all otherness. As Scott Warren summarizes Hegel's conclusion in *Phenomenology of Spirit,* thought unifies Kant's split between the subject and object, and "absolute knowledge is only attained when subject and object become totally identical and the opposition between knowing and all objecthood is superceded."[28]

In Hegel's philosophical system, objecthood is superceded and otherness is dissolved in the progress of reason; this illustrates the fact that the attempts to overcome Kant's dilemma of the chasm between subject and object were at least as problematic as Kant's dilemma itself and were subject to as much criticism. Sören Kierkegaard, Hegel's self-proclaimed archenemy, attracted little attention in his own day with his anti-Hegelian writings, but at least he had the satisfaction of dying in

1855 with the knowledge that idealism was already "in full retreat."[29] What philosophy, even in its left-wing and right-wing Hegelian forms, was retreating back to only 20 years after the death of Hegel was a thought more chastened by the epistemological and ontological limits of Kant's critical philosophy. By 1865, Otto Liebman in *Kant und die Epigonen* uttered the cry of the neo-Kantians: "Back to Kant."[30]

Husserl's Rigorous Science of Pure Consciousness

Despite the many efforts and the many ways proposed in the latter quarter of the eighteenth century and in the nineteenth century to solve Kant's problem, continental philosophers even at the beginning of the twentieth century still inherited it as a problem to be solved. This is clearly apparent if we analyze the evolution of Husserl's philosophy. Here we can see that Kant's problem of the chasm between subject and object was a primary concern for Husserl; while he neither agreed with it nor attempted to disprove it, he eventually developed a philosophy on a scientific basis that enabled him to evade the problem.

From the very beginning, Husserl shared Kant's ideal of making philosophy scientific, yet he distances himself as far as possible from Kant in his early writings. In a series of lectures he gave in 1907, Husserl declared: "We do not say as Kant did in 1774: 'Upon what ground rests the relation of that which we call representation in us to an object existing in itself?'"[31] His phenomenological rallying cry uttered in his 1911 work, *Philosophy as a Rigorous Science*, "to the things themselves," seems to defy Kant, redirecting philosophy into a mode and a region of inquiry Kant would not even think possible. In 1913, in the foreword to the second edition of *Logical Investigations*, Husserl insists that his Investigations

> . . . are attempts at genuinely executed fundamental work on the immediately envisaged and grasped things [Sachen]; and even where they proceed critically, they do not lose themselves in discussions of standpoint, but rather leave the last word to the things themselves and to the work on them.[32]

Despite Husserl's un-Kantian language, it would be incorrect to suppose that even in the earlier works he is proposing a return to a pre-Kantian realism or objectivism.[33] This would be so if Husserl maintained that the process of return to things involved *Erfahrung*, or experience only of real things, rather than *Anschauung*, or "looking at" either real or imaginary or intuited things or essences.[34] Husserl thereby included "ideas" or "essences" in his definition of things. Even in *Philosophy as a Rigorous Science* he insisted:

> But one must never abandon one's radical lack of prejudice and identify such things [Sachen] with empirical facts [empirische Tatsachen], thus remaining blind to ideas, which are, after all, to such a great extent absolutely given in immediate intuition.[35]

Husserl gave a clear indication of how far this definition of things removed him from a pre-Kantian realism with the publication in 1913 of *Ideas Concerning Pure Phenomenology and Phenomenological Philosophy*. By a "pure phenomenology," he meant a phenomenology purified of all assertions about reality other than that of intentional consciousness. He achieved this by the methodological innovation he introduced in *Ideas* and which he forever after insisted was absolutely central to the phenomenological method—the phenomenological reduction. By means of the phenomenological reduction, all questions of the reality of things outside consciousness were bracketed, or put out of play, put aside. Husserl's slogan of return "to the things themselves" became, rather, return to the consciousness that is always consciousnes of something, and phenomenology became not the science of phenomena in themselves but the science of "pure consciousness."[36]

Husserl's decidedly subjectivist turn cannot be attributed primarily to the influence of Kant.[37] It is probably much more attributable to Husserl's desire to construct his philosophy as an absolutely certain science. But Husserl maintained that in order to have an absolutely certain science, questions of the physical universe have to be bracketed, demonstrating that he is an heir to Kant as well as to Descartes. In fact, Husserl confesses his growing appreciation of and affinity for Kant when he says in *Ideas* that Kant's "greatest intuitions" became quite clear to him only after he "brought the distinctive features of the phenomenological field into the focus of full consciousness."[38] It was Kant, he said, whose "mental gaze rested on this [the phenomenological] field."[39]

But it would be wrong to think that Husserl saw the phenomenological reduction as a concession to Kant. By bracketing out the natural world, Husserl saw himself as opening up a field of inquiry that could yield absolutely certain knowledge, knowledge not of things in themselves of the natural world, but of the constitution of essences by the consciousness, knowledge of what Husserl termed "essential Being." According to Husserl, the chasm between subject and object posited in *The Critique of Pure Reason* enabled Kant to gaze upon the phenomenological field, but in thinking that this chasm constituted some type of crisis for thought and in trying to bridge this chasm, Kant failed to "appropriate" and "recognize" the phenomenological field "as the center from which to work up on his own line a rigorous science of Essential Being."[40] This is precisely what Husserl thought he himself had done, or rather was continuously doing, and in his rigorous science of essential Being, the Kantian question of whether consciousness actually penetrated things in themselves was bracketed out in order to get at the more primordial and more certain region of intentional consciousness.[41]

Husserl maintained, then, not that he had the answer to Kant's question, but that answering it was not necessary to come to absolute certainty about the region of phenomena philosophy should make its field of inquiry—pure consciousness. Husserl might have said that in gazing upon the phenomenological field, Kant had the *experience* of pure consciousness but missed the *meaning*. The meaning of pure consciousness as always consciousness of something was what Husserl was endeavoring to describe. Thus, Husserl's phenomenology does not constitute a concession to Kant as much as it constitutes a way to avoid Kant's problem of the in-itself, because for Husserl the true field of phenomenological inquiry lies elsewhere than in speculation about the in-itself.

Heidegger's Different Starting Point

This avoidance of Kant's problem via the phenomenological reduction is exactly where Heidegger, Husserl's greatest student and the one to whom Husserl looked to to carry on his rigorous science of pure consciousness, broke with the master. No avoidance of Kant was possible for Heidegger because he aimed at a phenomenological description not of pure consciousness but of Being. Phenomenology in its Heideggerian form, or phenomenological ontology, had to come to terms with and oppose Kant in a way Husserl did not have to. Heidegger's definition of phenomenology in *Being and Time* makes this quite obvious.

Appealing to the Greek word *phanaesthai*, which means "to show itself," Heidegger said phenomenology means "to let that which shows itself be seen from itself."[12] He said that by defining phenomenology in this way, he was stating nothing other than what Husserl expressed in the maxim "to the things themselves." But whereas Husserl meant things as they are constituted by and in the consciousness, Heidegger meant things as they actually are in their being.[43] Phenomenology for Heidegger was a method of "intuitive grasping" of things in their being, a way in which the being of things could be wrested away from their disclosure and hiddenness and laid bare.[44] Much bolder than Husserl and leaping over rather than avoiding the Kantian chasm between subject and object, Heidegger insists that we "must venture forward into the most primordial problematic of the 'things themselves' to get such nuances straightened out."[45]

Heidegger criticized philosophy for either forgetting or misunderstanding Being, and in this rather sweeping condemnation he certainly included Kant. Kant's problem of the chasm between subject and object was for Heidegger symptomatic of a more profound failure that Kant shared with the dominant philosophical tradition "to master the basic problem of Being."[46] The primary reason Kant and the rest of the tradition didn't understand Being was, according to Heidegger, that it took the wrong path or access to Being. The world and *Dasein* and entities within-the-world are, says Heidegger, "the ontologically constitutive states which are closest to us; but we have no guarantee that we can achieve the basis for meeting up with these as phenomena by the seemingly obvious procedure of starting with the Things of the world . . ."[47] In interpreting Being, philosophy starts with the "seemingly obvious" starting point of things. The correct way to interpret and to understand Being, Heidegger insists, is to start with the analysis of *Dasein*. This is exactly what Kant, following Descartes, failed to do, and this is why the Being of the thing in itself is a problem for Kant and for other heirs of Descartes: "In taking over Descartes' ontological position Kant made an essential omission: he failed to provide an ontology of *Dasein*. This omission was a decisive one in the spirit of Descartes' ownmost tendencies."[48]

It is crucial to understand what Heidegger believed Kant could have learned if he had begun his interpretation of Being with *Dasein* and, thus, what Heidegger thought his own phenomenological ontology discovered. Kant's dilemma of whether the being of the thing can ever be known is no longer a dilemma if you analyze the being of *Dasein*, for if you do you will discover, according to Heidegger, that "understanding of Being is itself a distinctive characteristic of *Dasein*'s Being. *Dasein* is ontically distinctive in that it is ontological."[49] The analysis of the Being of *Dasein* is the key to the question of Being in general for ". . . only because *Dasein* is as constituted by disclosedness (that is, by understanding) can anything like Being be understood; only so is it possible to understand Being."[50] It is of the very Being of *Dasein* that it already exists in and is open to and understands the World.[51] That is why for Heidegger the most primordial affirmation of the Being of *Dasein* is Being-in-the-World. This means that there is no understanding of *Dasein* that isn't also an understanding of the world: ". . . the world is disclosed essentially along with the Being of *Dasein*."[52]

Heidegger's conception of *Dasein* as always already Being-in-the-World and as a Being who understands the Being of entities enables him to dispense with Kant's problem of the thing in itself. Discussing Kant's attempts to prove the reality of the world outside the self, Heidegger states that if one began with Kant's presuppositions of the "whole distinction between the inside and the outside," then even the possibility of any and every proof "would collapse."[53] Heidegger quickly asserts that the fault is not in the proofs. The error is that ". . . the kind of Being of the entity which does the proving and makes request for proofs has not been made definite enough." He then adds that ". . . if *Dasein* is understood correctly," these proofs are absolutely unnecessary ". . . because, in its Being, it [*Dasein*] already is what subsequent proofs deem necessary to demonstrate for it."[54] In Heidegger's view, if Kant had understood *Dasein* correctly, he should never have troubled himself with the "whole distinction" between subject and object.

Levinas's Contribution to this Tradition

As we have already shown, Levinas's philosophy must be considered within the tradition of Husserl's phenomenology transmuted into phenomenological ontology by Martin Heidegger. Levinas's dissertation on Husserl, in which he parts from Husserl for the same reasons as Heidegger, as well as Levinas's own phenomenological descriptions of being and of the being of the existent in "De l'evasion," *Existence and Existents, Time and the Other* and *Totality and Infinity*, demonstrate that he is much more a phenomenologist after the manner of Heidegger than of Husserl. But if Heidegger's extension of phenomenology to an analysis of *Dasein* showed Levinas the true fruitfulness of the phenomenological method,[55] it also provided him with a region of being that he felt necessary to interpret otherwise than did Heidegger. As I have argued before, Levinas's philosophy is misunderstood as philosophy if it is not made clear that his philosophical project is an interpretation of being in but otherwise than Heidegger's own phenomenological ontology.

Levinas and Heidegger's most fundamental point of disagreement in their analyses of the being of the existent is their different starting points. Both analyze *Dasein* or the being of the existent at what they see as the most primordial point, but they disagree as to what this point is.

Heidegger analyzes *Dasein* at the point at which its Being is already characterized by sociality or, in other words, at a point prior to the individuation of *Dasein*. Thus, in Heidegger's analysis, *Dasein* is always already Being-With, so that thought about the relation between one individuated *Dasein* and another is a second-order thought about a second-order relation, thought that does not break through to the constitution of *Dasein*'s Being. For Heidegger, then, thought concerning the intersubjective relation is secondary and derivative, and the existential analytic of *Dasein* must go past or beyond it to be able to describe both the Being of *Dasein* and Being itself.[56]

Levinas, on the other hand, begins by insisting on the absolute solitude of the existent and, correspondingly, on the separation of one existent from the other. This enables him to describe the phenomenon wherein the subject and the other person, always separated and distinct, come into contact—or in Levinas's own words, into proximity with one another in the intersubjective relation. Levinas posits that there is always already in the phenomenon of the subject's response to the Other an obligation, an indebtedness, a responsibility implicit within the response. Levinas insists that all recourse to words already takes place in this context of response, which is responsibility, so that language itself bears the weight of ethical obligation.[57] There is then no understanding of the Other's being that does not always already involve and is directed by the ethical obligation to the Other.

For Levinas, ethical obligation is not the most primordial state of the being of the existent, but it is the most primordial state of the intersubjective relation and gives direction and sense (*sens*) to all thought, even thought of what is more primordial than ethics itself.[58] This is what Levinas means by saying that the ethical obligation to the Other "is the first intelligible," before culture and history.[59] Thus, while for Levinas ethical obligation isn't the most primordial state of the being of the existent, it is ethics that presides over and gives direction to thought. This is why for Levinas "ethics is first philosophy,"[60] or as he says in a different way, "morality presides over the work of truth."[61]

Perhaps now that we have placed Levinas's admittedly very unusual ethical phenomenology in relation not only to Heidegger but to the larger tradition of modern continental philosophy, we can evaluate Levinas's distinctive contribution to that tradition. By transmuting continental philosophy's central question of the relation between the subject and its other into a question of the relation between the subject and the other person, Levinas has raised all the old issues of the limitations and potentialities of human knowing, but he has raised them all in a very new way. It is certainly not that Levinas is the only person who has raised the question of this relation. But this question was treated merely as a subset of the more comprehensive question of how or whether the subject knows for certain the existence and being of the thing.

In Descartes, Kant, Husserl and Heidegger, as well as in the philosophical tradition of the Problem of Other Minds,[62] the question is almost entirely how the subject knows the existence of the other person and how the other person enters into the consciousness of the subject. In Husserl, for instance, the question is how the other person is constituted in the consciousness of the subject,[63] and as Theunissen says, Heidegger's treatment of this issue is only a "modified repetition" of Husserl.[64] Even in the anti-Husserlian, dialogical philosophy of Martin Buber, the issue of primary concern is the mutual constitution of the subject by the other and the other by the subject. Theunissen's work, in fact, makes clear that although Buber proposes quite different answers to the question of the constitution of the other than do Husserl and Heidegger, Buber is united with Husserl and Heidegger in asking the same question. For all of them, the question of the other person is the question of how the self and the other are constituted in consciousness.

Part of Levinas's originality and contribution to the tradition lies in the fact that he did not think the phenomenon of the other person through the question of the constitution of the other. Instead, Levinas has pondered a different question concerning the nature of human knowing. Levinas has thought what really has gone largely unthought in the history of philosophy—that knowing takes place always within the context of the intersubjective relation. Levinas's question is not: How does the solitary subject know the other person when the two initially confront one another? Instead, Levinas's question is: What is the significance of the fact that knowing occurs within and is a result of the intersubjective relation? How does this fact affect our conception of knowing? Levinas has consistently thought out this question and, consequently, devised a novel and radical reinterpretation of the process of human knowing and what it means to know.

Levinas has shifted the focus of philosophical thought away from the constitution of the other and the self in consciousness and to the relationship between the self and the Other in which all knowing occurs. He has made clear that the question of the being of the other person is not merely a subset of the question of the being of things other than the subject, precisely because the other person is that being external to the subject who is a face, who expresses him/herself and who attends and directs his/her expression.[65] The encounter with the Other involves on the part of the subject not only the active moment, the cognitive attempt to comprehend the Other's being, but also the passive moment, the attending to the Other's expression. The other person not only is something to be understood, but also something to be responded to. The attempt at understanding the being of the other person is always already some kind of response to the Other's originary expression. The being of the Other is different from the being of things because the expression of the Other is also a solicitation, a summons to respond: "The face summons me."[66] Because the face is a summons to respond, it is also a summons to the subject to assume responsibility for the Other. As Levinas says, the response of the subject ". . . is the response of responsibility."[67] The subject is indebted to the Other for the Other's expression, an indebtedness which comes in the form of obligation. To see the face is, for Levinas, to be called into responsibility for it. This is what Levinas means by saying that the expression of the face is the command "Don't kill me." There is no expression of the face, no giving over or offering up of the Other to the subject's understanding, without this ethical appeal.

Levinas presents a very interesting and unique interpretation of the process of knowing based on what is for him the phenomenological and ontological fact that the face of the Other calls the subject to responsibility. Because the expression of the face is also a command to respond and a call to responsibility, it provides the subject with a certain directedness or orientation to the subject's response to the Other. Levinas uses the word *sens*, which signifies both "meaning" and "direction," to express this orientation that the Other provides the subject. Since this orientation is rooted in the Other's calling the subject to responsibility, an ethical sense or orientation directs the process whereby the subject comes to know the other person. For Levinas, the fact that knowing occurs within the intersubjective relation means that knowing has an ethical sense or orientation.

Levinas clarifies what he means by this ethical orientation or sense in knowing in his 1964 essay "Meaning and Sense." Here Levinas begins by observing that it is possible for a French person to learn to speak Chinese and so to appreciate the Other's culture. However, adds Levinas, "what has not been taken into consideration in this case is that an orientation which leads the Frenchman to take up learning Chinese instead of declaring it to be barbarian (that is, bereft of the real values of language), to prefer speech to war, is needed.[68] His point is that there is an orientation that directs the process of knowing, an orientation that directs the French individual to learn Chinese so as to appreciate and to respect the Other's culture rather than to dismiss it and ultimately to oppress it as barbarian.

Levinas says we are blind to this orientation in our knowing, and we reason as though our appreciation of the richness of cultures is merely a result of our coming into contact with them. Levinas reminds us, however, that "incomprehension, war, and conquest" also derived from "the contiguity of multiple expressions of being" of diverse cultures. Our "peaceful coexistence" with other cultures and our recognition of their riches are "themselves the effects of an orientation of an unequivocal sense in which humanity stands."[69] That humanity stands in this ethical orientation is, for Levinas, the meaning of the fact that in the face-to-face relation the expression of the Other is also the summons of the subject into responsibility for the Other. In the intersubjective relation, response is responsibility, and knowing is directed by the ethical sense: ". . . in a relationship with a face, in the ethical relationship, there is delineated the straightforwardness of an orientation, or sense."[70]

Interpreting the process of knowing through the analysis of the subject and the other person rather than the subject and the other in general, Levinas makes a very important contribution to philosophical reflection concerning knowledge of what is external to the self by introducing the discussion of ethics within the process of knowing. Levinas claims to find within the intersubjective relation obligation to and responsibility for the Other, which gives direction or sense to the process of knowing. Thus, knowledge not only includes ethics, but ethics gives directionality to the process of knowing. Knowledge involves not only the capacity of the mind, but the mind directed by, oriented by, the ethical sense. Because Levinas finds in the intersubjective relation the ethical obligation that orients or directs thought, he claims that ethics is not a branch of philosophy but first philosophy, because it orients or directs the process of knowing. This is precisely what he means by saying that "morality presides over the work of truth."[71]

Through his phenomenology of the other person, Levinas brings the question of ethics and of the relation of ethics to knowing and to philosophy to the forefront of philosophical inquiry. If Theunissen is correct in saying that the "problem of the Other has certainly never penetrated as deeply as today into the foundations of philosophical thought,"[72] then surely Levinas is chiefly responsible for making the problem of the Other as a questioning of philosophy at its foundations also a problem of ethics, a problem of the relation between ethics and philosophy. We have already seen how Levinas constructed his phenomenology by interpreting in but otherwise than Heidegger to critique Heidegger's ontology and to exalt ethics. As we suggested earlier, however, Levinas's phenomenology also represents a radical questioning of and a challenge to all previous philosophical thought. Does philosophy pursue knowledge for knowledge's sake? Does it aimlessly follow the thread of Being or of consciousness, or does it have a direction? Is it oriented by an ethical sense? And if philosophy is directed by its own ethical orientation, is it able, or does it even try, to excavate the meaning of its own ethical sense? By declaring that ethics is first philosophy, Levinas issues a challenge to philosophy to question itself as to whether it is oriented by an ethical sense and to question whether philosophy has thought through the meaning and significance of ethics for philosophy. Levinas's phenomenology of the Other asks philosophy the basic question of whether morality presides over and directs the work of truth, the work of philosophy.

Historical exigency is the force behind Levinas's ethical phenomenology. "The moment," says Levinas, "when philosophy becomes suspect is not just any moment."[73]

For Levinas, the Holocaust is the moment, the event that necessitates a radical questioning and revision of the task and essence of philosophy. Whatever can be said about philosophy and its reflections on human existence, meaning, political order, ethics, etc., before the Holocaust, what must be said after the Holocaust is that not only were all of the West's philosophical, ethical and religious teachings and reflections unable to prevent Auschwitz, but they also may have provided a certain legitimation to the devaluation and desecration of human life.[74] To Levinas, this is what philosophy after the Holocaust—whatever it may look like—must never forget, and this is what must give philosophy an ethical sense, an orientation toward the Good. As Stephen Smith correctly asserts, "the full weight" of Levinas's philosophy ". . . is a question of opposing the philosophy that produced and underwrote the colonial arrogance of Europe and the totalitarian cruelties of Hitler and Stalin."[75]

Levinas's philosophy, however, not only opposes the philosophy that underwrote the Holocaust and other nightmares of history, but it also raises the question of what kind of philosophy can be written after the Holocaust. As Blanchot says, the question of "how can one philosophize after Auschwitz is the thought that transverses the whole of Levinas's philosophy and that he proposes to us without saying it."[76] Levinas's own philosophical response to the Holocaust is unequivocal: Ethics must no longer be considered a branch of philosophy, but first philosophy, which is to say that philosophy must realize and insist that ethics orients and gives direction to knowing.

But the question then must become: Is contemporary philosophy written in the shadow of Auschwitz? Further, is it sufficiently chastened by the Holocaust, and is it more concerned with ethics than the philosophy written before? What is more, does contemporary philosophy even when it exhibits ethical concerns have within itself the philosophical resources to explicate the meaning of ethics? These are all vital questions Levinas's work puts to philosophy after Auschwitz.

I shall attempt to discuss these questions by analyzing the work of three contemporary philosophers whose works in some way exhibit a certain concern for ethical issues. I shall discuss first Theodor Adorno and his contention that philosophical thought after the Holocaust has to be negative dialectics; then I shall discuss Jacques Derrida and his increasing concern for the deconstruction of social, political and educational institutions; and finally, I shall discuss Jean-Francois Lyotard's concern for the just adjudication of language games. I shall thereby attempt to show that although these three thinkers are very much concerned with ethical issues, yet even they are all in some way incapable of explicating the meaning of ethics within the terms of their own philosophy. It is Levinas, I shall argue, who has responded to the historical crises of the Holocaust and similar manifestations of the harsh reality of physical violence by creating a philosophy that not only is preoccupied with ethical concerns, but that also explicates the meaning of ethics in the language of philosophy.

Theodor Adorno and Critical Theory

Few contemporary philosophers are as concerned with the Holocaust as is Adorno or interpret its significance as radically as he does. For Adorno, the Holocaust is the event that requires that all philosophy, all knowing and all language be reinterpreted in its light. As he says in *Negative Dialectics*: "After Auschwitz there is no word tinged from on high, not even a theological one, that has any right unless it underwent a transformation."[77] In Adorno's own philosophy, the Holocaust serves as the model of the fact that experience exceeds all concepts, so that a version of theory or of conceptuality that is believed to fully express or capture reality is a form of violence. The Holocaust represents the fact that philosophy must show "the untruth of identity, the fact that the concept does not exhaust the thing conceived."[78] Adorno even insists that if thought does not take its lessons from the Holocaust and does not permit itself to be "measured by the extremity that eludes the concept, it is from the outset in the nature of the musical accompaniment with which the SS liked to drown out the screams of its victims."[79]

With its emphasis both on the Holocaust and on the inability of the concept to capture and exhaust the alterity of the real, Adorno comes closer to the main thrust of Levinas's philosophy than perhaps any other contemporary thinker.[80] Yet there are some major differences between the two. The most important one is that Adorno's critical philosophy, although it is directed by an ethical sense, has no capacity to explore the deeper meaning of its own ethical sense.

Following Horkheimer's distinction between traditional and critical theory, Adorno attempts to develop a philosophy that would entirely avoid the former type of theory and fulfill the latter. Adorno's critical theory is designed, then, to be entirely critical, an entirely negative or destructive strategy of reflection, a reflection aimed at a radical critique and negation of any totalizing truth claims or traditional theories.

Adorno's critical theory is useful for Levinas in that it criticizes other theories that claim to fully represent the unrepresentable. Yet insofar as Adorno's philosophy sees itself as the one critical theory or negative strategy capable of criticizing all other theories, it is for Levinas still a philosophy dominated by theory rather than by the actual experience of the face-to-face encounter. Although Levinas's philosophy is theoretical and is not a protest against all theory, it embraces a theory directed by and in the service of that which exceeds theory—ethics. Because Levinas's philosophy is dominated by the face-to-face encounter, it is dominated by ethics, by the relation in which the call to ethical responsibility is heard. Consequently, theory in Levinas's philosophy is not merely critical; rather, theory is in the service of the ethical orientation or sense that Levinas describes in his phenomenology. Theory directed by and in the service of ethics is theory superceded. Reflection that has discovered in reflection something more important than reflection, and which orders and directs reflection, is reflection superceded by ethics—reflection dethroned, unavoidable and necessary, but no longer primary. This is part of what Levinas means by saying "ethics is not a branch of philosophy, but first philosophy" and "morality presides over the work of truth."[81] Derrida is also right in saying that "the notion of primacy, employed so frequently by Levinas, well translates the gesture of his entire critique."[82]

This dethroning of theory is precisely the concession to Marx that Adorno, the philosopher of critical reflection, maintained philosophy could not make: "Anyone who still philosophizes can do so only if he rejects the Marxist thesis that reflection has been superceded."[83] In Adorno's philosophy, reflection is not superceded because it is always critical reflection, negative dialectics. Aimed at opposing all theories that eliminate absolute otherness, Adorno's philosophy responds to the demand to be always on guard against totalizing theories; as such, it is directed by an ethical sense. However, because his philosophy is an entirely negative strategy of reflection, an entirely critical theory, it cannot excavate the meaning of its own ethical sense. It can stand on guard, but it cannot explain why it feels the compulsion to stand on guard. As critical theory, as theory that can only criticize other theories, Adorno's philosophy cannot explicate the meaning of that which directs its own theory—its ethical sense. Because it cannot describe the meaning of the ethical, Adorno's philosophy cannot see what Levinas insists upon—that the ethical command both directs and supercedes theory.

Jacques Derrida and the Deconstruction of Institutions

Adorno is not the only contemporary thinker who shares Levinas's concern for otherness. Although Derrida's project of deconstruction is often taken to task for being absolutely detached from the real world and consequently unable to adequately address or affect issues of ethical, political or social import,[84] it must be seen as a concern for otherness that owes a great deal to Levinas's own ethical phenomenology. We can see that Derrida's concern for otherness is at the very root of his own philosophical program if we analyze carefully one of Derrida's earliest works, his 1964 essay on Levinas entitled "Violence and Metaphysics."

In 1963, two years after the publication of *Totality and Infinity*, Levinas published an essay entitled "The Trace of the Other," in which he clarifies what he means by the Other as absolutely or infinitely other. The Other comes to us in the face-to-face encounter out of the depths of a past that can never be entirely recovered. This means, as we have seen, that even in the expression of the face, the Other is never fully given, never entirely present in the full depths of the Other's alterity. Thus, what the subject becomes aware of in the face-to-face encounter is the impossibility of an absolute or totally exhaustive relation with the Other. The subject becomes aware that, in fact, the Other is present only as an infinite absence that can never be made present. The face to face is a relation wherein the Other's presence is a trace of the Other's infinite alterity, wherein the Other is present only as a trace. The trace signifies the infinite alterity of the Other that can never be retrieved in the present but is always already an irretrievable past, "an immemorial past,"[85] a past "always past."[86]

It is important to see that Derrida does not argue with Levinas's "thematic of the trace." Far from it, he adopts it and uses it for a purpose of his own that is quite in keeping with Levinas's own purpose—to preserve the sense of radical otherness. What is more, Derrida employs the concept of the trace in an attempt to heighten the sense of radical otherness it expresses. Levinas's concept of the trace prompts Derrida to observe that the absolute otherness of the Other is better expressed not as speaking, where the speaker is present to attend and direct his/her expression, but as writing. In this, the writer, after imparting his/her traces, disappears from the scene. Derrida suggests that since the author withdraws and disappears, writing is a better expression of the other's nonpresence, of the other's presence only as past, as a trace of having once been there. Thus, is not writing a better expression of the other's infinite alterity never to be made present? Is it not true that the writer, who as writer must absent himself, "expresses himself better as other?"[87] Levinas's thematic of the trace, concludes Derrida, "should lead to a certain rehabilitation of writing. Is not the `He' whom transcendence and generous absence uniquely announce in the trace more readily the author of writing than of speech?"[88]

"Violence and Metaphysics" makes clear what is so often overlooked about Derrida's concern for and preoccupation with issues of writing as the key to language in general—that it springs from a concern he shares with Levinas for preserving otherness from its elimination via a totalizing view of the referential capacity of language. Thus, Derrida's project of dismantling or deconstructing the metaphysics of presence via an analysis of the foundation of language stems from an ethical concern.[89] Language does not capture reality and eliminate all otherness because it is—and here Derrida is taking his cue from Saussure—a system of differential relations without any positive terms, a purely arbitrary play of signifiers. Language is a system of pure differences without any center to limit the play of signifiers.[90] Conceiving of language in this way enables Derrida in his deconstructive project to call everything into question, and this, he tells us, is the best way to oppose the violence that would eliminate otherness.[91]

In 1966, when Derrida delivered his lecture "Structure, Sign, and Play" at Johns Hopkins, he began to spell out the philosophical consequences of thinking of language as a system of differential relations. He said that philosophy could interpret this in two ways: it could either live off the dream of and the nostalgia for full presence and the center, which governs and assures the end of play, or it could determine "the noncenter otherwise than as loss of center."[92] This second interpretation would be the positive, indeed "joyous affirmation of the play of the world and of the innocence of becoming, the affirmation of a world of signs without fault, without truth, and without origin."[93] As such, this affirmation would also be the affirmation of the inability of language and of thought to capture otherness.

In "Violence and Metaphysics," Derrida says that questions about the possibility, the future, and the death of philosophy ". . . should be the only questions today capable of founding the community, within the world, of those who are still called philosophers."[94] In "Structure, Sign, and Play," he writes that ". . . the passage beyond philosophy does not consist in turning the page of philosophy (which usually amounts to philosophizing badly), but in continuing to read philosophers in a certain way."[95] Much of Derrida's early work is preoccupied with philosophizing beyond and within the death of philosophy by reading philosophy in a certain way, by deconstructing the history of philosophy through showing that philosophical truth claims depend upon the onto-theological language of presence. Thus, Derrida's early writings, and especially the three works of 1967—*Writing and Difference, Of Grammatology* and *Speech and Phenomenon*—attempt to think the end of philosophy by advancing a certain method of reading texts. In these early works, deconstruction means deconstruction of texts; it entails a preoccupation with a certain method of reading. As Derrida himself says, between 1963—when he was beginning to write the essays such as "Violence and Metaphysics" that were later published in book form in 1967—and 1968, he was trying to work out ". . . a sort of strategic device, opening onto its own abyss, an unclosed, unenclosable, not wholly formalizable ensemble of rules for reading, interpretation and writing."[96] In fact, in his early writings Derrida's program of deconstruction is so preoccupied with reading, interpretation and texts that deconstruction entered the American academic scene primarily via departments of English and literary criticism rather than through philosophy departments.[97]

Derrida's project of deconstruction must inevitably go beyond its initial preoccupation with written texts, however, for certainly the repercussions of the contention that language is a system of purely arbitrary differences extend beyond merely literary and philosophical texts. The same logocentrism that establishes unequivocality in texts is certainly at the foundation of social and political institutions. This is what Derrida realized increasingly especially after the events in Paris in 1968. After 1968, says Derrida,

> . . . I came to understand better to what extent the necessity of deconstruction (I use this word for the sake of convenience, though it is a word I have never liked and one whose fortune has disagreeably surprised me) was not primarily a matter of philosophical contents, themes or theses, philosophemes, poems, theologemes or ideologemes, but especially and inseparably meaningful frames, institutional structures, pedagogical or rhetorical norms, the possibilities of law, of authority, of evaluation, and of representation in terms of its very market.[98]

Although the points of reference for Derrida's work have remained primarily philosophical and literary (Kant, Hegel, Husserl, Heidegger, Benjamin), Derrida's recent works, especially *Truth in Painting* (1979) and *The Post Card* (1979), are concerned not only with deconstructing texts but with deconstructing institutions. In other words, there is in Derrida's own work a progression from a celebration of the free and open mere playing of language to the purposeful employment of language within a social and political critique.[99] In 1980, Derrida wrote that his philosophy involved the deconstruction not only of language, but also of French educational institutions. He confessed, in fact, that for him the deconstruction of institutions was an "ineluctable responsibility."[100] He also stated that his writings in the seventies placed the greatest emphasis

> on rights and on what is proper, what is one's own, on the rights of property, on copyright, on the signature and the market, on the market for painting or, more generally, for culture and all its representations, on speculation on what is proper, one's own, on the name, on destination and restitution, on all the institutional borders and structures of discourses, on the whole machinery of publishing and on the media.[101]

In these writings, Derrida shows that for him, despite the apolitical reception of deconstruction in the United States, the deconstruction of language leads to the deconstruction of institutions. Derrida's deconstructive philosophy is, then, as Bernstein says, "an ethico-political critique"[102] and "a way of taking a position not separable from the political institutional problematic."[103] Rick Roderick is even more emphatic in stating that in Derrida's philosophy "what is at stake is political in the last analysis—the overthrow of current modes of thinking and living, the 'reinvention of revolution.'"[104]

Interestingly, when Derrida discusses the political and institutional concerns of his works of the seventies, he admits that at times he felt at odds with his own earlier writings. When he became more interested in the deconstruction of institutions, he would have liked to "have been able to shape both my discourse and my practice . . . to fit the premises of my earlier undertakings. In fact, if not in principle, this was not always easy, not always possible, at times indeed very burdensome in a number of ways."[105] As we have seen, one of the primary premises of Derrida's early work is that language is a system of differences without positive terms. Thus, there is no center, no *arche* that would provide a *sens*, or direction, to language, so that language is merely free play. Consequently, Derrida insists that his own writing never knows where it is going but is an aimless drifting or, as he says, an "erring" in language.

The critique of this view of language made by the semiotician and psychoanalyst Julia Kristeva, among others, can illustrate to us how Derrida's deconstruction of institutions does not necessarily fit the premises of his earlier writings. Kristeva charges that a view of language as free play ignores how language actually arises in human situations. For Kristeva, Derrida's view of language is inapplicable in the therapeutic situation in which she cannot merely play with language freely but is constrained to employ a certain language so as to respond to and to treat her patients.[106] Language as the free play of signifiers might be an adequate account of what language is in theory, but it doesn't account for the meaning language has as it is used in human existence.

If the progression of Derrida's work is taken into account, Kristeva's insight that language cannot be merely the free play of signifiers but has to be conscripted in the service of responding to certain situations may not be as foreign to Derrida's own work as it appears. Certainly Derrida, just like Kristeva, has felt the necessity of responding to certain situations in particular ways. Certainly his own work demonstrates, too, that which his view of language is accused of disregarding—that "the world constrains . . . our talk about the world."[107] He responded to the need for a criticism and a deconstruction of French political, social and educational institutions not by merely playing freely with language, not by merely saying anything he wished to say. Certainly the situation to which he felt he had to respond and for which he felt a "responsibility ineluctable" directed his language use. And what else is an ethical *sens* or direction in language but this feeling that one is required to respond to a particular situation, even obligated to respond by choosing and using a certain language rather than another? Is this one way in which Derrida felt it was "not always possible" and sometimes "very burdensome" to make his deconstruction of institutions fit his earlier writings' premises about language? In any case, since Derrida's later work does seem to be a response to a certain situation for which he feels responsible, so that he feels he is obligated to respond in a certain way and not another, it is difficult to see how even his own work can be seen as playing aimlessly with language, as free and unconstrained erring.

Derrida's most recent works in the eighties, in which the motif of responsibility constantly resurfaces,[108] make even more obvious how his own work does not fit with his earlier premises concerning language. Clearly, his language use in his 1980 essay on Levinas entitled "At this Very Moment in this Work Here I Am," and in his 1988 essay "The Politics of Friendship,"[109] as well as in works in defense of Heidegger and Paul de Man, is very much at odds with his theory of language as free and unconstrained erring.

Derrida certainly admits in "At This very Moment in this Work Here I Am" not only that his language is constrained, but that the essay itself is written out of the experience of being constrained by Levinas's texts: "*il aura oblige*" (he will have obligated).[110] Here Derrida states quite clearly that he writes out of an obligation to respond to Levinas and that his response, as a response, rather than being free and arbitrary, is constrained by what it is responding to: "One must respond to it [Levinas's work] and even respond for it, not by means of what one understands by work according to the dominant interpretation of language, but according to what his work says, in its manner, of Work."[111]

Derrida further explores this fact of being constrained "at this very moment" in his language use by a sense of responsibility in his 1988 essay "The Politics of Friendship." He begins by quoting Montaigne on friendship, and then asks if he is responsible for quoting these words another has said: "Am I completely irresponsible for what I have said when I am not responsible for what I have said?"[112] Derrida then admits that you [the reader] "hold me responsible, personally responsible, for the simple fact that I am speaking, and, for example, for the fact of quoting Montaigne in order to begin in place of and before saying anything else."[113] Then, in order to explore and to explain this mysterious and unavoidable assignation of responsibility, Derrida asks: "What is happening at this very moment?"[114] His answer, that we are caught in a primordial situation of obligation toward the Other, shows that Derrida's own language use is far from unconstrained free play. In fact, his answer here shows that Derrida's view in the eighties of the scene of language is much closer to the views espoused by Levinas than to his own earlier views:

> . . . before even having taken responsibility for any given affirmation, we are already caught up in a kind of asymmetrical and heteronomical curvature of the social space, more precisely, in the relation to the Other prior to any organized socius, to any determined "government," to any "law" . . . This heteronomical and asymmetrical curvature of a sort of originary sociality is a law, perhaps the very essence of the law. What is taking place at this moment, the disquieting experience we are having, is perhaps just the silent unfolding of that strange violence that has since forever insinuated itself into the origin of the most innocent experiences of friendship or justice.

> We have begun to respond. We are already caught, surprised [pris, surpris] in a certain responsibility, and the most ineluctable of responsibilities—as if it were possible to conceive of a responsibility without freedom. We are invested with an undeniable responsibility at the moment we begin to signify something (but where does that begin?). This responsibility assigns us our freedom without leaving it with us, if one could put it that way. And we see it coming from the Other. It is assigned to us by the Other, from the Other, before any hope of reappropriation permits us to assume this responsiblility in the space of what could be called autonomy.[115]

Certainly Derrida's recent work on Heidegger entitled *Of Spirit* also illustrates that Derrida's own work is not in keeping with his earlier view of language. In this work Derrida attempts to defend Heidegger from the charge that he put his philosophy in the service of Nazism. By a careful and meticulous reading of the ways in which Heidegger uses the words *geist* and *geistig* in both his philosophical and political writings, Derrida labors to show that Heidegger clearly undercut any attempt to implicate his philosophy in any determinate politics. Obviously Derrida's language in defending Heidegger, far from being free play, is constrained by the necessity to interpret Heidegger's texts accurately and meticulously in order to render justice to their author.

Perhaps it is Derrida's recent defense of Paul de Man, however, that most clearly shows the disparity between Derrida's actual use of language and his theory of language as free play. In his essay "Paul de Man's War," Derrida defends de Man against accusations of complicity with the Nazis when he was editor of a Belgian newspaper during World War II. Derrida again admits from the beginning that his language in the essay will be constrained "by a responsibility [to de Man] which would never be cancelled."[116] He then tries to fulfill his responsibility by launching into a long, labored, and at times highly improbable defense of de Man.[117] Derrida insists that this issue must involve a very careful rereading of de Man's work that must begin "by listening, to try to hear what he said to us . . ."[118] To analyze how de Man experienced the war, to interpret the war as Paul de Man's war, warns Derrida, "will require patient, careful, minute and difficult research."[119] Anything less, any attempt to settle the issue not constrained by the necessity for such difficult research, "would be unjust, abusive and irresponsible. I would even say, given the gravity of these things, indecent."[120]

It is obvious from many of Derrida's writings—but especially from these three most recent ones—that his language use does not accord with his view of language in that it is not mere playing and aimless wandering. More and more, Derrida's own language is constrained by situations to which he must respond, for which he feels responsible, for which he even admits an "ineluctable responsibility." Thus, even Derrida's own language use seems to have a certain ethical *sens* or direction to it.

It is a *sens* or direction, however, that cannot be accounted for within the premises of Derrida's early theory of language. Derrida views language as a system of differences. Without doubt, Derrida is quite correct in this, but this is not all language is, and this is why Derrida cannot account for all of even his own language use. Language is more than a system of differences because, as Levinas has seen more clearly than anyone, it is a system of differences that arises within the face-to-face encounter. Because Derrida interprets language as what it is in theory rather than in its actual incarnation in human interaction, he sees language as a "game" and as "play."[121] Levinas, on the other hand, analyzes language as it arises within the face-to-face encounter between persons, so that for him, "Language is not a game but bears the weight of the responsibility for the other."[122]

It would be wrong to say of Derrida that he has never

felt this responsibility. In fact, as we have seen, his philosophy testifies again and again to the weight of responsibility as it bears upon and constrains language use. Derrida's theory of language, however, as Derrida himself intimates, is incapable of taking the weight of responsibility into account. What is more, since it fails to take the weight of responsibility into account, Derrida's view of language, contrary to his language use, is incapable of being transformed by the weight of responsibility to which it testifies.[123]

Jean-Francois Lyotard and the Gaming of the Just

Certainly one contemporary French philosopher who does not share Derrida's truncated view of language is Jean-Francois Lyotard. He is one of the few philosophers who combines continental philosophy's concern for language as system with Anglo-American philosophy's concern with language use. In fact, one of the central issues of Lyotard's philosophy is the adjudication of Wittgensteinian language games in order to bring about what Lyotard refers to as "just gaming."[124]

Although Lyotard's philosophy owes a great deal to Wittgenstein, it is in some ways a Wittgenstein in reverse. The goal of Wittgenstein's *Philosophical Investigations* was to resolve philosophical disputes by an analysis of ordinary language use. By asking the question, "what do we mean when we say a certain thing?", Wittgenstein sought in linguistic analysis the way to unravel philosophical puzzles, to untie the knots in our thinking. The goal of philosophy, then, according to Wittgenstein, is not the pronouncement of propositions but "no knots."[125] Thus, knots can be untied, consensus can be reached by analyzing how words are ordinarily used. For Lyotard, on the other hand, the knots cannot be untied and no consensus can be reached, because language use entails a plurality of language games, all played by rules distinct to each particular game.[126] The plurality of language games means that phrases are forever in dispute, and that any resolution of the dispute is always at the expense of one or both parties of the dispute, always involves imposing the rules of one language game upon another language game. Thus, consensus for Lyotard involves a certain violence.[127] Philosophy should shun this violence and leave phrases in dispute. Philosophy should concern itself not with untying knots but with witnessing to the phrases in dispute, to the differend, which is a "case of conflict, between (at least) two parties, that cannot be equitably resolved for lack of a rule of judgment applicable to both parties."[128]

Lyotard's philosophy, then, is preoccupied not only with the analysis of different language games, but with an explicitly ethical concern to avoid violence by leaving phrases in dispute. Lyotard's ethical concern is his distinction, absolutely vital especially in his most recent work, between just and unjust gaming. Undeniably rhetorical, Lyotard's work attempts to bring philosophy closer to what he refers to as "just gaming," understood as "the gaming of the just." But what is just gaming? It begins with the realization that the various language games are all played by their own rules so that, for instance, ". . . it is not possible to decide from the viewpoint of the prescriptive game about matters of denotative or narrative games."[129] Just gaming, then, amounts to not imposing the rules of one language game on another. "The Idea of justice," says Lyotard, "will consist in preserving the purity of each game" by preventing the "infiltration" of one game by another.[130] In just gaming, no one language game is favored over, or is dominant over another, and truth is not the absolute truth of one exalted language game but is the individual truth of each "specific" language game.

The question Lyotard's philosophy brings upon itself, however, is: Is not such an obviously rhetorical philosophy as this, which argues and insists that the equality and purity of language games must be preserved, itself guilty of favoring one particular language game, the prescriptive, over the others? As both Lyotard's conversation partner in *Just Gaming*, Jean-Loup Thebaud, and the author of the book's Afterword, Samuel Weber, have noted, Lyotard's contention that just gaming means that no language game is to be dominant over any other involves him in a contradiction, for this injunction is itself a prescriptive language game. This is why Thebaud says that when Lyotard insists on this, he is "talking like the great prescriber himself."[131] Weber makes the same point in a different way, asserting that Lyotard's

> . . . concern with "preserving the purity" and singularity "of each game" by reinforcing its isolation from the others gives rise to exactly what was intended to be avoided: "the domination of one game by another," namely the domination of the prescriptive. For without a "great prescriber," no purity, no specificity, no incommensurability, even identified, could be preserved as such.[132]

Lyotard's philosophy, then, unwillingly points to a certain necessity that Levinas more than any other contemporary philosopher has recognized, and which Lyotard himself attempts to deny—the necessity for there to be a formulated prescriptive if the play of language is to be just. Lyotard's distinction between just and unjust gaming and his desire that gaming be the gaming of the just requires that a prescriptive—in this case, something like "let no one language game dominate the others"—preside over the playful nonresolutions of the differends. Lyotard's just gaming is, then, a good example of what Levinas means when he says that there is an ethical orientation (*sens*) in knowing, or that morality presides over the work of truth, or that ethics is first philosophy.

One of the reasons Lyotard himself cannot recognize the necessity of the prescriptive to guide the nonresolution of the differends if the gaming is to be just—even though his own philosophy illustrates it so clearly—is that he wants to distance himself from what he interprets as the dominance of the prescriptive in Levinas's philosophy. This desire to distance himself proceeds, however, from a misinterpretation of the relation between the prescriptive and the descriptive language games in Levinas's ethical philosophy. Lyotard says that in his own philosophy each game is preserved in its purity, "each game is played as such."[133] This means for Lyotard that no game is seen as "the game of all the other games or as the true one."[134] He says that this is a "betrayal of" and is "alien to" Levinas's philosophy, in which the prescriptive, "the lived experience of obligation," is "truth itself." He then goes on to say that in Levinas this truth is not ontological truth, but ethical truth, and asserts that for Levinas this ethical truth is the only truth. This ethical truth, or what he takes to be the prescriptive language game in Levinas, cannot be the truth for Lyotard; he believes that there are also other truths in other language games, and he refers to truths in the narrative language game as an example. Lyotard then says that "privileging a language game above others"—which is what Levinas does, according to Lyotard, when he takes the prescriptive language game as the truth—"would be something like saying: The only important game, the only true one, is chess. That is absurd."[135]

Levinas's philosophy makes clear, however, that the prescriptive language game and the descriptive language game coincide. Indeed, to think with Lyotard that the prescriptive language game is the only true language game or that ethical truth is the only truth is to misunderstand Levinas's entire philosophical project as philosophy. It is to fail to see that Levinas's philosophy is phenomenology, which means that it proceeds predominantly via a descriptive language game. Far from seeing truth only as ethics, it sees truth in phenomena, as does Heidegger's phenomenological ontology. And it finds in the face-to-face encounter the phenomenon of the prescriptive, the ethical command. Quite different from Lyotard's insistence on the separateness of language games, the prescriptive language game is for Levinas a phenomenon capable of being described in the descriptive language game because the prescriptive announces itself in the face of the Other.[136] But he also insists that the prescriptive, once it is found via the descriptive language game, announces its own authority, demands privilege in the sense of priority or primacy—ethics is first philosophy.

This priority of the prescriptive language game, however, does not mean for Levinas what Lyotard thinks it means for him. Levinas does not say that the prescriptive, or the ethical, is the only important language game, the only true one, or the only truth. Levinas does say, however, that the prescriptive, or the ethical, orients and presides over the work of truth, which in Lyotard's language means that it orients other language games, including the descriptive one. This prioritizing of the prescriptive language game is exactly what Lyotard himself does when he says that no one language game should dominate the others if the gaming is to be just. Thus, Lyotard's interpretation of what Levinas means by privileging the prescriptive language game is incorrect. Ironically, Levinas's insistence that morality presides over the work of truth, on his prioritizing of the prescriptive language game, is exactly what Lyotard reluctantly discovers that he himself must do if the gaming he recommends and seeks is to be the gaming of the just.

CONCLUSION

Adorno, Derrida and Lyotard are all explicitly postmodern philosophers. As such, they have all tried to think within the end of philosophy, an end whose beginning has been brought about in part by an awareness, felt within the shadow of the Holocaust, of the totalizing nature of traditional philosophy. All three philosophers exhibit clearly a certain concern for otherness, a concern to avoid the violence involved in reducing otherness to the realm of the same. Thus, the philosophy written at the end of philosophy by Adorno, Derrida and Lyotard embraces and is even written out of explicitly ethical concerns.

As we have seen, however, these philosophies are incapable of explicating the meaning of their own ethical concerns. Adorno's critical theory is an entirely negative strategy of critical reflection and, as such, cannot explicate the positive meaning of the ethical concerns that drive its negative dialectics. Similarly, Derrida's theory of language as the arbitrary play of signifiers does not accord with, nor can it account for, the many ways in which his sense of ethical responsibility constrains his language use. And Lyotard, in insisting that just gaming consists in maintaining the purity and equality of language games, is blind to the fact of the primacy of the prescriptive in his own philosophy. All three philosophers grapple very seriously with the reality of and the radical need for ethics, but none can explicate the meaning of ethics in the terms of their own philosophy.

This clarifies, perhaps, Levinas's most important contribution to contemporary philosophy. Among those philosophers who have tried to write at the end of philosophy, perhaps the only one who has both experienced the command of ethics and attempted to explicate the meaning of the ethical command for philosophy is Levinas. "We have, very largely if not entirely," states Alisdair McIntyre, "lost our comprehension, both theoretical and practical, of morality."[137] It is Levinas who has felt the full import of this loss and has attempted to respond to this challenge and to rectify this situation. It is Levinas who not only has philosophized at the end of philosophy and in the shadow of the Holocaust out of and cognizant of an ethical sense, but has also tried to interpret the meaning of the ethical sense. Consequently, he has provided us with what we may well need most—a philosophical explication of the meaning of the ethical exigency other contemporary philosophers certainly have felt but have so far proven unable to explain and account for, especially in the language of philosophy.

NOTES

Notes to Introduction

1. Recent translations of Levinas's work include: *Ethics and Infinity*, trans. Richard Cohen, (Pittsburgh: Duquesne University Press, 1985); *Time and the Other*, trans. Richard Cohen, (Pittsburgh: Duquesne University Press, 1987); *Collected Philosophical Papers*, trans. A. Lingis, (The Hague: Martinus Nijhoff, 1987); *The Levinas Reader*, ed. Sean Hand (Oxford: Basil Blackwell, 1989); *Nine Talmudic Readings*, trans. Annette Aronowicz, (Bloomington: Indiana University Press, 1990); *Difficult Freedom*, trans. Sean Hand, (Baltimore: Johns Hopkins University Press, 1990).

Recent books on Levinas include: Steven Smith, *The Argument to the Other: Reason Beyond Reason in the Thought of Karl Barth and Emmanuel Levinas* (Chico, CA: Scholars Press, 1983); Salmon Malka, *Lire Levinas* (Paris: Les Editions Du Cerf, 1984): Richard Cohen, ed., *Face to Face with Levinas* (Albany: State University of New York Press, 1986); Francois Poire, *Emmanuel Levinas: Qui etesvous?* (Lyon: La Manufacture, 1987); Robert Bernasconi and David Wood, eds., *The Provocation of Levinas* (London: Routledge, 1988); Klaas Huizing, *Das Sein und der Andere. Levinas' Auseinandersetzung mit Heidegger* (Frankfurt-am-Main: Athenaum, 1988); Andrius Valevicius, *From the Other to the Totally Other* (New York: Peter Lang, 1988); *Re-reading Levinas*, eds. Robert Bernasconi and Simon Critchley (Bloomington: Indiana University Press, 1991); Susan Handelman, *Fragments of Redemption* (Bloomington: Indiana University Press, 1991).

2. Carl Jung, *Essays on Contemporary Events: The Psychology of Nazism* (Princeton: Princeton University Press, 1989), 71.

3. See the interview with Levinas entitled "The Paradox of Morality" in *The Provocation of Levinas,* 175.

4. This includes: Levinas's dissertation *The Theory of Intuition in Husserl's Phenomenology,* A. Orianne, tr. (Evanston: Northwestern University Press, 1973); *Meditations Cartesiennes,* Emmanuel Levinas and Michelle Pfeiffer, trs. (Paris: Colin, 1931); and a series of articles on Husserl and Heidegger resulting in Levinas's *En decouvrant l'existence avec Husserl and Heidegger,* 2nd ed. (Paris: Vrin, 1967).

5. All biographical information about Levinas was obtained from Levinas's article "Signature," ed. Adriaan Peperzak, trans. Mary Ellen Petrisko *Research in Phenomenology,* 8 (1978): 175-89.

6. Emmanuel Levinas, *Existence and Existents,* trans. A. Orianne (The Hague: Martinus Nijhoff, 1978).

7. See Simone de Beauvoir, *Le Deuxieme Sexe,* 2 vols. (Paris: Gallimard, 1949), 1:15, translated by H. M. Parshley as *The Second Sex* (New York: Random House, 1952), p. xix. Here de Beauvoir criticizes Levinas for writing a sexist philosophy deliberately from a man's point of view to affirm masculine privilege.

8. Emmanuel Levinas, *Totality and Infinity,* trans. Alphonso Lingis (Pittsburgh: Duquesne University Press, 1969).

9. See Jacques Derrida's, "Violence and Metaphysics" in *Writing and Difference,* trans. Alan Bass (Chicago: The University of Chicago Press, 1978), 151.

10. Langdon Gilkey, "Comments on Emmanuel Levinas' *Totality and Infinity,*" *Algemeen Nederlands Tijdschrift voor Wijsbegeerte,* 64 (1972): 26–38.

11. See Rudolf J. Gerber, "Totality and Infinity: Hebraism and Hellenism—the Experiential Ontology of Emmanuel Levinas," *Review of Existential Psychology and Psychiatry,* 7, no. 3 (1967): 177–88. It should be noted that in 1970–71, Levinas was awarded the Schweitzer Prize at Leiden, naming him the leading phenomenological philosopher in Europe, a fact I learned through private conversations with Langdon Gilkey.

12. Harold Durfee, "War, Politics, and Radical Pluralism" in *Foundational Reflections* (Dordrecht: Martinus Nijhoff, 1987), 208.

13. This is true of Derrida's initial essay on Levinas, "Violence and Metaphysics," and of several other essays: Steven Gans, "Ethics or Ontology: Levinas and Heidegger," *Philosophy Today,* 16, no. 2 (Summer 1972): 117–21; Luk Boukaert, "Ontology and Ethics," *International Philosophical Quarterly* 10 (1970): 402–19; C. D. Keyes, "An Evaluation of Levinas' Critique

of Heidegger," *Research in Phenomenology*, 2 (1972): 121–42. Bernasconi and Critchley also observe this in their introduction to *The Levinas Reader* when they say that "the initial reception of Levinas's work has been to a great extent determined by *Totality and Infinity*" (p. xii).

14. For a discussion of this see below, chapter 3.

15. Boukaert, 405.

16. F. P. Ciglia, "Du Neant A L'Autre. Reflexions sur le theme de la mort dans la pense de Levinas" in *Les Cahiers de la nuit surveillee*, no. 3 (Lagrasse: Verdier, 1984), 146.

17. See Guy Petitdemange's essay "L'un ou l'autre. La querelle de l'ontologie: Heidegger-Levinas" in *Les Cahiers de la nuit surveille*, 46.

18. Allain David, "Le nom de la finitude" in *Les Cahiers de la nuit surveillee*, 248.

19. Adriaan Peperzak, "From Intentionality to Responsibility: On Levinas's Philosophy of Language" in *The Question of the Other*, Arleen Dallery and Charles Scott, eds. (Albany: State University of New York Press, 1989), 3.

20. Bernasconi, "Levinas and Derrida: The Question of the Closure of Metaphysics" in *Face to Face With Levinas*, 185.

21. Bernasconi and Wood, 3.

22. Valevicius, 100.

23. Adriaan Peperzak, "Emmanuel Levinas: Jewish Experience and Philosophy," *Philosophy Today*, vol. 27, no. 4 (Winter 1983): 300.

24. See Levinas's discussion of Heidegger's *Being and Time* in *Ethics and Infinity*, 37–41.

25. Bernasconi and Critchley, Introduction to *Re-reading Levinas*, xii.

26. The straightforwardness with which Levinas announces in 1930 that it is Heidegger, and not Husserl, who is opening up the true richness of the phenomenological method contrasts sharply with Cohen's reading of the relation Levinas bears to Heidegger and to Husserl in his "Non-indifference in the Thought of Rosenzweig and Levinas" in *Graduate Faculty Philosophy Journal* vol. 13, no. 1, pp. 141–53. Here Cohen states that in his dissertation "Levinas attributes to Husserl a theory of consciousness grounded in representation and a theory of consciousness grounded in presence to being. In so doing, Levinas avoids mentioning Heidegger while crediting Husserl with being a Heideggerian! For those who know better, it is clear that Levinas is praising and blaming both thinkers at the same time." Certainly, Levinas does mention Heidegger directly in his dissertation, and while it is clear that

Levinas is praising Heidegger, I fail to see how he is blaming Heidegger for anything in 1930.

27. Levinas, *Existence and Existents,* 19.

28. Mark Taylor, in a project similar in some ways to my own, has shown that the relation Kierkegaard's thought bears to Hegel's is not merely an oppositional one, even though Kierkegaard's writings often give this impression. In his *Journeys to Selfhood: Hegel & Kierkegaard* (Berkeley: University of California Press, 1980), Taylor has shown the great extent to which Kierkegaard is indebted to Hegel even while constantly arguing against him.

29. Levinas's philosophy is, then, an excellent example of the truth Edward Said expresses when he says in *The World, The Text, and The Critic* (Cambridge: Harvard University Press, 1983), 45, that ". . . all texts essentially dislodge other texts or, more frequently, take the place of something else."

30. Levinas, *Totality,* 304.

31. See Reed's essay "Levinas' Question" in *Face to Face,* 74.

32. Derrida, "Violence and Metaphysics," 82.

33. See Levinas's essay "Le nom de Dieu d'apres quelques textes talmudiques" in *L'analyse du langage theologique,* ed. E. Castelli, (Paris: Aubier, 1969).

34. Steven Smith, "Reason As One for Another" in *Face to Face With Levinas,* 68.

35. See Levinas's 1948 essay "Reality and its Shadow" in *Collected Philosophical Papers,* 45.

36. This fact is rarely mentioned in Levinas scholarship and, as far as I know, Levinas never mentions it himself in published interviews. It is, perhaps, partly revealed in Levinas's dedication to *Otherwise Than Being* (The Hague: Martinus Nijhoff, 1981): "To the memory of those who were closest among the six million assassinated by the National Socialists . . ." This fact was confirmed by M. Levinas in a private conversation I had with him on 10 November 1989.

37. Levinas, *Existence and Existents,* 54–109. He also clearly makes this point in "Ideology and Idealism" in *The Levinas Reader* (247) when he says of the Other that "of course we have power to exploit and oppress him, but the relation cannot be totally suppressed." He admits in the interview entitled "Ethics and Politics" in the same volume (294) that "in alterity we can find an enemy, or at least then we are faced with the problem of knowing who is right and who is wrong, who is just and who is unjust. There are people who are wrong."

38. Levinas, *Totality,* 199.

39. Jean Greisch, "The Face and Reading: Immediacy and Mediation" in *Re-reading Levinas,* 79.

40. Maurice Blanchot, "Our Clandestine Companion," *Face to Face,* 50.

Notes to Chapter One

1. Emmanuel Levinas, "De l'evasion," *Recherches Philosophiques* 5 (1935–36): 373–92.

2. In fact, until 1935 the only work Levinas published that did not deal explicitly with Husserl and/or Heidegger is his 1934 article on Hitler entitled "Quelques reflexions sur la philosophie de l'hitlerisme" in *Esprit* 2 (1934): 199–208.

3. Levinas said in "Questions et reponses" in *Le Nouveau Commerce,* nos. 36–37 (1977), 2: "In spite of everything, I think that what I do is phenomenology, even if it is not according to the rules laid down by Husserl, even if the entire Husserlian methodology is not observed." Allain David, one of Levinas's most insightful French critics, notes in his essay "Le Nom de la Finitude" (247): "Levinas ne cesse pas de designer dans la phenomenologie la methode de la philosophie."

4. Derrida, "Violence and Metaphysics," 97–98.

5. This contrasts with Cohen's contention in "Levinas, Rosenzweig, and the Phenomenologies of Husserl and Heidegger" (122) that "Levinas always prefers phenomenology in its Husserlian form." Certainly in some ways Levinas prefers phenomenology in its Husserlian form, but *Husserl's Theory of Intuition* leaves little doubt that Levinas's phenomenology is cast essentially in a Heideggerian, not a Husserlian, mode.

6. Our contention is that we can better understand Levinas's relation to Husserl and Heidegger by a close reading of Levinas's early texts and that this will help clarify misunderstandings that have arisen due to the fact that Levinas scholarship thus far has focused almost exclusively on *Totality and Infinity* and *Otherwise Than Being.* One example of such a misunderstanding is Richard Cohen's remark in his "Absolute Positivity and Ultrapositivity: Hussserl and Levinas" in *The Question of the Other* (38) that Levinas attacks the positivity of Husserlian phenomenology by a positivity greater than phenomenological positivity through the notion of the face and that this necessitates breaking the boundaries of the Husserlian reduction.

7. Emmanuel Levinas, "Sur *les Ideen* de M. E. Husserl," *Revue Philosophique de la France* 54 (1929): 230–65.

8. Martin Heidegger, *Being and Time,* trans. J. Macquarrie and E. Robinson, (New York: Harper & Row, 1962); also, see Emmanuel Levinas's comments on *Being and Time* in *Ethics and Infinity,* 37.

9. For an account of the relationship between Husserl and Heidegger, see Herbert Spiegelberg, *The Phenomenological Movement* I (The Hague: Martinus Nijhoff, 1960), 271–353.

10. Spiegelberg, 297. The lecture notes from these courses comprise Heidegger's *The Basic Problems of Phenomenology* (Bloomington: Indiana University Press, 1982).

11. Spiegelberg, 281–82.

12. See Hans-Georg Gadamer, *Philosophical Hermeneutics* (Berkeley: University of California Press, 1977), 133.

13. See Walter Biemel's article entitled "Husserl's *Encyclopedia Britannica* Article and Heidegger's Remarks Thereon" in *Husserl Expositions and Appraisals,* Frederick Elliston and Peter McCormick, eds. (Notre Dame: University of Notre Dame Press, 1977), 286–303.

14. Levinas, *The Theory of Intuition,* xxv–xxvi.

15. Notice, for example, that Levinas stresses in *The Theory of Intuition* (149) that the phenomenological *epoche* is not temporary but absolutely central in Husserlian phenomenology, and Levinas fully realizes how different this makes Husserl's phenomenology of consciousness from Heidegger's phenomenological ontology.

16. Heidegger, *Being and Time,* 63.

17. Heidegger, *Being and Time,* 63.

18. Heidegger, *Being and Time,* 50.

19. Heidegger, *Being and Time,* 63.

20. Biemel, 300.

21. Heidegger, *Being and Time,* 43.

22. Quentin Lauer, *Phenomenology: Its Genesis and Prospect* (New York: Harper & Row, 1958), 129.

23. See Michael Murray, ed., *Heidegger and Modern Philosophy* (New Haven: Yale University Press, 1978), 285, fn. 12.

24. According to Macquarrie and Robinson, Heidegger takes the Husserlian formula of *"die Sachen Selbst"* as a slogan for phenomenology.

25. In his Preface to W. R. Boyce Gibson's translation of *Ideas* (New York: The MacMillan Company, 1931), Husserl declared that "a philosophy with problematic foundations, with paradoxes which arise from the obscurity of the fundamental concepts, is no philosophy, it contradicts its very meaning as philosophy."

26. Husserl, *Ideas,* (1931).

27. Paul Ricoeur, "On Interpretation" in *Philosophy in France Today,* Alan Montefiore, ed. (Cambridge: Cambridge University Press, 1983), 189.

28. Edmund Husserl, *Logical Investigations* 2 vols., trans. J. N. Findlay, (New York: Humanities Press, 1970).

29. Edmund Husserl, *Ideas Pertaining to a Pure Phenomenology and to a Phenomenological Philosophy* 2 vols., trans. F. Kersten (The Hague: Martinus Nijhoff Publishers, 1982).

30. Husserl, *Ideas* (1982), 73.

31. Levinas, *The Theory of Intuition,* 41.

32. Quoted by Richard Cohen in "Absolute Positivity and Ultrapositivity: Husserl and Levinas," 216.

33. Husserl, *Ideas,* (1982), 216.

34. Husserl, *Ideas,* (1982), 11.

35. Husserl, *Ideas,* (1982), 61.

36. Ricoeur, "On Interpretation," 188.

37. Husserl, *Ideas,* (1982), 65–66.

38. See Biemel, 294. This is why the phenomenological *epoche* is so crucial to Husserl's phenomenology. In *Ideas* (1931), 23, in fact, he says that to view the reduction as unnecessary is to "destroy the whole meaning of my work and of my phenomenology."

39. Husserl, *Ideas,* (1931), 187.

40. According to Quentin Lauer in *Phenomenology: Its Genesis and Prospect* (129), Heidegger posits that Husserl is concerned only with that which is, not with Being.

41. Levinas deals with the same problem in *En decouvrant l'existence avec Husserl et Heidegger.*

42. Levinas, *The Theory of Intuition,* xxiv.

43. This is a claim also made by Stanislaus Breton in "From Phenomenology to Ontology," *Philosophy Today* (Winter 1960), 112–45.

44. Levinas, *The Theory of Intuition,* 89.

45. Husserl, *Ideas* (1982), 65.

46. Husserl, *Ideas* (1982), 65.

47. Husserl, *Ideas* (1982), 114. Levinas states in *The Theory of Intuition* (34) that by calling consciousness "absolute" Husserl means that consciousness ". . . is itself being, and that it is here that the notion of existence must be sought."

48. Levinas, *The Theory of Intuition,* 149. Levinas adds here life (vie) as a synonym for "absolute being," an unfortunate choice of words if it be not understood that Levinas means by life "life of consciousness." On this see Lauer, 79.

49. Husserl, *Ideas* (1982), 113.

50. De Doer, "An Ethical Transcendental Philosophy" in

Face to Face With Levinas, 85.

51. Levinas, *The Theory of Intuition,* 37.

52. Levinas, *The Theory of Intuition,* xxxiv. This is one of the quotations Cohen overlooks when he argues that in *The Theory of Intuition* Levinas "avoids mentioning Heidegger while crediting Husserl with being a Heideggerian." See Cohen's "Absolute Positivity and Ultrapositivity: Husserl and Levinas," 126.

53. Biemel, 298. Here the key word expressing the fact that both Husserl and Heidegger are concerned with Being is "ontology"; this should not obscure the fact that what Husserl and Heidegger mean by "Being" is quite different, as is indicated by Husserl's use of the word "eidetic," meaning that the Being he is interested in is investigated only via the series of reductions he proposes and which Heidegger abandons.

54. Biemel, 300.

55. Lauer, 170.

56. Hence, in *Being and time* (43) Heidegger retains the original Greek meaning of phenomenon, *phaenesthai,* that which shows or reveals itself.

57. Biemel, 300. Thus, Biemel is correct when he says that both Husserl and Heidegger make specifically human being the problem, but that their answers to the problem are extremely different.

58. Biemel, 300.

59. Levinas, *The Theory of Intuition,* xxxiv.

60. Levinas, *The Theory of Intuition,* xxxiv.

61. Levinas, *The Theory of Intuition,* xxxiii.

62. Levinas, *The Theory of Intuition,* xxxiii.

63. Levinas, *The Theory of Intuition,* 94.

64. levinas, *The Theory of Intuition,* 119.

65. Levinas, *The Theory of Intuition,* 149.

66. Levinas, *The Theory of Intuition,* 149.

67. Levinas, *The Theory of Intuition,* 154.

68. Levinas, *The Theory of Intuition,* 155. Levinas charges that Husserl's excessively theoretical phenomenology "seems as independent of the historical situation of man as any theory that tries to consider everything *sub specie aeternitatis.*" A few years later, in *Discovering Existence With Husserl and Heidegger* (49), Levinas thus sums up "the difference between Husserl and Heidegger. For Heidegger, life isn't simply a game which is played in the last analysis for thought. He is dominated by history, by his origin in which he had nothing to do, since he is thrown into the world."

69. Levinas, *The Theory of Intuition,* 155.

70. Steven Smith in *The Argument to the Other* (67) also maintains that the early Levinas departed from Husserl in the company of Heidegger: "Levinas agreed with Heidegger's reversal of phenomenology—saying first philosophy is to inquire into the meaning of being instead of bracketing being."

71. Levinas, "De l'evasion," 374.

72. Levinas, "De l'evasion," 374.

73. Heidegger, *Being and Time,* 22 and ff.

74. Levinas, "De l'evasion," 374.

75. Levinas, "De l'evasion," 378.

76. See *Being and Time,* especially 67 and ff. *Dasein* literally means "Being-There," and refers particularly to that aspect of being in general which is human being as it is thrown into the world.

77. Heidegger, *Being and Time,* 229.

78. Heidegger, *Being and Time,* 294.

79. Heidegger, *Being and Time,* 295.

80. Levinas, "De l'evasion," 379.

81. Levinas, "De l'evasion," 376.

82. See Lingis's introduction to *Existence and Existents,* 10. Similarly, in the introduction to *Collected Papers (xii),* Lingis points again to the differences within the similarities between Levinas and Heidegger when he says that in Heidegger concern is for "*Zeug,* others, Being, and only as a phase of these outer-directed movements, care for oneself. For Levinas, there is a care for oneself prior to other concerns: one's own existence is a burden. It is not the menace of nothingness that makes life a care, but the weight its own existence is for itself."

83. Levinas, "De l'evasion," 377–78.

84. Levinas, "De l'evasion," 379.

85. Levinas, "De l'evasion," 380.

86. Levinas, "De l'evasion," 388.

87. Levinas, "De l'evasion," 380.

88. Levinas, "De l'evasion," 380.

89. Levinas, "De l'evasion," 382.

90. Levinas, "De l'evasion," 383.

91. Levinas, "De l'evasion," 383.

92. Levinas, "De l'evasion," 385.

93. Levinas, "De l'evasion," 384.

94. Levinas, "De l'evasion," 385.

95. Levinas, "De l'evasion," 388. Levinas, in fact, considers this a "banal" truth.

96. Levinas, "De l'evasion," 386–87.

97. Levinas, "De l'evasion," 389.

98. Levinas, "De l'evasion," 391.

99. Levinas, "De l'evasion," 391.
100. Levinas, "De l'evasion," 391–92.
101. Levinas, "De l'evasion," 391–92.
102. Levinas, *Existence*, 17.
103. Levinas, *Existence*, 17.
104. Levinas, *Existence*, 19.
105. Levinas, *Existence*, 19.
106. Heidegger, *Being and Time*, 32.
107. George Steiner, *Martin Heidegger*, 81.
108. Levinas, *Existence*, 101.
109. See Heidegger, *Being and Time*, 219 and ff.
110. Levinas, *Existence*, 57.
111. In his autobiographical essay entitled "Signature," (181), Levinas states that he stressed the impersonality of *il y a* because "no generosity, which the term *es gibt* is said to express, showed itself between 1933 and 1945. This must be said!"
112. Breton in "From Phenomenology to Ontology" Part II, (66–67) says Heidegger's notion of *es gibt* expresses "a fundamental generosity which is the foundation of all being, a primordial gushing forth."
113. Levinas, *Existence*, 58.
114. Breton, 66.
115. See Heidegger, *Being and Time*, 67 and ff.
116. Levinas, *Existence*, 23.
117. Heidegger, *Being and Time*, 181.
118. Heidegger, *Being and Time*, 180.
119. Heidegger, *Being and Time*, 181.
120. Levinas, *Existence*, 20.
121. Edith Wyschogrod, *Emmanuel Levinas and the Problem of Ethical Metaphysics* (The Hague: Martinus Nijhoff, 1974), 78.
122. Levinas, *Existence*, 46.
123. Levinas, *Existence*, 76.
124. Levinas, *Existence*, 79.
125. Levinas, *Existence*, 29.
126. Heidegger, *Being and Time*, 223.
127. Heidegger, *Being and Time*, 264.
128. De Boer, "An Ethical Transcendental Philosophy," 92.
129. Levinas, *Existence*, 45.
130. Heidegger, *Being and Time*, 96 and ff.
131. Heidegger, *Being and Time*, 103.
132. Heidegger, *Being and Time*, 97.
133. Levinas, *Existence*, 43.
134. Lingis, introduction to *Collected Papers*, xxviii.
135. Lingis, introduction to *Collected Papers*, xxviii.

136. Heidegger, *Being and Time,* 160–61.
137. Heidegger, *Being and Time,* 160.
138. Heidegger, *Being and Time,* 162.
139. Levinas, *Existence,* 95.
140. Heidegger, *Being and Time,* 315–16. Peter Elliston in *Heidegger's Existential Analytic* (New York: Harper & Row, 1974, 172) states that the relation of listening to the other person is primary for Heidegger and that it "even constitutes the primary and true openness of *Dasein* for its possibilities to be with others, that is, to hear the voice of a friend." However, as this passage from *Being and Time* clearly shows, the fact that *Dasein* listens to the other has not only a positive, but also a very negative significance. It is the voice of the other that tempts *Dasein* to lose itself in the They-self.
141. Heidegger, *Being and Time,* 264. I use the term "either/or" quite purposefully exactly because of its Kierkegardian resonances. Certainly much of what Heidegger says about "fallenness" and the negative influence of the "they" is influenced by Kierkegaard. As Hans-George Gadamer says in *Philosophical Hermeneutics* (Berkeley: University of California Press, 1977), 122, these notions of Heidegger's "reflect a passion for Kierkegaard, who had such a profound influence on the thought of our generation."
142. Heidegger, *Being and Time,* 235.
143. Levinas, *Existence,* 94.
144. Levinas, *Existence,* 95.
145. Levinas, *Existence,* 95.
146. Levinas, *Existence,* 95.
147. Levinas, *Existence,* 96.
148. Levinas, *Existence,* 99.
149. Levinas, *Existence,* 45.
150. Levinas, *Existence,* 40.
151. Levinas, *Existence,* 58.
152. Levinas, *Existence,* 43.
153. Levinas, *Existence,* 42.
154. Levinas, *Existence,* 40.
155. Levinas, *Existence,* 41.
156. Levinas, *Existence,* 93.
157. Levinas, *Existence,* 83.
158. Levinas, *Existence,* 75–76.

Notes to Chapter Two

1. Heidegger, *Being and Time,* 40.

2. Heidegger, *Being and Time,* 39. Heidegger also declares (40) that "Being itself is made visible in its temporal character."

3. Heidegger, *Being and Time,* 19.

4. See Lingis's introduction to Levinas's *Collected Philosophical Papers,* xxiv.

5. Levinas, *Existence,* 98.

6. Richard Cohen, in his introduction to *Time and the Other* (5), says Levinas shares the classical notion that "instants exclude one another, are separate, monadic, but contrary to the classical theory he conceives the instant concretely as the very 'accomplishment of existence.'"

7. Levinas, *Existence,* 98.

8. Levinas, *Existence,* 79.

9. Levinas, *Existence,* 83.

10. Levinas, *Existence,* 78.

11. Levinas, *Existence,* 81.

12. Levinas, *Existence,* 82.

13. Levinas, *Existence,* 97.

14. Levinas, *Existence,* 79.

15. Levinas, *Time,* 39.

16. F. P. Ciglia in his article "Le Mort de L'Autre" in *Les Cahiers de la nuit surveille* (147) points out that Levinas's interpretation of death constitutes one of the fundamental points of his anti-Heideggerian polemic.

17. *Time,* 76. Levinas says in *Totality and Infinity* (28) that Rosenzweig's *The Star of Redemption* is "too often present in this book to be cited."

18. Heidegger, *Being and Time,* 292: "If 'death' is defined as the 'end' of *Dasein*—that is to say, of Being-in-the-world—this does not imply any ontical decision whether 'after death' still another Being is possible, either higher or lower, or whether *Dasein* 'lives on' or even 'outlasts' itself and is 'immortal.'"

19. Heidegger, *Being and Time,* 286. Heidegger adds the proviso that "Ending does not necessarily mean fulfilling oneself." This may or many not be the case for each individual *Dasein,* but death as the end of *Dasein* means that every *Dasein* becomes "no-longer-*Dasein.*"

20. Heidegger, *Being and Time,* 70.

21. Heidegger, *Being and Time,* 302.

22. Heidegger, *Being and Time,* 297.

23. Heidegger, *Being and Time,* 298.
24. Heidegger, *Being and Time,* 284.
25. Heidegger, *Being and Time,* 294.
26. Heidegger, *Being and Time,* 289.
27. Heidegger, *Being and Time,* 294.
28. Heidegger, *Being and Time,* 294.
29. Heidegger, *Being and Time,* 302.
30. Lingis, introduction to *Collected Papers,* x, fn. 7.
31. Levinas, *Time,* 71. In his footnote to this passage, Richard Cohen takes Levinas's use of the word "evasion" to refer to Levinas's early article, "De l'evasion." This work, however, has nothing to do with death. It therefore seems much more likely, especially if one is convinced as I am that Levinas's entire phenomenological project—and not merely *Totality and Infinity*—is a constant interpreting in but otherwise than Heidegger, that Levinas's use of the word *evasion* refers here not to his own earlier work, but to *Being and Time,* in his attempt to interpret death otherwise than does Heidegger.
32. Levinas, *Time,* 70.
33. Lingis, introduction to *Collected Papers,* xxiii, fn. 19.
34. Levinas, *Totality,* 233. Levinas shows how his interpretations, developed by arguing in but otherwise than Heidegger, are consistent with his Judaism when he states in his essay "La Laicite et La Pensee d'Israel" in *La Laicite* (Paris: Presses Universitaires de France, 1960), 50: "The prophet never speaks of the tragedy of man determined by death, and he does not concern himself with the immortality of the soul. The unhappiness of man is in the misery which destroys and rends society. Murder is more tragic than death." Quoted by Charles McCollester in his "The Philosophy of Emmanuel Levinas" (*Judaism,* 1974, 354).
35. Lingis, introduction to *Collected Papers,* xxxvii.
36. Levinas, *Time,* 70.
37. Levinas, *Time,* 74.
38. Levinas, *Time,* 75.
39. Levinas, *Time,* 75.
40. Levinas, *Time,* 74.
41. Lingis, introduction to *Collected Papers,* xxvi: "The futurity of death, finally, approaches as pure menace, time to come that is completely ungraspable."
42. Levinas, *Time,* 76–77.
43. Levinas, *Time,* 81.
44. Levinas, *Time,* 79.
45. Cohen, introduction to *Time and the Other,* 10.

46. This is not to say that the erotic relationship is not unique, but its uniqueness is in how the lovers relate to others, not in how they relate to one another. Levinas does assert that *eros* is the opposite of the social relation in that "it excludes the third party" (*Totality*, 261). But *eros* is also the model of the relationship between the subject and the other because it is a relationship of proximity. Thus, one should not deduce too much from the fact that Levinas discusses the erotic relationship in *Time* and in *Totality*, but drops it in his later works in favor of discussing the relationship between the subject and the other in general, which he characterizes as "proximity." We could say that in *eros* proximity is experienced as voluptuosity, whereas in the later works proximity is experienced as responsibility, but this does not by any means indicate that ethics is Levinas's concern only in his later works.

47. Alphonso Lingis in his *Libido: The French Existential Theories* (Bloomington: Indiana University Press, 1985, 68) explains Levinas's notion of voluptuousness "as longing for the remote, fascination with what remains other."

48. Levinas, *Totality*, 265.

49. Lingis, introduction to *Collected Papers*, xvi.

50. Adriaan Peperzak perhaps does not see that Levinas's description of eros is very important in that it enables him to make the rhetorical move from the other to the totally and infinitely other. It is the other I know best that gives to me the idea of the other as totally other. Quite to the contrary, Peperzak says in "Some remarks on Hegel, Kant, and Levinas" in *Face to Face* (213) that "Because the other would not be fully other if he/she were my parent, husband or wife, sister or brother or friend, the other is a stranger."

51. Levinas, *Time*, 86.

52. Jacques Derrida, in his essay on Levinas entitled "At this very Moment in this Work here I Am" in *Rereading Levinas*, accuses Levinas of subordinating sexual difference to the difference between people in general: "E.L.'s work seems to me to have always rendered secondary, derivative, and subordinate, alterity as sexual difference, to the alterity of a sexually non-marked wholly other. It is not woman or the feminine he has marked secondary, but sexual difference" (40). While it is undeniable that Levinas after *Totality and Infinity* does not discuss the relationship between self and other through sexual difference and instead insists that every other, and not just the sex opposite of what I am, is infinitely other, Derrida's criticism can at least be rightly accused of

overlooking the fact that sexual difference is absolutely central for Levinas in his very significant rhetorical move from the other to the totally, absolutely, and infinitely Other. It is sexual difference itself that enables him to make this move. Given the significance of sexual difference for Levinas's early work, it is hard to agree with Derrida that Levinas's work has "*always* rendered secondary" sexual difference. Even in the later Levinas, Levinas's insistence that every other is absolutely other to me need not necessarily entail that he makes sexual difference secondary. It would be consistent with Levinas's hyperbolic rhetoric to say that for Levinas the male philosopher all other males are infinitely other, whereas all females are even more infinitely other, just as the set of numbers from 10 to infinity is infinite, whereas the set of numbers from 5 to infinity could be said to be more infinite. For a discussion of Derrida's critique of Levinas on this point, see the essays by Bernasconi and Critchley in *Re-reading Levinas*. For a discussion of the role sexual difference plays in the thought of Heidegger, see Derrida's essay "Geschlecht: sexual difference, ontological difference" in *Research in Phenomenology*, vol. 13 (1983): 65–83.

53. This is exactly what Simone de Beauvoir has accused Levinas of doing. In *Le Deuxieme Sexe*, vol. 1 (15), de Beauvoir charges that Levinas's philosophy is in continuity with traditional patriarchal thought because he "deliberately takes a man's point of view" by labeling certain qualities as feminine and by referring to the feminine as "the other." Although de Beauvour's charges are not completely without foundation, it is certainly true that she has failed to understand that for Levinas every other person is "the other" and that the feminine is only an image of this otherness. For a discussion of this issue, see Tina Chanter's essay "Feminism and the Other" in *The Provocation of Levinas*, 32–56, as well as my own essay entitled "Thinking the Other Without Violence: Levinas' Relation to Feminism "in *The Journal of Speculative Philosophy*, vol. 5, no. 2, 1991, pp. 132–43.

54. Levinas, *Time*, 36.

55. Levinas, *Time*, 87.

56. Levinas, *Time*, 88.

57. Levinas, *Totality*, 260.

58. Levinas, *Totality*, 277.

59. Levinas, *Time*, 90.

60. Levinas, *Time*, 88.

61. Smith in *The Argument to the Other* (69) states this very clearly and shows that this is an argument against Heidegger:

"Temporality, the advent of an other instant really other than the present instant, can only be produced in relation with an other. The temporal dialectic is the dialectic of sociality. Actual time distinct from the eternally repeated instant requires the interval of nothingness that only occurs between the self and other persons. Traditional philosophy, even Heidegger and Bergson, miss this by conceiving time as belonging to, or affecting, the self in its solitude."

62. Derrida also makes this point in "Violence and Metaphysics" (91): "Because [phenomenology and ontology] do not think the other, they do not have time. Without time, they do not have history. The absolute alterity of each instant, without which there would be no time, cannot be produced—constituted—within the identity of the subject or existent. It comes into time through the other."

63. Lingis, introduction to *Collected Papers,* xxiv.

64. Levinas, *Totality,* 266.

65. Levinas, *Totality,* 282.

66. Levinas, *Totality,* 268.

67. Levinas, *Totality,* 247.

68. Levinas, *Totality,* 284.

69. See Levinas's essay "Meaning and Sense" in *Collected Papers,* 92.

70. Levinas writes in the Preface to *Totality and Infinity* (21): "Everyone will readily agree that it is of the highest importance to know whether we are not duped by morality." Levinas finds his assurance in infinite time.

71. Levinas, *Totality,* 284.

72. Lingis, introduction to *Collected Papers,* xvi.

73. Levinas, *Totality,* 283.

74. Levinas, *Totality,* 284.

75. Heidegger, *Being and Time,* 443.

76. Heidegger, *Being and Time,* 444.

77. Richard Cohen, introduction to *Time and the Other,* 12.

78. It is important to recognize the dual identity of the Other as both you and third person. Roland Blum misses this important point in his "Emmanuel Levinas' Theory of Commitment" (*Philosophy and Phenomenological Research* vol. 44, no. 2, December 1983, 25) when he says that when the third person appears, the "unlimited initial responsibility has been abandonned." The appearance of the third person brings the ajudication of the subject's competing responsibilities which Levinas calls politics, but it does not mean the responsibility is abandonned. Blum thinks the responsibility is abandonned when the subject looks on the Other as "only

a third party." But the Other is never only a third party, but remains a you, remains my Other, even when the Other becomes also a third party.

79. See Levinas's essay entitled "Phenomenon and Enigma" in *Papers,* 71. Also, in *Otherwise Than Being* (103) Levinas says: "Through a trace, the irreversible past takes on a profile of a he, illeity."

80. Levinas, "Phenomenon and Enigma," 71.

81. Levinas, "Diachrony and Representation" in *Time and the Other,* 103.

82. Levinas, *Otherwise Than Being,* 89.

83. See Levinas's essay "Humanism and Anarchy" in *Papers,* 131.

84. Levinas, *Otherwise Than Being,* 37.

85. See "Beyond Being" by Adriaan Peperzak in *Research in Phenomenology,* vol. 8 (1978): 247: "The realm of the Said is the realm of ontology, synchrony."

86. See Levinas's essay "Meaning and Sense" in *Papers,* 104–05.

87. Levinas, "Meaning and Sense," 106.

88. Lingis, introduction to *Collected Papers,* xxvii.

89. Levinas, *Otherwise Than Being,* 38.

90. Levinas, *Otherwise Than Being,* 13.

91. Levinas, *Otherwise Than Being,* 10.

92. Levinas, *Otherwise Than Being,* 103.

93. See Levinas's essay "God and Philosophy" in *Collected Papers,* 168.

94. Levinas, "Philosophy and the Idea of Infinity" in *Collected Papers,* 53.

Notes to Chapter Three

1. According to Bernasconi and Critchley in their introduction to *Re-reading Levinas* (xii), any rereading of Levinas must acknowledge two facts about the initial reception of Levinas: "First, the initial reception of Levinas's work has been to a great extent determined by *Totality and Infinity.* Second, the questions addressed to *TI* by this initial reading have been largely and particularly in the English-speaking world determined by Derrida's "Violence and Metaphysics."

2. Levinas, *Totality,* 20.

3. Richard Cohen, "Non-indifference in the Thought of Rosenzweig and Levinas," 143.

4. F. P. Ciglia, "Du Neant A L'autre" in *Les Caheirs de lan*

nuit Surveille, 146.

5. Pettitdemange, 41.

6. Levinas, *Totality*, 304.

7. Luk Boukaert, in his essay "Ontology and Ethics"(407), at least catches some of the dialectical relationship between Levinas and Heidegger when he says that Levinas's relation to Heidegger should not be seen exclusively as ethics vs. ontology and points to interpretations of being Levinas offers that are a direct response to some of Heidegger's interpretations.

8. In "Ethics or Ontology" (118), Steven Gans obscures this important point in saying that "the development of an ethical standpoint is the basis for Levinas' opposition to Heidegger."

9. Harold Durfee in his excellent essay on Levinas entitled "War, Politics, and Radical Pluralism" in *Foundational Reflections*, 218, observes that Levinas attacks ontology "while still speaking from within the phenomenological movement."

10. Steven Smith, "Reason as One for Another" in *Face to Face With Levinas*, 58-59. Smith also correctly insists (69) that according to Levinas "the moral quality of life . . . is that with which we are more intimately acquainted than anything else."

11. Levinas, *Totality*, 303.

12. Levinas, *Totality*, 45–47.

13. Derrida in "Violence and Metaphysics" (97), says quite insightfully that "the notion of primacy, employed so frequently by Levinas, well translates the gesture of his entire critique." In this essay (81–83), Derrida outlines what he sees as Levinas's three most fundamental points of opposition between himself and Heidegger: 1) Levinas's thought seeks to liberate itself from the Greek domination of the Same and the One; 2) Levinas's thought seeks to define itself as metaphysical; 3) It calls upon the ethical relationship to the other person to open up the possibility of metaphysics.

14. C. D. Keyes in his "An Evaluation of Levinas' Critique of Heidegger" (122), insists that one of the "most interesting, and perhaps questionable implications of Levinas' argument" is that Heidegger's totalizing ontology "necessarily leads to totalitarian ways of acting."

15. Keyes, 125.

16. Derrida, "Violence and Metaphysics," 145.

17. Thus I will try to show how even such an astute critic of Levinas's as Robert Bernasconi underestimates Levinas's comprehension of Heidegger when he says in *Re-reading Levinas* (152): "Levinas is at his weakest when he sets himself up

against individual philosophers or philosophy in general."

18. Heidegger, *Being and Time*, 37.
19. Heidegger, *Being and Time*, 58.
20. Heidegger, *Being and Time*, 257.
21. Heidegger, *Being and Time*, 262.
22. Heidegger, *Being and Time*, 60. It is important to note also that Heidegger in *Being and Time* (130) criticizes Descartes on precisely this point—that he fails to let what shows itself in sensation present itself in its own kind of Being.
23. Keyes, 142.
24. Gans, p. 121.
25. Gans, 119.
26. Derrida, "Violence and Metaphysics," 146.
27. Derrida, "Violence and Metaphysics," 137.
28. Derrida, "Violence and Metaphysics," 142.
29. Lingis, introduction to *Otherwise Than Being*, xi. Lingis also says, however, that responsibility in Heidegger "appears as a prodigy" since it is assumed only by authentic *Dasein* whereas for Levinas responsibility is "transcendent, inexplicable in ontological terms, deduced from the empirical and expressed as its condition of possibility." (xii).
30. Cohen, Introduction to *Ethics and Infinity*, 2.
31. Gibson Winter demonstrates in his *Liberating Creation* (New York: Crossroad, 1981) that Heidegger's philosophy is not divorced from ethics and can even be instrumental in developing an ethical philosophy. Winter is heavily indebted to Heidegger for his terminology, and Winter is certainly trying to develop an ethic concordant with Heidegger's analysis of human dwelling. This does not mean, however, that Heidegger would necessarily agree with Winter when he says such things as "the moral imperatives of dwelling issue from symbolic disclosures of right, justice, good faith, and peace" (90), and "the overarching symbol for the ethic of dwelling is justice" (122). Heidegger does constantly talk about disclosure, but never about disclosure of peace, right, good faith and justice.
32. Levinas, *Totality*, 45.
33. Derrida, "Violence and Metaphysics," 97. It must be stated that Derrida keeps the notion of primacy in mind much more than most other critics of Levinas do.
34. Heidegger, *Being and Time*, 35.
35. Hans-Georg Gadamer, *Philosophical Hermeneutics*, liv.
36. Heidegger, *Being and Time*, 130.
37. Heidegger, *Being and Time*, 260.
38. Heidegger, *Being and Time*, 261.

39. Heidegger, *Being and Time,* 262.

40. Heidegger, *Being and Time,* 262. Heidegger appeals to Heraclitus to show that he has only appropriated the tradition more primordially.

41. On this point, Luk Boukaert in "Ontology and Ethics" (417) quotes R. Boehm, who asks if Heidegger's repudiation of truth as *adequatio intellectus et rei* constitutes anything other than a return to the foundation of the philosophical tradition. We have, in essence, raised the same question with a view to showing that Heidegger's relation to the philosophical tradition does not entail that he defines the essence of philosophy as anything other than knowledge of something, which means that he does give priority to knowledge of Being over ethics.

42. This is confirmed by Heidegger's own statement in his *Letter on Humanism* in *Basic Writings of Heidegger,* ed. David Krell, (New York: Harper & Row, 1978), 213, wherein he declares: ". . . in the determination of the humanity of ek-sistence what is essential is not man but Being . . ."

43. In *The Letter on Humanism* (232–36), Heidegger writes that "the thinking that inquires into the truth of Being and so defines man's essential abode from Being and toward Being is neither ethics nor ontology. Thus the question about the relation of each to the other no longer has any basis in this sphere." Heidegger then goes on to ask if thinking of Being yields to us "directives that can be readily applied to our active lives," and concludes: "The answer is that such thinking is neither theoretical nor practical. It comes to pass before this distinction. Such thinking is, insofar as it is, recollection of Being and nothing else. . . Such thinking has no result. It has no effect."

44. Edith Wyschogrod rightly warns in her *Spirit in Ashes: Hegel, Heidegger, and Man-Made Mass Death* (New Haven: Yale University Press, 1985, 159) that in reading Heidegger we should not interpret authenticity as a virtue, for "Heidegger claims his analysis lies outside the moral domain because from his perspective the moral is a derivative sphere."She also states that Heidegger's concept of guilt "is tied not to *Dasein*'s social existence, but to its finitude." Thus, according to Wyschogrod, Heidegger's notion of a "call to conscience is essentially a monologue" concerning individual *Dasein*'s own possibilities of being and not being" (173).

45. William Richardson, *Companion to Being and Time,* 171. Heidegger has been much criticized for giving ethics a secondary and derivative status. Theodore de Boor, for instance,

in "An Ethical Transcendental Philosophy" in *Face to Face With Levinas* (108), states that one thing remains constant in Heidegger's philosophy—" its ethical indifference." For a review of the literature on Heidegger's *Letter on Humanism* and its statements on ethics, see Robert Cousineau's *Heidegger, Humanism and Ethics* (Louvain: Nauwelaerts, 1972).

46. Gans in "Ethics or Ontology" (119) also makes this argument.

47. Quoted in Keyes, 141.

48. Keyes, 141.

49. Heidegger, *Being and Time,* 160–61.

50. Heidegger, *Being and Time,* 163.

51. Heidegger, *Being and Time,* 162.

52. Heidegger, *Being and Time,* 162.

53. Heidegger, *Being and Time,* 163.

54. Heidegger, *Being and Time,* 168.

55. Heidegger, *Being and Time,* 166.

56. Heidegger, *Being and Time,* 168.

57. Even Warnock, who insists in his *Existentialist Ethics* (35) on the ethical dimension in Heidegger's thought, is critical of Heidegger's treatment of the social relation: "other people come into his picture of life only as part of the scenery, part of the human situation, which each one of us has voluntarily to accept. There is a sort of heroism in this attitude, but very little humanity." Lingis is similar when he says that morality for Heidegger's involves *Dasein*'s resolute taking on itself its own possibilities in which "what is at stake is first courage and cowardice."

58. Elliston, 153.

59. Steven Smith in his "Reason as One for Another" in *Face to Face With Levinas* (68) states quite insightfully that in the philosophical tradition rhetoric is not appreciated sufficiently and adds that "it is precisely to the problematic appreciation of rhetoric that Levinas makes a great contribution, for his entire philosophy is deliberately and self-consciously rhetorical."

60. Levinas, *Totality*, 79.

61. Derrida, "Violence and Metaphysics," 140.

62. Petitdemange, 48.

63. Derrida in "Violence and Metaphysics" (137) expresses well this consolation of Heidegger's philosophy when he says that Heidegger's thought of Being "is the only thought which no anthropology, no ethics, and above all, no ethico-anthropological analysis will ever enclose."

64. Levinas, *Totality*, 46.

65. Derrida, "Violence and Metaphysics," 135.

66. See Levinas, *Time and the Other,* 46. For Levinas, a truism means something that is so obviously true that it really doesn't tell you anything. Thus, he doesn't argue with Heidegger's notion of *Geworfenheit,* or his notion that one has to comprehend the Being of an existent to know the existent, but he is arguing with the conclusions Heidegger draws from them and with how he uses these notions in his philosophy.

67. Derrida in "Violence and Metaphysics" (128) refers to this violence as ontological violence and says that Levinas, too, would regard this as violence. For Levinas, however, the selfsame's understanding of the other in terms of Being is not itself violent but is the condition for nonviolence, for the summoning of the selfsame by the other to responsibility, ethics, and nonviolence. An entire critique of Derrida's reading of Levinas could be done based upon Derrida's various definitions of violence, which include nearly everything except that which for Levinas is really the sole definition of violence—physical violence.

68. Derrida, "Violence and Metaphysics," 144.

69. Derrida, "Violence and Metaphysics," 144. For Derrida this necessity is violence itself, what he calls "ontological violence." Derrida assumes Levinas would agree with this, but far from calling the intentional modification of the ego violence, Levinas sees it as the opportunity for the other to command the self and institute nonviolence. As Levinas says in "Freedom and Command" (*Collected Papers,* 22): "To be in a relation with a face, with being itself, is to situate oneself in a transitivity without violence which is that of creation."

70. Derrida, "Violence and Metaphysics," 125.

71. Derrida, "Violence and Metaphysics," 125. Derrida notices, however, that in Levinas's philosophy he "must suppose and practice the precomprehension of Being" (141).

72. Levinas not only never denies the necessity of ontological language, but he actually turns the table on Derrida in his essay "Wholly Otherwise" (*Re-reading Levinas,* 5) when he points out the impossibility of deconstructive discourse to do without ontology: "What remains constructed after the deconstruction is, certainly, the stern architecture of the deconstructing discourse which employs the present tense of the verb to be in predicative propositions." Bernasconi has also observed this in his "Skepticism in the Face of Philosophy (*Re-reading Levinas,* 158): "In 'Wholly Otherwise,' Levinas also threatens Derrida with the same argument which 'Violence and Metaphysics' used against him." Also, even in using the

phrase "otherwise than being" in his work of that title, Levinas does so quite hesitantly and raises the possibility of the impossibility of escaping ontological language: "One immediately wonders if in the formula 'otherwise than being' the adverb otherwise does not inevitably refer to the verb to be, which simply has been avoided by an artificially elliptical turn of phrase" (*Otherwise Than Being,* 4). We could say the same thing about the title of our present project and wonder if even in interpreting otherwise than Heidegger Levinas is not in some way interpreting being as verb, the verbality of the verb 'to be', thereby returning inevitably, perhaps somewhat reluctantly, not only to the language of ontology, but also to the language of Heidegger.

73. Derrida, "Violence and Metaphysics," 151.

74. That Levinas says this in a minor key is in keeping with one of the rhetorical goals of his work, which is to distance his own philosophy from and dichotomize his philosophy against that of Heidegger. Bernasconi in his "Skepticism in the Face of Philosophy" (*Re-reading Levinas,* 154), quotes this passage from *Otherwise Than Being* to make the point that Levinas never denies ontological language: "The very discussion that we are at this moment elaborating about signification, diachrony and the transcendence of the approach beyond being, a discussion that means to be philosophy, is a thematizing, a synchronizing of terms, a recourse to systematic language, a constant use of the verb 'to be,' a bringing back into the bosom of being all signification allegedly conceived beyond being."Then Bernasconi adds quite correctly: "So when Levinas in *Otherwise Than Being* allows that his language is a thematization, he is doing more than repeating a point he had already conceded in *Totality and Infinity.*" Levinas insists on the necessity of thematization most insistently in his essay on Derrida entitled "Wholly Otherwise" (*Re-reading Levinas,* 6): "One can see nothing without thematization. . . even when it is a question of the nonthematizable."

75. Quoted by Derrida in "Violence and Metaphysics," 125.

76. This issue of what Levinas means by "absolutely and infinitely other," and Derrida's misunderstanding of this because he interprets Levinas's hyperbolic language literally, is a very good example of Smith's excellent point that "it is precisely to the problematic appreciation of rhetoric that Levinas makes a great contribution." Richard Cohen is one of the few who realize the importance of hyperbolic rhetoric within Levinas's philosophy. In his essay "Non-indifference

in the Thought of Rosenzweig and Levinas" (*Graduate Faculty Philosophy Journal* vol. 13, no. 1, p. 147) he states: "Levinas's point . . . lies in a . . . piercing, an emphasis, an hyperbole, an inspiration which exceeds even the most determinate thought . . ."

77. Levinas, "Meaning and Sense" in *Collected Papers*, 98.

78. Cohen, "Non-indifference in the Thought of Rosenzweig and Levinas," 142.

79. Smith, *Argument to the Other*, 188.

80. Levinas, *Totality*, 50.

81. Cohen, "Absolute Positivity and Ultrapositivity: Husserl and Levinas" in *The Question of the Other*, 41.

82. Richard Cohen is most insightful in analyzing the hyperbolic character of Levinas's thought. In his introduction to *Face to Face* (6) he states: "The ethical situation is excessive. The originality of Levinas' ethical philosophy lies in the very exorbitance of its claims." He then points out four important components of Levinas' philosophy, stating that "all four components are excessive: 1) the other's alterity 2) the passivity of the self 3) the other's command 4) my responsibility."

83. In *The Ethics of Rhetoric* (Chicago: Regenery-Gateway, 1953), 19–20, Richard Weaver says "the exaggeration which the rhetorician employs is not caricature but prophecy; and it would be a fair formulation to say that true rhetoric is concerned with the potency of things. The literalist . . . is troubled by its failure to conform to a present reality. What he fails to appreciate is that potentiality is a mode of existence, and that all prophecy is about the tendency of things." Quoted in Megill, 244–45.

84. Levinas, *Totality*, 174.

85. Levinas, *Totality*, 174.

86. Levinas, *Totality*, 174.

87. Levinas, *Totality*, 206.

88. Levinas, *Totality*, 171.

89. Lingis, introduction to *Otherwise Than Being*, xvii.

90. Levinas, *Totality*, 203.

91. Levinas, *Totality*, 203.

92. Levinas, *Totality*, 98.

93. Levinas, *Totality*, 51.

94. Lingis, introduction to *Otherwise Than Being*, xvii.

95. Lingis, introduction to *Otherwise Than Being*, xiii. In his book *Libido*, Lingis describes other ways of seeing a face, ways which are overthrown according to Levinas when the face expresses him/herself: "When a face faces me, it shows color, shape, and relief; it exhibits density and elasticity, solidity

and weight. It is like a surface with which any sensible object spreads out in the light and becomes a phenomenon" (58).

96. Levinas, *Totality*, 199.

97. In *Totality*, Levinas writes of "the order of responsibility," which he will later expand upon and make the basis of his concept of the saying in *Otherwise Than Being*. In his Introduction to *Otherwise Than Being*, Lingis states that in *Totality and Infinity* Levinas insists that "the locus where responsibility is articulated is the face" (xiii).

98. Levinas, "Freedom and Command" in *Collected Papers*, 22. Richard Cohen observes in his Introduction to *Ethics and Infinity*: "The surplus of the other's nonencompassable alterity . . . is the way ethics intrudes, disturbs and commands being—from height and destitution" (10).

99. Lingis, introduction to *Collected Papers*, xiv.

100. Levinas, *Collected Papers*, 40.

101. Fabio Ciaramelli states in his essay "Levinas's Ethical Discourse between Individuation and Universality" (*Re-reading Levinas*), 85, that "For Levinas, 'ethics' means an anarchical assignation of the particular subject to morality by the appeal of the other."

102. Levinas, *Totality*, 181.

103. Levinas, "Beyond Intentionality" in Montefiore, 103.

104. Levinas, "Beyond Intentionality," 103.

105. Levinas, *Totality and Infinity*, 302.

106. Levinas will heighten his rhetoric in *Otherwise than Being* by saying that the subject is a hostage to the other and is seized by responsibility.

107. Levinas, *Totality*, 291.

108. Levinas, *Totality*, 291.

109. Levinas, *Totality*, 291.

110. Levinas, *Totality*, 290.

111. Levinas, *Totality*, 72.

112. Levinas, *Totality*, 303.

113. Levinas, *Totality*, 302.

114. Cohen, introduction to *Face to Face*, 1.

115. Levinas, *Totality*, 304.

116. Lyotard uses this phrase in his essay "Levinas' Logic" in *Face to Face*, 152.

117. Cohen, *Face to Face*, 2.

118. Cohen, *Face to Face*, 5.

119. Levinas, *Totality*, 90.

120. Even when Levinas attempts to distance himself from ontological language in *Otherwise Than Being*, he wonders whether the return to ontological language is inevitable.

121. Levinas, *Totality*, 303.

122. Levinas, *Totality*, 290. We should keep in mind here the subtitle Levinas gives to *Totality* : "An Essay in Exteriority."

123. Levinas, *Totality*, 302.

124. Levinas, *Totality*, 47. Levinas writes that if ontology is impossible, "it is because the comprehension of Being in general cannot dominate the relationship with the Other. The latter relationship commands the first."

125. In his "Memorial Address" to honor the celebration of the 175th birthday of the German composer Conradin Kreutzer in 1955, Heidegger distinguishes between "calculative thinking" and "releasement toward things" and "openness to the mystery," which occur in "meditative thinking." "The issue," says Heidegger, "is keeping meditative thinking alive." This address is included in Heidegger's *Discourse on Thinking* (New York: Harper & Row, 1966), 56.

126. In his *Letter on Humanism*, Heidegger maintains the "the thinking that inquires into the truth of Being and so defines man's essential abode from Being and toward Being is neither ethics nor ontology." See Heidegger's *Basic Writings*, 235–36.

127. Edith Wyschogrod states rightly in her *Man-Made Mass Death* (167) that *Being and Time*'s "analysis of guilt offers no frame of reference for making moral determinations."

128. This is precisely the basis of Hans Jonas's criticisms of Heidegger, so similar to Levinas's, in his essay "Heidegger and Theology" in *The Phenomenon of Life* (Chicago: University of Chicago Press, 1966), 247: "But as to Heidegger's being, it is an occurrence of unveiling, a fate-laden happening upon thought: so was the Fuhrer and the call of German destiny under him: an unveiling of something hidden, a call of being all right, fate-laden in every sense: neither then nor now did Heidegger's thought provide a norm by which to decide how to answer such calls—linguistically or otherwise: no norm except depth, resolution, and the sheer force of being that issues the call. But to the believer, ever suspicious of this world, depth may mean the abyss, and force, the prince of this world. As if the devil were not part of the voice of being! Heidegger's own answer is, to the shame of philosophy, on record and, I hope, not forgotten."

129. Cohen, introduction to *Ethics and Infinity*, 12.

130. Levinas writes in *Difficile Liberte*: "Not to submit the law of justice to the implacable course of events, to denounce them when necessary as senseless or insane—this is what it means to be a Jew." Quoted in McCollester, 351.

131. Blum rightly sums up in his "Emmanuel Levinas' Theory of Commitment" one of the ways in which Levinas attacks Heidegger when he says that Levinas accuses Heidegger "of treating persons as merely occasions for the revelation of being, thereby depriving them of any reality of their own" (4).

132. Levinas, *Totality*, 290.

133. Levinas in fact says in *Totality* (79) that "the establishing of this primacy of the ethical, that is of the relationship between man and man . . . is one of the objectives of the present work."

134. It is important to see that for Levinas a thought that is dominated by the good, by alterity or exteriority, may still be a philosophical thought. As Adriaan Peperzak says in "Presentation" (*Re-reading Levinas*), 65: "Responsibility is better than reflection, but philosophy cannot give up reflecting upon its extradition to the better. As long as responsibility remains reflexive, it cannot evade philosophy."

135. Hans Jonas, in his essay "Heidegger and Theology," (247), says that this personal fact of Heidegger's life is of immense philosophical significance. If so, philosophy certainly has not so far recognized this fact. Levinas's philosophy may, in fact, be seen as the only philosophical attempt to deal with the philosophical significance of Heidegger's Nazism.

136. Philipe Lacoue-Labarthe, *La Fiction du politique: Heidegger, l'art et la politique* (Paris: Christian Bourgois, 1987).

137. Victor Farias, *Heidegger et le Nazisme* (Paris: Lagrasse, 1987).

138. See Habermas's essay "Back from Syracuse" in *Critical Inquiry* 15, no. 2 (Winter 1989): 456.

139. Quoted by Maurice Blanchot in "Thinking the Apocalypse" in *Critical Inquiry* 15, no. 2 (Winter 1989): 476. Lowith's account, written in 1940, was published by Lowith's widow in 1986 in *Mein Leben in Deutschland vor und nach 1933: ein Bericht*.

140. See Habermas, 451.

141. See Karsten Harries's translations of Heidegger's "The Self-Assertion of the German Universities" and "The Rectorate 1933–34: Facts and Thoughts" in *Review of Metaphysics* 38 (1985): 470-502. Arnold Davidson states the question well in his essay "Questions Concerning Heidegger: Opening the Debate" in *Critical Inquiry* 15, no. 2 (Winter 1989): 417: ". . . the problem here . . . is whether Heidegger unfolds his rector's rhetoric and his official vocabulary and structure of concepts so as to secure their derivation from, or display their harmony

with, the philosophical writings that preceded and came after the episodes of 1933–34."

142. See Derrida's essay "Of Spirit" in *Critical Inquiry* 15, no. 2 (Winter 1989): 472. Heidegger's concept of spiritual leadership is expressed in the following excerpt from an article Heidegger wrote in 1933 which Davidson cites in his essay: "Doctrines and 'ideas' shall no longer be the rules of your being. The Fuhrer, and he alone, is the present and future of German reality, and its law." In his essay, Derrida says Heidegger's use of *Geist* is "the most fatal figure" of the return of metaphysics, and he classifies this as an evil along with the sanctioning of Nazism (470).

143. See Davidson, 419.

144. Davidson, 419.

145. See Harries, "Heidegger as a Political Thinker," in Murray, 312.

146. See the excerpt from Lacoue-Labarthe's book in *Critical Inquiry* 15, no. 2 (Winter 1989): 482.

147. Quoted by Blanchot in "Thinking the Apocalypse," 477. Note that in *Being and Time, Geschicklichkeit* involves the communal destiny of a people: "Destiny is not something that puts itself together out of individual fates, any more than being-with-one-another can be conceived as the occurring together of several subjects. Our fates have already been guided in advance, in our being with one another in the same world and in our resoluteness for definite possibilities. Only in communicating and struggling does the power of destiny become free. *Dasein*'s fateful destiy in and with its 'generation' goes to make up the full authentic historicizing of *Dasein*" (*Being and Time,* 436). In a private conversation with M. Levinas on 10 November 1989, I asked him if he thought Heidegger's political activity was consistent with his philosophy. He replied in quite strong terms that there was no difference between the two.

148. DeBoer says in "An Ethical Transcendental Philosophy" in *Face to Face* that the fundamental difference between Heidegger's and Levinas's philosophy is "the ethical indifference of Heidegger's philosophy" (108).

149. Edith Wyschogrod in *Sprit in Ashes* charges that Heidegger's priorities, as they can be discerned from what he said and wrote, are "astounding": "Such facts as the damning of the Rhine are devastating, but the camps go unmentioned" (188). She also charges that Heidegger is more concerned with "bligted landscapes" than with "the destruction of persons [which] is for him a secondary phenomenon" (203).

150. Quoted by Levinas in "As if Consenting to Horror" in *Critical Inquiry* 15, no. 2 (Winter 1989): 487.

151. Levinas, "As if Consenting to Horror," 477.

152. Levinas, "As if Consenting to Horror," 488.

153. Derrida, "Violence and Metaphysics," 142.

154. See Blanchot's "Thinking the Apocalypse," 476.

155. Bernasconi perhaps writes out of this sense of exigency when he asks in "Levinas and Derrida: The Question of the Closure of Metaphysics" (197) "whether the human face ever reverberates in our dealings with the history of philosophy?" Bernasconi suggests that this happens when we call into question what we do as philosophers. Then he asks, "Would we be wrong to suppose that in recent times this questioning has become more widespread?"

156. Steven Smith, "Reason as One for Another," 67. Durfee also points to the historical phenomenon behind Levinas's philosophy when he says: "The social movements to constrain war will be of little effect if the very philosophical foundation of war is left unclarified" (218).

157. Blanchot, "Our Clandestine Companion," 50.

158. Levinas, "As if Consenting to Horror," 488.

159. Robert Bernasconi in his "Habermas and Arendt on the Philosopher's 'Error': Tracking the Diaboliical in Heidegger" in *Graduate Faculty Philosophy Journal*, vol. 15, no. 2 (1991): 3–24, concludes that Heidegger brought about the end of philosophy by "showing what for too long had gone unsuspected—that great thoughts can under the mask of nobility lead us astray."

160. Levinas, "As if Consenting to Horror," 488.

161. In *Otherwise Than Being* Levinas will refer to this wisdom as "the wisdom of love." Greish in "The Face and Reading: Immediacy and Mediation" points out the reversal, the counter option this involves: "It is essential to size up the reversal that takes place here. Philosophy is no longer philo-sophia, love of wisdom, but wisdom of love. To read Levinas is to attempt the thought of this reversal" (77).

162. Emil Fackenheim, *To Mend the World* (New York: Schocken Books, 1982), 266.

163. Jean-Francois Lyotard, *Le Differend* (Paris: Minuit, 1983), 134-35. For a discussion of Lyotard on this point see David Carroll's *Paraesthetics* (New York: Metheun, 1987), 169–73.

164. Richard Cohen in his Introduction to *Time and the Other* (25-26) also makes this point when he says that Levinas shows that there are responsibilities "greater than the infinite responsibility to think and be on one's own (not just a rigorous

attention to evidence), greater, then, than all the traditional philosophic responsibilities, greater because better."

165. See our discussion of these terms in chapters 1 and 2.

166. I have in mind here the fact that Heidegger's most important heir in contemporary philosophy is Jacques Derrida, whose poststructuralist philosophy has often been accused of being detached from real historical issues, whether they be political, social or ethical in character. Although Levinas does not criticize Derrida on this point in the only essay he writes explicitly about Derrida's thought, "Wholly Otherwise," he write in *Otherwise Than Being* of "the insignificant signs of a language in dissemination. . . ." According to Bernasconi in "Levinas and Derrida: The Question of the Closure of Metaphysics" (197), Levinas refers here to Derrida and that Derrida's philosophy is "a clear revelation of the poverty of philosophy, and the human sciences generally, with their 'impossible indifference with regard to the human.'" See Edward Said's *The World, the Text, and the Critic,* (Cambridge: Harvard University Press, 1983), as one example of the criticism of Derrida on this point. I also have in mind Emil Fackenheim's accusation in his *To Mend the World,* 11, that neither philosophy nor theology has been sufficiently transformed by the Holocaust: "To this day philosophers keep on acting as if, philosophically, there is no difference between the six million and one child dying of cancer, just as theologians keep on acting as if, theologically, the 'case' of Auschwitz were 'covered' by Good Friday or the ninth of Av. So far as most philosophers and theologians are concerned, there simply is no Holocaust."

167. Derrida says in "Violence and Metaphysics" (143) that in opening up the ontological difference, Heidegger's thought "permits the emergence of every possible difference."

Notes to Chapter Four

1. Blum states in his "Emmanuel Levinas' Theory of Commitment" (24–25) that the way Levinas describes the other, as an infinitely other to whom I have an infinite responsibility, is a "God-like other."

2. A good example would be this quotation from Levinas's *Difficult Freedom* in *The Levinas Reader* (205): "Man is not therefore a being (etant) among beings (etants), a mere receiver of sublime message. He is, at the same time, the person to whom the word is said, and the one through whom there

is a Revelation. Man is the site of transcendence, even if he can be described as 'being there' or *Dasein.*"

3. Steven Smith observes in *The Argument to the Other* (205) that "the positive presentation of the Infinite in *Totality and Infinity* becomes the glorification of God in *Otherwise Than Being.*"

4. Alan Megill, *Prophets of Extremity* (Berkeley: University of California Press, 1985), 308. Adriaan Peperzak is also certainly correct when he states in his "'Emmanuel Levinas: Jewish Experience and Philosophy" (298) that Levinas's "criticism of the occidental way of life and thought would probably have been impossible if he had not been educated as a Jew."

5. Quoted by Derrida in "Violence and Metaphysics," 103.

6. Derrida, "Violence and Metaphysics," 103.

7. See, for example: *Difficile Liberte* (Paris: Albin Michel, 1963); *Quatre lectures talmudiques* (Paris: Editions de Minuit, 1968); *Du sacre au saint* (Paris: Editions de Minuit, 1977); *De Dieu qui vient a l'idee* (Paris: Vrin, 1982).

8. McCollester is absolutely correct when he says of Levinas that "there is no discontinuity between the ideas developed in his philosophical writings and his vision of Judaism" (350).

9. See Levinas's interview with Richard Kearney in Kearney's *Dialogues With Contemporary Continental Thinkers* (Manchester: Manchester University Press, 1984), 174.

10. Kearney, 174.

11. Lingis makes this important distinction in his introduction to *Otherwise Than Being* (xv) that Levinas's phenomenology of the face in *Totality and Infinity* is a "quasi-phenomenology, for a face is not so much a mode of appearing of the other as a trace where alterity passes." Similarly, Adriaan Peperzak maintains that though the Face is "the closest and most intimate reality of our lives," its presence is unique in that it "is present without being a phenomenon." See Peperzak's "Emmanuel Levinas: Jewish Experience and Philosophy," 303.

12. Bernasconi in his "Re-reading *Totality and Infinity*" in *The Question of the Other* (23) states that the question that most preoccupies Levinas scholars today is: "What status is to be accorded the face to face relation." He says the question is answered in two ways: 1) Levinas's claim regarding the face to face relation is seen as a transcendental claim, i.e., the ethical is the foundation of all experience but is itself beyond experience; 2) Levinas's claim is empirical, i.e., the command in the face is found in our actual experience in and of the

world. DeBoer in his "An Ethical Transcendental Philosophy" expounds the first view. Levinas is certainly making a transcendental claim, but as Bernasconi, Lingis, Lyotard, Smith, McCollester, Blum and many others point out, Levinas also claims that the command to ethics in the face is actually "a concrete experience in our lives" (Bernasconi, 24). As Bernasconi says, what is for Levinas "beyond totality and objective experience is reflected within the totality and history, within experience (Bernasconi, 23–24). Lingis clearly gives his answer to this central question in his Introduction to *Otherwise Than Being*: "The relation with alterity is presented by Levinas both as an experience and as an apriori to all experience" (xxii).

13. Derrida, "Violence and Metaphysics," 151.

14. See Andrew Tallon's "Review of Edith Wyschogrod's *Emmanuel Levinas and the Problem of Ethical Metaphysics*" in *Philosophy Today* (Spring 1986), 60. According to Tallon, he asked Levinas to justify his claim that we are ethically responsible for each other, and Levinas responded that he found the need and the call for the justification "completely paradoxical," for this is just the way things are, and Levinas used the Cain and Abel story as an example.

15. Jean Greisch, "The Face and Reading: Immediacy and Mediation" in *Re-reading Levinas*, 76.

16. Levinas, who is so dissimilar to Kant in so many ways, admires Kant for the central role the categorical imperative has in his philosophy. Levinas expresses his paradoxical relation to Kant quite well when he says in *Otherwise than Being* (129) that he'd like to keep the categorical imperative and nothing else in Kant. Allain David in his "Le Nom de la Finitude" says that Levinas's exposition of the other is similar to Kant because "the grandeur of Kantianism" is that it explicates temporality as respect for persons (279). Petitdemange in his "Le Neant de L'Autre" also says that Levinas's insistence on the ethical command in the face of the other "could be interpreted as an empiricism. A just title perhaps, despite the pejorative connotations of the word, but Kant also spoke of the fact of the practical reason" (44).

17. Immanuel Kant, *The Critique of Practical Reason*, trans. L. Beck (Indianapolis: Bobbs-Merrill, 1965), 122.

18. See Kristeva's essays "The True-Real" and "A new Type of Intellectual: The Dissident" in *A Kristeva Reader*, ed. Toril Moi (New York: Columbia University Press, 1986); also see Moi's introduction to this volume.

19. Derrida, "Punctuation: The time of a Thesis" in Montefiore, 47.

20. Derrida, "At This Very Moment in this Work Here I Am," *Re-reading Levinas*, 11–48.

21. Bernasconi and Critchley, Editor's Introduction to *Re-reading Levinas*, xiv.

22. Derrida, *Of Spirit* (chicago: The University of Chicago Press, 1989).

23. Derrida, "Paul de Man's War," *Critical Inquiry* 14 (Spring 1988): 590–652.

24. Derrida, "Paul de Man's War," 590 and ff. Also see on the topic of Derrida's sense of responsibility Jon Wiener, "The Responsibilities of Friendship: Jacques Derrida on Paul de Man's Collaboration" *Critical Inquiry* 14 (Spring 1988): 797–803.

25. Megill, 308.

26. Lingis points out that "Levinas is not purely exalting human relations. He rather means to locate the meaning of God in the ethical bond" (introduction to *Otherwise Than Being*, xxxiii).

27. Levinas, *Difficile liberte*, 33.

28. Levinas, *Transcendance et intelligibilite* (Geneva: Editions Labor et Fides, 1984), 38–39.

29. Levinas, *Transcendance et intelligibilite*, 39.

30. Levinas, "Diachrony and Representation" in *Time and the Other*, 137.

31. Levinas, *Difficile liberte*, 33.

32. Levinas, *Totality*, 79.

33. Levinas, *Totality*, 303.

34. Levinas, Beyond Intentionality," 115.

35. Levinas, "Beyond Intentionality," 113. Levinas declares his opposition to logical proofs and certainty in *Otherwise Than Being* (99): "Certainty is the guide and guarantee of the whole spiritual adventure of being. But this is why this adventure is no adventure."

36. See Kearney, 67. Lingis points out in his introduction to *Otherwise Than Being* (xxxiii) that Levinas's notion of the trace means that God is not revealed in ethical phenomenology "but that God is the non-phenomenal force of the other, that God exists in his voice."

37. Although Levinas insists that thought of God must be in an ethical and not an ontological perspective, he still declares that the ethical dimension of the relationship between persons in which God comes to the idea emerges in the "phenomenologocial-ontological perspective." As Levinas says in his dialogue with Richard Kearney entitled "Ethics of the Infinite" (56–57): "The interhuman is thus an interface: a double axis where what is 'of the world' qua phenomenological intelli-

gibility is juxtaposed with what is 'not of the world' qua ethical responsibility. It is in this ethical perspective that God must be thought and not in the ontological perspective of our being-there or of some Supreme Being and Creator correlative to the world, as traditional metaphysics often held. God, as the God of alterity and transcendence, can only be understood in terms of the interhuman dimension which, to be sure, emerges in the phenomenological-ontological perspective of the intelligible world, but which cuts through and perforates the totality of presence and points towards the absolutely Other. . . . I would maintain, against Heidegger, that philosophy can be ethical as well as ontological, can be at once Greek and non-Greek in its inspiration."

38. Levinas, *Difficile Liberte*, 33.

39. Levinas, "Beyond Intentionality," 113.

40. This interview with Levinas took place on 31 December 1982 and is as yet unpublished. Thanks are due to Professor Wyschogrod for providing me with a transcript of the interview.

41. Wyschogrod interview, 6.

42. Levinas, "Beyond Intentionality," 113.

43. Levinas, *Totality*, 79.

44. Levinas, *Totality*, 77.

45. Megill, 308.

46. This has led Robert Herrera in his "Modern Jewish Thought and the Problem of God" in *Philosophy Today* to make the rather odd statement that "Levinas' God is hardly a religious God: a pious sense of uncanniness is noticeably absent." While uncanniness is certainly missing from Levinas's conception of God, his view of God entirely through ethics can be considered not religious only if one does not consider certain elements of Rabbinic Judaism religious.

47. In "Meaning and Sense" (89–90), Levinas discusses the traditional economy between God and the world and states that "when history gives lie to this economy, this did not refute the supernatural providence any more than the deviation of the stars refuted the Ptolemaic astronomy. . . . This religion which the person required for himself, rather than feeling himself required by this relgion, . . . has lost much of its influence over men."

48. See Levinas's essay entitled "God and Philosophy" in *Papers*; also see Edith Wyschogrod's essay "God and 'Being's Move in the Philosophy of Emmanuel Levinas, *The Journal of Religion*, 62, no. 2 (Winter 1982): 145–55.

49. Levinas, "God and Philosophy," 155.

50. Levinas, "Revelation in the Jewish tradition," *The Levinas Reader,* 208. Peperzak says in his "Beyond Being" (241) that ontology "transforms God and humans and the subject into moments or adventures of Being."

51. See Levinas's essay entitled "Useless Suffering" originally published in *Les cahiers de la nuit.* This essay was recently translated by Richard Cohen and included in *The Provocation of Levinas,* 156–67.

52. Levinas's treatment of the Holocaust is similar to Jean-Francois Lyotard's treatment of it in terms of excess in *The Differend,* 4–19.

53. Levinas, "Useless Suffering," 161–62. Levinas addresses the issue of theodicy in his essay "Prayer Without Demand" in *The Levinas Reader,* 227–34. Here Levinas ask, "Is it right for us to ask, in our prayers, for human suffering to be eased?" He sin." But then he adds what is certainly a very significant footnote, so significant in fact that it is puzzling why he relegates it to a footnote: "A phrase which, after Auschwitz, has become unacceptable. Preaching it to others is intolerable. But does this prevent one from saying it to oneself?" This forces us to ask what status this answer has, this answer that affirms that "the meaning of suffering is the expiation of sin," when one says it to oneself even while knowing not only that it is disproven by the Holocaust, but also that it is intolerable to say it to someone else. Perhaps for Levinas it is morally acceptable to say this, but only to oneself, because it induces one to analyze the wrongs one might have committed. This perhaps reveals the radical extent to which Levinas says the self is commanded to be more concerned with the sin I commit than the sin the other commits against me.

54. Levinas, "Useless Suffering," 156–67. Interestingly enough, Arnold Davidson says Levinas's philosophy is an attempt to retrieve the human and God after Nietzsche's and Heidegger's proclamation of the death of God. Levinas does mention Nietzsche's proclamation of the death of God but, as we have already seen, he says that it is not humans but history, meaning the Holocaust and other atrocities, that kills the traditional conception of God. See Davidson's "Questions Concerning Heidegger: Opening the Debate," 424–26.

55. See the interview with Levinas entitled "The Paradox of Morality," 175.

56. Levinas, "Useless Suffering," 163.

57. Levinas, "The Paradox of Morality," 176.

58. Levinas, *Totality,* 21.

59. Levinas, "The Paradox of Morality," 176.

60. Quoted by Richard Cohen in his introduction to *Face to Face,* 3.

61. Levinas, "Meaning and Sense," 122.

62. Levinas, "Meaning and Sense," 177.

63. This statement is not made any less true by the fact that Levinas even before the Holocaust, in his 1935 essay "De l'evasion," was very concerned with the reality of physical violence and other horrors of being. Indeed, a case could be made, based upon the warnings and the dire forecast of violent things to come that Levinas issues in his 1934 essay "The Philosophy of Hitlerism," that his thought from the very first is a response to Nazism and to what at first the specter and then became the only too real fact o the Holocaust.

64. Davidson in "Opening the Debate" (426), for example, says that at the event of the Holocaust ". . . questioning must stop."

65. Fackenheim discusses the Holocaust as the rupture which ruptures philosophy in his *To Mend the World.*

66. See, for example, Fackenheim's discussion of Eichmann's appeal to Kant's Categorical Imperative during his trial (270–71).

67. See, for example, Richard Rubenstein's *After Auschwitz* (New York: MacMillan Publishing Co., 1966).

68. In *Totality* (305–06), Levinas defines goodness as transcendence, the fact that there is a transcendent I capable of responding to the command of the other: ". . . goodness is transcendence itself. Transcendence is the transcendence of an I. Only an I can respond to the injunction of a face." Goodness is produced as the relation of pluralism and of peace between the I and the other.

69. Steven Smith in *The Argument to the Other* (205) says that similar to Descartes, for Levinas "the Good is too Good (and too Other) not to call God; analysis yields to adoration. The analogy holds only up to a point, for the God of Levinas is adored only in the third person, never face to face. That may be the difference between the Catholic and a Jew."

70. Llewelyn begins his article "Am I obsessed by Bobby? (Humanism of the Other Animal)" in *Re-reading Levinas* (234–45) by recounting a story Levinas tells of being cheered up by a dog who would excitedly greet Levinas and his fellow prisoners when they returned to camp from their day of forced labor during World War II. Llewelyn is encouraged by this story, but he concludes with dismay that "we fail to find any evidence that Levinas allows the dog to have a face that says

'Don't kill me.'"

71. The fact that Levinas restricts the good to the relationship between persons is evidence of the fact that although Levinas's philosophy can aid in restoring ethics to a more central position in contemporary philosophy, it does remain within contemporary philosophy's dominant anthropocentrism. For a critique of contemporary philosophy on this point see Vincent Descombes' *Modern French Philosophy* (Cambridge: Cambridge University Press, 1980), 14–15.

72. We might find scriptural warrant for this in a passage from Numbers that Levinas cites in the interview "Ethics and Politics," 296–97. In this biblical passage, Moses sends out a search party to explore the land the people of Israel must enter. The explorers villify the land and, for this, are punished with death. Levinas says of this that the explorers' calumny of the land merits death, so certainly there must be some ethical relation between people and the land for this penalty to be merited. Levinas does not draw this consequence, however, but cites a Talmudic commentary that states that the text above all "should teach us the gravity of calumny concerning persons. For if calumny of that which is 'but stones and trees' already merits death, then how serious, *a fortiori*, must be calumny relating to human beings." This indicates as well as anything can that Levinas simply is not going to allow himself to be pushed to open up the dimension of the ethical and the good to the relation between people and the cosmos. Ironically, perhaps, the work of Martin Heidegger, despite its shortcomings concerning questions of ethics, is much more fruitful in this regard, as Gibson Winter among others has shown.

73. Catherine Challier makes this point about God's ethical bond not only with humans but with the earth in *Alliance avec La Nature*. In the chapter entitled "La Signification Ethique De La Creation" she says: "Si le coeur obtus de ce puple s'humilie, s'il expie son iniquite alors Dieu se souviendra de Son Alliance avec Jacob, commed de celle avec Isaac et de celle avec Abraham, Il se souviendra aussi de la terre" (172). Levinas says in "Prayer Without Demand" (232) that the fact that God's command to responsibility between persons is anterior to being equals "the ethical meaning of creation."

74. See Levinas's essay "As if Consenting to Horror," 488.

75. This is most clearly seen in Levinas's essay "Meaning and Sense" wherein he says that the ethical command is "the orienting sense in being" before history and cultures and is that by which history and cultures can be judged.

76. Levinas, *Transcendence and Intelligibilite,* 41.
77. Levinas, "Revelation in the Jewish Tradition" in *The Levinas Reader,* 207.
78. Levinas expresses his suspicion of language as noun when he asks in "Revelation in the Jewish Tradition" (209): "Can we convert transcendence as such into answers without losing it in the process?"
79. Levinas, *Otherwise Than Being,* 34.
80. We could contrast what Levinas is saying here about religious language with Tillich's attempt to find some language to name in a nonsymbolic way "the God beyond God." In his *Systematic Theology* vol. 1 (Chicago: The University of Chicago Press, 1951) he maintains that all language about God is symbolic except the name of God as the Ground of Being. For an explication of this see Langdon Gilkey's *Gilkey on Tillich* (New York: Crossroad, 1990).
81. Edith Wyschogrod intimates that there may be different types of religious language for Levinas when she states in "God and 'Being's Move' in the Philosophy of Emmanuel Levinas" (154) that for Levinas, "Religious language for the most part intends to bring something about." She perhaps overlooks the great significance of the fact that for Levinas there are two types of religious language and that one has priority over the other. This is a point that must be understood in order to see what kind of religious language Levinas is recommending and, indeed, producing himself.
82. Derrida, "Violence and Metaphysics," 97: "The notion of primacy well translates the gesture of Levinas' entire critique."
83. Boukaert, 121.
84. Levinas, *Debats sur le langage theologique,* 69.
85. Steven Smith, "Reason as One for the Other," 57.
86. See Kierkegaard's explication of the Abraham and Isaac myth as "a teleological suspension of the ethical" in his *Fear and Trembling* (Princeton: Princeton University Press, 1941).
87. Levinas, "As if Consenting to Horror," 488.
88. It should be pointed out that as a twentieth century Jewish thinker, Levinas is keenly aware of the history of religious persecution. In *Transcendence et intelligibilite* (55), for example, he states that ". . . the figure of the cross was that which brought the crosses. The crucified will command the crusades! The memories are very lively, especially since they also live from the Shoa."
89. Levinas, "Beyond Intentionality," 115.
90. Levinas, *Transcendence et intelligibilite,* 41.

91. See, for example, *Liberacion Latino Americana Y Emmanuel Levinas* by Enrique Dussel and Daniel Guillot (Buenos Aires, Editorial Bonum, 1975).

92. Levinas, *Difficult Freedom* in *A Levinas Reader,* 252.

93. Levinas, "The Ego and the Totality" in *Collected Papers,* 44.

94. Derrida is correct in "Violence and Metaphysics" (95) when he says that for Levinas "the ethical relation is a religious relation. Not a religion, but the religion, the religiousity of the religious."

95. Levinas, "Revelation in the Jewish Tradition," 209.

Notes to Chapter Five

1. In Kearney, 50, Levinas declares: "Indeed, from the point of view of philosophical method and discipline, I remain to this day a phenomenologist." Also, in "Questions et reponse" in *Le Nouveau Commerce,* nos. 36–37, p. 2, he says: "In spite of everything, I think that what I do is phenomenology . . ." Similarly, in "Transcendence et Hauteur" in *Bulletin de la Societe francaise de Philosophie,* 56 (1962): 110, Levinas insists: "My point of departure is absolutely nontheological. This is very important to me; it is not theology which I do, but philosophy." Adriaan Peperzak, in his review of *Otherwise Than Being* in *Research in Phenomenology,* vii (1978): 241, says that "we should thus read them [Levinas's philosophical works] as philosophical works which have won a place in contemporary philosophy."

2. Derrida, "Violence and Metaphysics," 89.

3. Levinas, "The Paradox of Morality," 174.

4. In his *Prolegomena to any Future Metaphysics* (Indianapolis: Hackett, 1977), 5, Kant pays to Hume his famous tribute: "I openly confess that my remembering David Hume was the very thing which many years ago first interrupted my dogmatic slumber and gave my investigations in the field of speculative philosophy a quite new direction."

5. Kant, *Prolegomena,* 4: "This was Hume's problem. It was a question concerning the origin of the concept, not concerning its indispensability in use."

6. Kant, *Prolegomena,* 3.

7. Kant, *Prolegomena,* 6.

8. Immanuel Kant, *Critique of Pure Reason,* trans. Norman Kemp Smith (New York: Macmillan & Co., Ltd., 1929), 41.

9. Kant, *Critique of Pure Reason,* 42.

10. Kant, *Critique of Pure Reason,* 43.
11. Kant, *Critique of Pure Reason,* 20.
12. Kant, *Critique of Pure Reason,* 22.
13. Kant, *Critique of Pure Reason,* 24.
14. Kant, *Critique of Pure Reason,* 74.
15. In his *Deconstruction in Context* (Chicago: University of Chicago Press, 1986), 7–8, Mark Taylor states that because in the Second Critique Kant "does not reconcile inclination and obligation," and because in the Third Critique the reconciliation of opposites is only a "regulative idea" that is never "concretely actualized in time and space," the last two critiques do not bridge the "gap between subject and object that undermines the very possibility of knowledge."
16. Paul Tillich, *Systematic Theology,* vol. 3 (Chicago: University of Chicago Press, 1963), 70. Quoted by Wayne Floyd, Jr. in *Theology and the Dialectics of Otherness* (Lanham, MD: University Press of America, Inc., 1988), 21.
17. See Levinas's essay "Meaning and Sense" in *Collected Papers,* 82.
18. Vincent Descombes, *Le Meme et l'Autre,* translated as *Modern French Philosophy* (Cambridge: Cambridge University Press, 1980).
19. Descombes, 216.
20. Taylor, 4.
21. For a treatment of the reactions against Kant, see Floyd, 15–17.
22. G. W. F. Hegel, *Phenomenology of Spirit,* trans. A. V. Miller (Oxford: Oxford University Press, 1979), 47.
23. Hegel, 48.
24. See Floyd, 26: "For Hegel, despite the appearance of a certain two-sidedness to knowledge, such distinctions as that between appearance and thing-in-itself, when they are drawn, must themselves be drawn within consciousness."
25. Hegel, 55.
26. Quoted in Floyd, 27.
27. Hegel, 55.
28. Scott Warren, *The Emergence of Dialectical Theory: Philosophy and Political Inquiry* (Chicago: University of Chicago Press, 1984), 35.
29. Floyd, 32. This is not to deny the dialectical relationship between Hegel and Kierkegaard. For the best treatment of the Hegel-Kierkegaard relationship, see Mark Taylor's *Journeys to Selfhood.*
30. Floyd, 33.
31. Quoted in John Scanlon's review of Husserl's *Ding und*

Raum: Vorlesungen 1907 in *Research in Phenomenology*, vi (1974): 130.

32. Quoted by John Sallis in "The Identities of the Things Themselves" in *Research in Phenomenology*, xii (1982): 116.

33. See Spiegelberg, vol. 1, 122.

34. Spiegelberg, 117.

35. Quoted in Sallis, 119.

36. *Ideas* (1982), 112.

37. This point is made firmly by John Scanlon, 30: "Husserl's Critique is not Kant's Critique, and Husserl's issues are not Kant's issues."

38. *Ideas* (1982), 183; also Spiegelberg, 126.

39. *Ideas*, (1982), 183.

40. *Ideas*, (1982), 183.

41. Ricoeur, 188.

42. Heidegger, *Being and Time*, 58.

43. Sallis (114) points out that Heidegger's question, "what remains unthought in the appeal to things?" leads directly to *Lichtung*, or the clearing of Being, "and this redetermination produces an abrupt rupture with the Husserlian project."

44. Heidegger, *Being and Time*, 61.

45. Heidegger, *Being and Time*, 127.

46. Heidegger, *Being and Time*, 127.

47. Heidegger, *Being and Time*, 134.

48. Heidegger, *Being and Time*, 46.

49. Heidegger, *Being and Time*, 32.

50. Heidegger, *Being and Time*, 272.

51. In his *Modern German Philosophy* (Cambridge: Cambridge University Press, 1983), 30, Rudiger Bubner says "*Dasein* as Being-in-the-World is prior to all distinctions of subject and object."

52. Heidegger, *Being and Time*, 247.

53. Heidegger, *Being and Time*, 249. Heidegger also states in *Being and Time* that the real scandal to philosophy is not that the question of the external world has not yet been answered, but that it is still asked. Theodore De Boor, in his essay "An Ethical Transcendental Philosophy" (99), calls such doubt about the external world "an apparently authentic experience which cannot be exorcised by Heidegger's remark."

54. Heidegger, *Being and Time*, 249.

55. See Kearney (51) wherein Levinas says: *Being and Time* . . . represents the fruition and flowering of Husserlian phenomenology. The most far-reaching potentialities of the phenomenological method were exploited by Heidegger in his early work . . ." Also, Levinas declared in *Ethics and*

Infinity (37) that *Being and Time* was one of the four or five most important books in the history of philosophy.

56. That Heidegger's notion of Being-With is derivative of Being-in is crucial to Edith Wyschogrod's critique of Heidegger in her *Spirit in Ashes*, 172. Also, Heidegger himself confirmed that his philosophy attributed a secondary status to subjectivity and, accordingly, to intersubjectivity, when he was asked if his philosophy was directed toward a social mission: "What is society? Today it is only the absolutization of modern subjectivity, and that from this perspective a philosophy which has overcome the stand-point of subjectivity is not even permitted to participate in the discussion"—in Murray, 304.

57. Levinas, *Totality*, 206: "all recourse to words take place already within the primordial face to face of language."

58. See Levinas, "Meaning and Sense."

59. See Levinas, "Signature," 188.

60. Levinas, *Totality*, 304.

61. Levinas, *Totality*, 304.

62. See Norman Malcolm's *Problems of Mind* (New York: Harper Torchbooks, 1971); John Wisdom's *Other Minds* (Oxford: Blackwell, 1952); and J. L. Austin's reply to Wisdom entitled "Other Minds" in *Classics of Analytic Philosophy*, ed. Robert Ammerman (New York: McGraw-Hill Book Company, 1965), 353–78.

63. See Husserl's *Cartesian Meditations*, trans. D. Cairns (The Hague: Martinus Nijhoff, 1973; also see Theunissen, 13–166.

64. Theunissen, 167–98.

65. See Levinas, *Totality*, 174; also see chapter 3 of the present work.

66. Levinas, "Beyond Intentionality," 110.

67. Levinas, "Beyond Intentionality," 110.

68. Levinas, "Meaning and Sense," 88.

69. Levinas, "Meaning and Sense," 88.

70. Levinas, "Meaning and Sense," 98.

71. Levinas, *Totality*, 304.

72. Theunissen, 1.

73. Levinas, "God and Philosophy" in *Collected Papers*, 172.

74. For an exploration of this question see Wyschogrod's *Spirit in Ashes* and Piotr Hoffmann's *Violence in Modern Philosophy* (Chicago: University of Chicago Press, 1989).

75. Smith, "Reason as One for the Other" in *Face to Face*, 67.

76. Blanchot, 50.

77. Theodor Adorno, *Negative Dialectics* (New York: The Seabury Press, 1973), 307.

78. Adorno, *Negative Dialectics*, 5.
79. Adorno, 307.
80. This point is made quite well in the as yet unpublished essay on Levinas and Adorno by Wayne Floyd.
81. Levinas, *Totality*, 304; also see chapter 3 above.
82. Derrida, "Violence and Metaphysics," 97.
83. Quoted by Bubner in *Modern German Philosophy*, 173. For a critical appraisal of Adorno's theoreticism, see Bubner's *Essays in Hermeneutics and Critical Theory* (New York: Columbia, 1988), 33–35. Here Bubner criticizes critical theory for sharing the Young Hegelian belief ". . . that a type of thought which was related in a particular way to its time and was negative in regard to the status quo was the same as real change."
84. The Marxist literary critic Terry Eagleton, in his *Literary Theory* (145), charges that deconstruction "commits you to nothing. It is radical in respect of everyone else's opinions, but conservative in every other way. It is blank ammunition." Edward Said also takes deconstruction to task for being apolitical in his *The World, the Text, and the Critic* (Cambridge: Harvard University Press, 1983). Mark Edmundson in his essay "The Ethics of Deconstruction" in *Michigan Quarterly Review*, vol. 27 (Fall 1988): 622–23, notes that "the fact that deconstruction possesses an ethical dimension is not something that is generally acknowledged, as treatments of the subject in publications ranging from *Newsweek* magazine to some of the more esteemed scholarly journals attest."
85. Levinas, "Diachrony and Representation" in *Time and the Other*, 103.
86. Levinas, "Meaning and Sense," 105.
87. Derrida, "Violence and Metaphysics," 102.
88. Derrida, "Violence and Metaphysics," 102.
89. Bernstein makes this important point about Derrida, although he perhaps overstates the case somewhat, when he says in "Serious Play: The Ethical-Political Horizon of Jacques Derrida" (*The Journal of Speculative Philosophy*, vol. 1, no. 2, 1987, p. 105) that "few contemporary thinkers have been so alert and perceptive about the dangers of violently crushing differences, otherness, alterity. Few writers have written with such nuanced understanding about the suffering, mourning other."
90. See Derrida's essay "Structure, Sign, and Play" in *Writing and Difference*, 278–93.
91. "Violence and Metaphysics" (141) makes clear that Derrida, like Levinas, is attempting in his work to avoid violence.

Derrida has his own ideas about how to accomplish this: "The best liberation from violence is a certain putting into question, which makes the search for an *archia* tremble."

92. Derrida, "Structure, Sign, and Play," 292.

93. Derrida, "Structure, Sign, and Play," 292.

94. Derrida, "Violence and Metaphysics," 79. Bernasconi says correctly in "Levinas and Derrida: The Question of the Closure of Metaphysics" (198) that Derrida's insistence on this point is evidence of his ethical concerns.

95. Derrida, "Structure, Sign, and Play," 288.

96. See Derrida's thesis defense, "The Time of a Thesis: Punctuations," which he presented to his jury (one of whom was Levinas) at the Sorbonne in 1980, in Montefiore, 40.

97. This fact accounts at least in part for the apolitical nature of deconstruction in America. Even Bernstein, while insisting on the ethico-political nature of Derrida's work, agrees in his "Serious Play" (148) that in America deconstruction has been elitist and even conservative: "the reception of deconstruction has been almost totally apolitical—except, of course, for that domestic parlour game called 'academic politics.'"

98. Derrida, "Punctuations," 44–45.

99. It is interesting to note that this progression of Derrida's philosophy is the exact opposite of Eagleton's account of the history of poststructuralism, which is so often equated with Derrida's philosophy. Eagleton suggests that poststructuralism had its roots in a political movement, the student revolt in Paris in 1968, and that the failure of this movement changed Poststructuralism from a political to an intellectual protest: "Poststructuralism was a product of the blend of hope and catastrophe which was 1968. Unable to break the structures of state power, poststructuralism found it possible instead to subvert the structures of language" (142).

100. Derrida, "Punctuations," 47.

101. Derrida, "Punctuations," 48–49.

102. Bernstein, 97.

103. Bernstein, 108.

104. Rick Roderick, "Reading Derrida Politically (Contra Rorty)," *Praxis International* vol. 4, no. 4 (January 1987), 448–49.

105. Derrida, "Punctuations," 49.

106. See Kristeva's essays "The True-Real" and "A new Type of Intellectual: The Dissident" and the editor's introduction in *The Kristeva Reader*.

107. Novitz, 48.

108. Bernstein says "such motifs such as responsibility keep

resurfacing in his texts" (94).

109. Jacques Derrida, "The Politics of Friendship," *The Journal of Philosophy* (1988): 632–44.

110. Derrida, "At this very Moment Here in this Work Here I am" in *Re-reading Levinas*, 11–48.

111. Derrida, "At this very Moment," 38.

112. Derrida, "The Politics of Friendship," 632.

113. Derrida, "The Politics of Friendship," 633.

114. Derrida, "The Politics of Friendship," 633.

115. Derrida, "The Politics of Friendship," 633–34.

116. Derrida, "Paul de Man's War," 596.

117. The strained and improbable nature of Derrida's defense is evident in many places. Perhaps the most glaring of them is when Derrida asks why de Man dissembled the fact of his editorship of a Nazi-run newspaper. Derrida concludes that de Man was very humble and did not like to talk about himself much. Besides, says Derrida, if de Man had taken the trouble to speak and write about his past, "it would have consumed his time and energy . . . and that would have deprived us of a part of his work" (639).

118. Derrida, "Paul de Man's War," 645.

119. Derrida, "Paul de Man's War," 594.

120. Derrida, "Paul de Man's War," 594.

121. In his essay entitled "Saussurian Theory and the Abolition of Reality" in *The Monist*, 69, no. 1 (January 1986): 142, Colin Falk points to the same error in Derrida's thought when he says: "The whole Saussurian tradition of linguistic and literary theory is philosophically adrift to the extent that it ignores, or has found no way to recognize (as well as perhaps having helped to suppress any awareness in us of a need to recognize), the necessities of human incarnation." Similarly, Mark Edmundson (635) points to Derrida's view of language as "infinite deferral" as the root of what he views as "one of the major drawbacks in Derrida's work, his difficulty in making positive interventions in contemporary political and ethical controversies."

122. Edith Wyschogrod in *Emmanuel Levinas: The Problem of Ethical Metaphysics* (174) says that Levinas's insistence that "communication is not a game but the assumption of responsibility for others" is an idea Levinas borrowed from the Talmud.

123. Bernstein says that because of Derrida's view of language, the question of how we can warrant our ethico-political decisions "is the question that Derrida never answers" (112).

124. Jean-Francois Lyotard, *Just Gaming* (Minneapolis: University of Minnesota Press, 1985), 60.

125. Ludwig Wittgenstein, *Philosophical Investigations* (New York: MacMillan & Co., 1953), 66.

126. Lyotard, *Just Gaming,* 14 and ff.

127. David Carroll in his *Paraesthetics* says that "consensus of any sort is the obstacle to Lyotard's politics of differends" (163).

128. Jean-Francois Lyotard, *The Differend* (Minneapolis: University of Minnesota Press, 1988), xi–xii.

129. Lyotard, *Just Gaming,* 96.

130. Lyotard, *Just Gaming,* 96.

131. Lyotard, *Just Gaming,* 100.

132. Lyotard, *Just Gaming,* 104.

133. Lyotard, *Just Gaming,* 60.

134. Lyotard, *Just Gaming,* 60.

135. Lyotard, *Just Gaming,* 60–61.

136. That for Levinas the prescriptive language game occurs within and can be described by the descriptive language game is what Lyotard cannot understand in his insistence that language games are essentially separate and, thus, that the way to just gaming is to keep them separate. Lyotard, then, makes a mistake that is absolutely crucial to the correct understanding of Levinas's philosophy as philosophy when he says in *Just Gaming* (53) that Levinas's philosophy is entirely a prescriptive language game and that "as far as being, and hypothesis about being, are concerned, all of this is without interest" to Levinas. Jan de Greef makes a similar mistake in his "Skepticism and Reason" (174) when he says that in Levinas "affirmation and negation must be understood not as declarations that admit of truth value but as proclamations, statements that engage and commit the one who has engaged himself by what he says."

137. Alisdair McIntyre, *After Virtue,* 2.

Selected Bibliography

Works by Emmanuel Levinas

"About Blanchot: an interview." *Substance* 14 (1976): 54–57.

"As if Consenting to Horror." *Critical Inquiry* 15, no. 2 (Winter 1989): 485–88.

"Beyond Intentionality." In *Philosophy in France Today*. Edited by A. Montefiore. Translated by Kathleen McLaughlin. Cambridge: Cambridge University Press, 1983, pp. 100–15.

Collected Philosophical Papers. Translated by A. Lingis. The Hague: Martinus Nijhoff, 1987.

De Dieu qui vient a l'idee. Paris: Vrin, 1982.

"De l'evasion." *Recherches Philosophiques* 5 (1935–36): 373–92.

Debats sur le langage theologique. Paris: Aubre-Montaigne, 1968.

Difficile Liberte. 2nd ed. Paris: Albin Michel, 1976. Translated by Sean Hand as *Difficult Freedom*. Baltimore: Johns Hopkins University Press, 1990.

En decouvrant l'existence avec Husserl et Heidegger. 2nd ed. Paris: Vrin, 1967.

Ethics and Infinity. Translated by R. Cohen. Pittsburgh: Duquesne University Press, 1985.

"Ethics and Politics." In *The Levinas Reader*. Edited by Sean Hand. Oxford: Basil Blackwell, 1989, pp. 289–97.

"Ethics of the Infinite." In *Dialogues With Contemporary Continental Thinkers* by Richard Kearney. Manchester: Manchester University Press, 1984, pp. 47–69.

Existence and Existents. Translated by A. Lingis. The Hague: Martinus Nijhoff Press, 1978.

Humanisme de l'autre homme. Montpelier: Fata Morgana, 1972.
"Ideology and Idealism." In *The Levinas Reader.* Oxford: Basil Blackwell, 1989, pp. 235–48.
"Il y a." *Deucalion* 1 (1946): 141–54.
"Judaism and the Feminine Element." Translated by Edith Wyschogrod. *Judaism* 18, no. 1 (1969): 30–38.
"Liberte et commandment." *Revue de Metaphysique et de Morale* 58 (1953): 264–72.
"Le nom de Dieu d'apres quelques textes talmudiques." In *L'analyse du langage theologique. Le nom de Dieu.* Edited by E. Castelli. Paris: Aubier, 1969.
Nine Talmudic Readings. Translated by Annette Aronowicz. Bloomington: Indiana University Press, 1990.
Noms Propre. Paris: Fata Morgana, 1976.
Otherwise Than Being or Beyond Essence. Translated by A. Lingis. The Hague: Martinus Nijhoff, 1981.
"The Pact." In *The Levinas Reader.* Oxford: Basil Blackwell, 1989, pp. 211–26.
"The Paradox of Morality." In *The Provocation of Levinas.* Edited by Robert Bernasconi and David Wood. London: Roultledge, 1988, pp. 168–80.
"Prayer Without Demand." In *The Levinas Reader.* Oxford: Basil Blackwell, 1989, pp. 227–34.
"Questions et reponses." *Le Nouveau Commerce* 36–37 (1977): 61–86.
"Quelques reflexions sur la philosophie de l'hitlerisme." *Esprit* 2 (1934): 199–208.
"Revelation in the Jewish Tradition." In *The Levinas Reader.* Oxford: Basil Blackwell, 1989, pp. 166–89.
Du sacre au saint. Cinq nouvelles lectures talmudiques. Paris: Minuit, 1977.
"Sur *les Ideen* de M. E. Husserl." *Revue Philosophique de la France* 54 (1929): 230–65.
The Theory of Intuition in Husserl's Phenomenology. Translated by A. Orianne. Evanston: Northwestern University Press, 1973.
Time and the Other. Translated by Richard Cohen. Pittsburgh: Duquesne University Press, 1987.
Totality and Infinity. Translated by A. Lingis. Pittsburgh: Duquesne University Press, 1969.

"Transcendance et Hauteur." *Bulletin de la Societe francaise de Philosophie* 56 (1962): 104–16.

Transcendance et intelligibilite. Geneva: Editions Labor et Fides, 1984.

"Useless Suffering." In *The Provocation of Levinas*. Edited By Robert Bernasconi and David Wood. London: Routledge, 1988, pp. 156–67.

Other Works

Adorno, Theodore. *Negative Dialectics*. Translated by E. B. Ashton. New York: Continuum, 1983.

Ammerman, Robert, ed. *Classics of Analytical Philosophy*. New York: McGraw-Hill Book Company, 1965.

de Beauvoir, Simone. *Le Deuvieme Sexe*, 2 vols. Paris: Gallimard, 1949. Translated as *The Second Sex* by H. M. Parshley. New York: Random House, 1952.

Bernasconi, Robert, and Wood, David, eds. *The Provocation of Levinas*. London: Routledge, 1988.

Bernasconi, Robert, and Critchley, Simon, eds. *Re-reading Levinas*. Bloomington: Indiana University Press, 1991.

Bernasconi, Robert. "Habermas and Arendt on the Philosopher's 'Error': Tracking the Diabolical in Heidegger. *Graduate Faculty Philosophy Journal,* vol. 14, no. 2 (1991): 3–24.

———. "Levinas and Derrida: The Question of the Closure of Metaphysics." In *Face to Face with Levinas*. Albany: University of New York Press, 1986, pp. 183–202.

———. "Rereading Totality and Infinity." In *The Question of the Other*. Albany: University of New York Press, 1989, pp. 23–34.

———. "Skepticism in the Face of Philosophy." In *Re-reading Levinas*. Bloomington: Indiana University Press, 1991, pp. 149–60.

Bernstein, Richard. "Serious Play: The Ethical-Political Horizon of Jacques Derrida." *The Journal of Speculative Philosophy* vol. 1, no. 2, 1987: 93–117.

Biemel, Walter. "Husserl's *Encyclopedia Britannica* Article and Heidegger's Remarks Thereon." In *Husserl Expositions and Appraisals*. Edited by Frederick Elliston and Peter McCormick.

Notre Dame: University of Notre Dame University, 1977, pp. 286–303.

Blanchot, Maurice. "Our Clandestine Companion." In *Face to Face with Levinas*. Albany: University of New York Press, 1986, pp. 41–52.

Blum, Roland. "Emmanuel Levinas' Theory of Commitment." In *Philosophy and Phenomenological Research* vol. 44, no. 2 (December 1983): 2–26.

Bouckaert, Luk. "Ontology and Ethics: Reflections on Levinas' Critique of Heidegger." *International Philosophical Quarterly* 10 (1970): 402–19.

Breton, Stanislaus. "From Phenomenology to Ontology." *Philosophy Today* (Winter 1960): 112–45.

Bubner, Rudiger. *Essays in Hermeneutics and Critical Theory*. New York: Columbia University Press, 1988.

———. *Modern German Philosophy*. Cambridge: Cambridge University Press, 1983.

Carroll, David. *Paraesthetics*. New York: Metheun, 1987, pp. 169–73.

Challier, Catherine. *L'Alliance avec la Nature*. Paris: Cerf, 1989.

———. "Ethics and the Feminine." In *Re-reading Levinas*. Bloomington: Indiana University Press, 1991, pp. 119–29.

Chanter, Tina. "Antigone's Dilemma." In *Re-reading Levinas*. Bloomington: Indiana University Press, 1991, pp. 130–46.

———. "Feminism and the Other." In *The Provocation of Levinas*. London: Routledge, 1988, pp. 32–56.

Ciaremelli, Fabio. "Levinas's Ethical Discourse between Individuation and Universality." In *Re-reading Levinas*. Bloomington: Indiana University Press, 1991, pp. 83–105.

Ciglia, F. P. "Du Neant A L'autre." In *Les Cahiers de la nuit surveille*, no. 3. Lagrasse: Verdier, 1984.

Cohen, Richard. "Absolute Positivity and Ultrapositivity: Husserl and Levinas." In *The Question of the Other*. Albany: University of New York Press, 1990, pp. 35–46.

———, ed. *Face to Face With Levinas*. Albany: State University of New York Press, 1986.

———. Introduction to *Time and the Other*. Pittsburgh: Duquesne University Press, 1987.

———. "Levinas, Rosenzweig, and the Phenomenologies of Husserl and Heidegger. *Philosophy Today* 32, no. 24 (Summer 1988): 165–78.

———. "Non-indifference in the Thought of Emmanuel Levinas and Franz Rosenzweig." *Graduate Faculty Philosophy Journal* vol. 13, no. 1: 141–53.

Cousineau, Robert. *Heidegger, Humanism, and Ethics*. Louvain: Nauwelaerts, 1972.

Critchley, Simon. "'Bois'—Derrida's Final Word on Levinas." In *Re-reading Levinas*. Bloomington: Indiana University Press, 1991, pp. 162–89.

Davidson, Arnold. "Questions Concerning Heidegger: Opening the Debate." *Critical Inquiry* (Winter 1989): 407–26.

de Boer, Theodor. "An Ethical Transcendental Philosophy." In *Face to Face with Levinas*. Albany: University of New York Press, 1986, pp. 83–116.

de Greef, Jan. "Skepticism and Reason." In *Face to Face with Levinas*. Albany: University of New York Press, 1986, pp. 159–80.

Derrida, Jacques. "At this very Moment In this Work Here I am." In *Re-reading Levinas* (Bloomington: Indiana University Press, 11–49.

———. "Geschlecht: sexual difference, ontological difference." *Research in Phenomenology* 13 (1983): 65–83.

———. "Like the Sound of the Sea Deep Within a Shell: Paul de Man's War." In *Critical Inquiry* 14 (Spring 1988): 590–652.

———. *Of Grammatology*. Translated by Gayatri Chakravorty Spivak. Baltimore: The Johns Hopkins University Press, 1976.

———. "Of Spirit." *Critical Inquiry* 15, no. 2 (Winter 1989): 457–74.

———. *Speech and Phenomena*. Evanston: Northwestern University Press, 1973.

———. "The Time of a Thesis: Punctuation." In *Philosophy in France Today*. Edited by Alan Montefiore. Cambridge: Cambridge University Press, 1983, pp. 34–50.

———. *Writing and Difference*. Translated by Alan Bass. Chicago: University of Chicago Press, 1978.

Descombes, Vincent. *Modern French Philosophy*. Cambridge: Cambridge University Press, 1980.

Durfee, Harold. *Foundational Reflections*. Dordrecht: Martinus Nijhoff, 1987.

Dussel, Enrique and Guillot, Daniel. *Liberacion LatinoAmericana Y Emmanuel Levinas*. Buenos Aires: Editorial Bonum, 1975.

Eagleton, Terry. *Literary Theory*. Minneapolis: University of Minnesota Press, 1983.

Edmundson, Mark. "The Ethics of Deconstruction." *Michigan Quarterly Review* 27 (Fall 1988): 622–43.

Elliston, Frederick and McCormick, Peter, eds. Notre Dame: University of Notre Dame Press, 1977.

Fackenheim, Emil. *To Mend the World*. New York: Schocken Books, 1982.

Falk, Colin. "Saussurian Theory and the Abolition of Reality." *The Monist* 69, no. 1 (January 1986): 132–44.

Farias, Victor. *Heidegger et le Nazisme*. Paris: Lagrasse, 1987.

Floyd, Wayne Whitson, Jr. *Theology and the Dialectics of Otherness*. Lanham, MD: University Press of America, 1988.

Gadamer, Hans-Georg. "Back from Syracuse?" *Critical Inquiry* (Winter 1989): 427–30.

———. *Philosophical Hermeneutics*. Berkeley: University of California Press, 1977.

———. *Truth and Method*. New York: Crossroads, 1975.

Gans, Steven. "Ethics or Ontology." *Philosophy Today* 16, no. 2 (1972): 117–21.

Gilkey, Langdon. "Comments on Emmanuel Levinas' *Totalite et infini*." *Algemeen Nederlands Tijdschrift voor Wijsbegeerte* 64 (1972): 26–38.

———. *Gilkey on Tillich*. New York: Crossroad, 1990.

Greisch, Jean. "The Face and Reading: Immediacy and Mediation." In *Re-reading Levinas*. Bloomington: Indiana University Press, 1991, pp. 67–82.

Habermas, Jurgen. "Work and Weltanschauung: The Heidegger Controversy from a German Perspective." *Critical Inquiry* 15, no. 2 (Winter 1989): 431–56.

Harries, Karsten. "Heidegger as a Political Thinker." In *Heidegger and Modern Philosophy*. Edited by Michael Murray. New York: Harper & Row, 1978, pp. 307–17.

Hegel, G. W. F. *Phenomenology of Spirit*. Translated by A. V. Miller. Oxford: Oxford University Press, 1979.

Heidegger, Martin. *The Basic Problems of Phenomenology*. Bloomington: Indiana University Press, 1982.

———. *Basic Writings*. Edited by David Krell. New York: Harper & Row, 1976.

———. *Being and Time*. Translated by John Macquarrie and Edward Robinson. New York: Harper & Row, 1962.

———. *Discourse on Thinking*. Translated by John Anderson and E. Hans Freund. New York: Harper & Row, 1966.

Herrera, Robert. "Modern Jewish Thought and the Problem of God." *Philosophy Today*, vol. 26, no. 1 (Spring 1982): 54–64.

Husserl, Edmund. *Cartesian Meditations*. Translated by D. Cairns. The Hague: Martinus Nijhoff, 1973.

———. *Ideas Pertaining to a Pure Phenomenology and to a Phenomenological Philosophy*. 2 vols. Translated by W. R. Boyce Gibson. New York: The MacMillan Company, 1931.

———. *Ideas Pertaining to a Pure Phenomenology and to a Phenomenological Philosophy*. 2 vols. Translated by F. Kersten. Martinus Nijhoff Publishers, 1982.

———. *Logical Investigations*. 2 vols. Translated by J.N. Findlay. New York: Humanities Press, 1970.

Irigaray, Luce. "The Fecundity of the Caress." In *Face to Face with Levinas*. Albany: University of New York Press, 1986, pp. 231–56.

———. "Questions to Emmanuel Levinas on the Divinity of Love." In *Re-reading Levinas*. Bloomington: Indiana University Press, 1991, pp. 109–18.

Jonas, Hans. *The Phenomenon of Life*. Chicago: The University of Chicago Press, 1966.

Kant, Immanuel. *Critique of Pure Reason*. Translated by Norman Kemp Smith. New York: Macmillan & Co., Ltd., 1929.

———. *Prologomena to any Future Metaphysics*. Translated by James Ellington. Indianapolis: Hackett Publishing Co., 1977.

Kearney, Richard. *Dialogues with Contemporary Continental Thinkers*. Manchester: Manchester University Press, 1984.

Kern, Stephen. *The Culture of Time and Space*. Cambridge: Harvard University Press, 1983.

Kristeva, Julia. *The Kristeva Reader*. Edited by Toril Moi. New York: Columbia University Press, 1986.

Lacoue-Labarthe, Philipe. *La Fiction du politique: Heidegger, l'art et la politique*. Paris: Christian Bourgois, 1987.

Lauer, Quentin. *Phenomenology: Its Genesis and Prospects*. New York: Harper & Row, 1958.

Lentricchia, Frank. *After the New Criticism*. Chicago: The University of Chicago Press, 1980.

Lingis, Alfonso. Introduction to *Collected Philosophical Papers of Levinas*. Boston: Martinus Nijhoff Publishers, 1987, pp. vii–xxxi.

———. Introduction to *Otherwise Than Being, or Beyond Essence*. The Hague: Martinus Nijhoff, 1987, pp. xi–xxxix.
———. *Libido*. Bloomington: Indiana University Press, 1985.
———. "The Sensuality and the Sensitivity." In *Face to Face with Levinas*. Albany: University of New York Press, 1986, pp. 219–30.
Llwelyn, John. "Am I Obsessed by Bobby? Humanism of the Other Animal." In *Re-reading Levinas*. Bloomington: Indiana University Press, 1991, pp. 234–45.
Lyotard, Jean-Francois. *The Differend: Phrases in Dispute*. Translated by Georges Van Den Abbeele. Minneapolis: University of Minnesota Press, 1988.
———. *Just Gaming*. Minneapolis: University of Minnesota Press, 1985.
———. "Levinas' Logic." In *Face to Face With Levinas*. Albany: State University of New York Press, 1986, pp. 117–58.
———. "Presentations." In *Philosophy in France Today*. Edited by Alan Montefiorc. Cambridge: Cambridge University Press, 1983, pp. 116–35.
Malcolm, Norman. *Problems of Mind*. New York: Harper Torchbooks, 1971.
Manning, Robert. "Thinking the Other without Violence: Levinas' Relation to Feminism." *The Journal of Speculative Philosophy*, vol. 5, no. 2 (1991): 132–43.
Megill, Alan. *Prophets of Extremity*. Berkeley: University of California Press, 1985.
Montefiore, Alan, ed. *Philosophy in France Today*. Cambridge: Cambridge University Press, 1983.
Murray, Michael, ed. *Heidegger and Modern Philosophy*. New York: Harper & Row, 1978.
Novitz, David. "The Rage for Deconstruction." *The Monist* 69, no. 1 (January 1986): 48–59.
Peperzak, Adriaan. "Beyond Being." *Research in Phenomenology* viii (1978): 239–61.
———. "From Intentionality to Responsibility: On Levinas's Philosophy of Language." In *The Question of the Other*. Albany: University of New York Press, 1986, pp. 3–22.
———. "Emmanuel Levinas: Jewish Experience and Philosophy." *Philosophy Today*, vol. 27, no. 4 (Winter 1983): 297–306.
———. "Presentation." In *Re-reading Levinas*. Bloomington: Indiana University Press, 1991, pp. 51–66.

———. "Some Remarks on Hegel, Kant, and Levinas." In *Face to Face With Levinas*. Albany: University of New York Press, 1986, pp. 205–18.

Petitdemange, Guy. "L'un ou l'autre. La querelle de l'ontologie: Heidegger-Levinas." In *Les Cahiers de la nuit surveille*, no. 3. Lagrasse: Verdier, 1984.

Poire, Francois. *Emmanuel Levinas: Qui etes-vous?* Lyon: La Manufacture, 1987.

Richardson, William. *Companion to Being and Time*. New York: Harper & Row, 1975.

Ricoeur, Paul. "On Interpretation." In *Philosophy in France Today*. Edited by Alan Montefiore. Cambridge: Cambridge University Press, 1983.

Rosenzweig, Franz. *The Star of Redemption*. Translated by William Hallo. Notre Dame: Notre Dame University Press, 1970.

Rubenstein, Richard. *After Auschwitz*. New York: MacMillan, 1966.

Said, Edward. *The World, the Text, and the Critic*. Cambridge: Harvard University Press, 1983.

Sallis, John. "The Identities of the Things Themselves." *Research in Phenomenology* 12 (1982): 113–19.

Scanlon, John. "Review of Husserl's *Ding und Raum: Vorlesungen 1907*" in *Research in Phenomenology* 4 (1974): 129–35.

Smith, Steven. *The Argument to the Other*. Chico, CA: Scholars Press, 1983.

———. "Reason as One for Another." In *Face to Face with Levinas*. Edited by Richard Cohen. Albany: State University of New York Press, 1986, pp. 50–65.

Spiegelberg, Herbert. *The Phenomenological Movement* 2 vols. The Hague: Martinus Nijhoff, 1960.

Tallon, Andrew. "Review of Edith Wyschogrod's *Emmanuel Levinas and the Problem of Ethical Metaphysics*." *Philosophy Today* (Spring 1986): 56–62.

Taylor, Mark. *Altarity*. Chicago: University of Chicago Press, 1987.

———. *Deconstruction in Context*. Chicago: University of Chicago Press, 1986.

———. *Journeys to Selfhood*. Berkeley: University of California Press, 1986.

Theunissen, Michael. *The Other*. Translated by Christopher Macann. Cambridge: MIT Press, 1986.
Tillich, Paul. *Systematic Theology*. 3 vols. Chicago: University of Chicago Press, 1963.
Valevicius, Andrius. *From the Other to the Totally Other*. New York: Peter Lang, 1988.
Warnock, Mary. *Existentialist Ethics*. New York: St. Martin's Press, 1967.
Warren, Scott. *The Emergence of Dialectical Theory: Philosophy and Political Inquiry*. Chicago: University of Chicago Press, 1984.
Weaver, Richard. *The Ethics of Rhetoric*. Chicago: Henry Regnery Company, 1953.
Wisdom, John. *Other Minds*. Oxford: Blackwell, 1952.
Wittgenstein, Ludwig. *Philosophical Investigations*. New York: MacMillan & Co., 1953.
Wyschogrod, Edith. *Emmanuel Levinas and the Problem of Ethical Metaphysics*. The Hague: Martinus Nijhoff, 1974.
———. "God and 'Being's Move' in the philosophy of Emmanuel Levinas." *The Journal of Religion* 62, no. 2 (1982): 145–55.
———. *Spirit in Ashes: Hegel, Heidegger, and Man-made Mass Death*. New Haven: Yale University Press, 1985.

INDEX